ALL ABOUT THEATRE

Property of
CUAdrama

Donated By
Jon Palmer Claridge

ALL ABOUT THEATRE

Helen Sheehy
Hamden Hall Country Day School
Hamden, Connecticut

Illustrations by
Elizbeth Griffin

SECOND EDITION

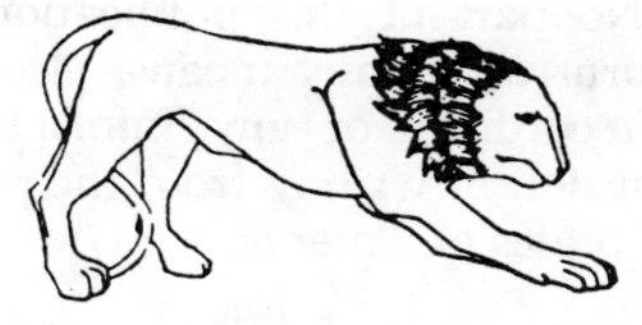

Independent School Press

Wellesley Hills Massachusetts

"The War Prayer" from EUROPE AND ELSEWHERE by Mark Twain, Copyright 1923, 1951 by The Mark Twain Company. Reprinted by permission of Harper & Row, Publishers, Inc.

Yale Center for British Art, Paul Mellon Collection

Box Lobby Loungers, Thomas Rowlandson, Aquatint, Hand Colored, 1786, After Wigstead, England, Print, William A. Sargent Fund. Courtesy, Museum of Fine Arts, Boston.

From "MEDEA" from THREE GREAT PLAYS OF EURIPIDES, translated by Rex Warner. Copyright 1944 by Rex Warner. Reprinted by arrangement with The New American Library, Inc., New York, New York.

From *A Doll's House* by Henrik Ibsen, translated by R. Farquharson Sharp and revised by Torgrim and Linda Hannas. An Everyman's Library Edition. Reprinted by permission of the publisher in the United States, E. P. Dutton.

Cover photograph: W.B. Carter
A Midsummer Night's Dream
Yale Repertory Theatre
New Haven, Connecticut

Copyright © 1981, 1986 by Independent School Press, Inc.

All rights reserved. No part of this publication may be reproduced or transmitted in any form or by any means, electronic or mechanical, including photocopy, recording, or any information storage or retrieval system, without permission in writing from the publisher.

Printed in the United States of America

0-88334-147-6

8687888990
1234567890

For T.W.

CONTENTS

ACKNOWLEDGMENTS

Many theatre people shared their knowledge, experience, and talents with me in the preparation of this text. I gratefully acknowledge their support and encouragement.

Thom Peterson, Designer and Professor of Theatre at Southern Connecticut State College, provided costume and set designs; Tom Hudak of C. B. C. Scenery contributed his technical expertise; Ron Wallace, Lighting Designer; Paul Huntley of Paul Huntley Designs; and Herman Russell of Costume Bazaar all generously shared their knowledge. Long Wharf Theatre, Rosalind Heinz, and Anthony Zerbe graciously allowed us to photograph CYRANO. Dr. Richard Welsbacher and Professor Joyce Cavarozzi of Wichita State University provided initial inspiration and encouragement.

A special thanks to Judith Kase who offered insight and support at every step, and a debt of gratitude to all my students who were the reason for the book in the first place.

Helen Sheehy

Part I.

PERFORMANCE SKILLS

Chapter 1

An Introduction

Playing frees the imagination and enables the mind and body to create. Every child knows how to play. It is as natural as breathing. Theatre is equally natural. It is the oldest of the arts and includes all of the arts. As a child you made theatre simply by saying the magic words "Let's play like . . . !" Basements and backyards were transformed into stages, faded jeans and discarded hats became costumes, and an adventure began that might last a lifetime. Children play and theatre endures for one primary reason - both are fun! Both give pleasure and nourish the human spirit.

In this text you will continue the process of learning to make theatre. Your tools are your mind and body - your method is practice and performance. When you have mastered the rules and techniques of theatre, you will be able to "play." It is no accident that "play" has many variations of meaning in theatre terminology. A play is a dramatic composition. One may play or act out a scene. A player is an actor who may be instructed to "play off" or relate to another actor. All of these ideas are built upon the spontaneous, natural "play like" games of childhood. You have the imagination, the mind, and the body to create the next logical step - theatre as a conscious art form.

Four basic elements are necessary for theatre as a conscious art form. All of these elements are present in a classroom.

1. an audience
2. players
3. a playing space
4. "something to act"

Without an *audience*, a theatrical performance is merely a rehearsal. Unlike the passive spectators of television and film, theatre audiences are engaged actively in the immediacy of each performance. A theatre audience is part of the creative process. Audience reaction - laughter, tears, yawns, applause - all help shape the performance. A film or television show may be viewed many times and the performances are frozen on film, but a theatrical performance is created afresh with each new audience.

In this course you will be called upon to be a member of an audience. You will be asked to give specific reactions and judgments. Therefore, you must learn the techniques of critical analysis in order to respond accurately and sensitively. You will learn about the various aspects of play production - acting, set design and construction, lighting, costuming, make-up, and script analysis. This knowledge will give you a more complete understanding of the complexities and relationships of the various production areas. Your judgments will be based on solid skills. You will ask questions about each play and classroom performance you observe. Did the performance hold my attention? Why? Why not? Why were certain choices made? Why that particular costume? that color paint? that lighting instrument? You will discover that each production involves a process of selection from a multitude of choices. Your function as a critical audience member is to decide if the choices made are compatible with the script and the production as a whole. In this process you will not only be enriching your own performance and production skills, but you will also be widening your experience and exposure to theatrical forms.

Players are the second element essential for theatre. When the Greek actor, Thespis, stepped out of the chorus and spoke lines, an acting tradition was born. All actors are called "Thespians" in honor of Thespis. Actors may act in written plays as Thespis did in sixth-century B.C., perform improvisationally as the Italian actors did in the commedia dell' arte, or interpret literature and tell stories as the wandering minstrels did during the Middle Ages. The player's primary purpose is always to communicate with the audience and create a theatrical reality. As a player you will act many parts. You must use your imagination, your voice, your body, and your mind with freedom and discipline.

Two basics of acting, *relaxation* and *concentration*, will be explored through exercises designed to aid you in developing your own technique. Becoming comfortable with your mind and body, freeing yourself from tension, *relaxing*, is the first step. Focusing your attention on a specific task or intention — *concentration* — is the next step. How many of you have seen an amateur production in which actors "broke character" and acted like themselves instead of their characters? Too often young actors aren't taught the basics of relaxation and concentration. Freedom to "play" can only occur if you first learn discipline. You will discover techniques by playing within the limits of the game, learning rules, practicing, and performing. The process is progressive and circular.

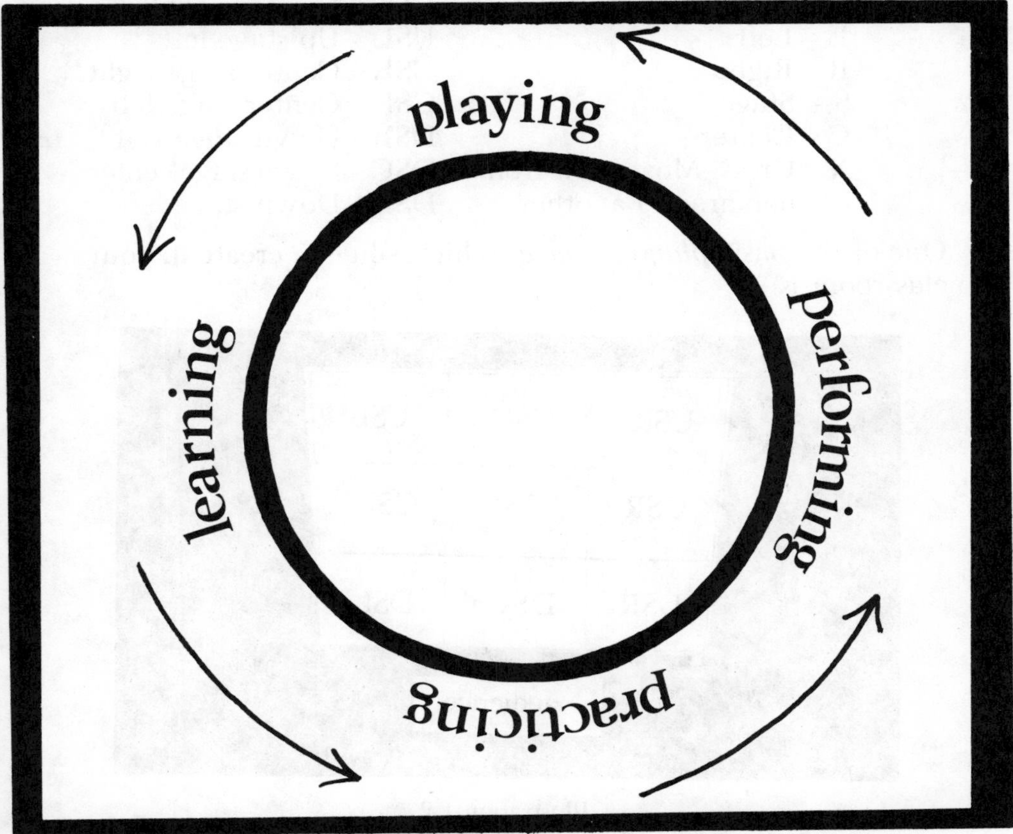

Illustration 1-1

The *playing space*, the third essential element, has a dual meaning. First, it is simply a place to perform. It might be a Broadway stage, a barn, a basement, or your classroom. The playing space, or stage, has many different shapes. In the past, stages used to be "raked" or slanted toward the audience. Thus, when an actor walked toward the audience he walked "down" stage. When he walked away from the audience, he literally walked "up" stage. Stage right is always the actor's right as he stands onstage facing the audience. Stage left is always the actor's left as he stands onstage facing the audience. The use of abbreviations enables theatre people quickly to establish areas of the stage in giving written or verbal directions. For example,

D - Down	USR - Up stage right
U - Up	USC - Up stage center
L - Left	USL - Up stage left
R - Right	CSR - Center stage right
S - Stage	CSL - Center stage left
C - Center	DSR - Down stage right
X - Cross, Movement from one area to another	DSC - Down stage center
	DSL - Down stage left

One of the basic *playing spaces* which you can create in your classroom is:

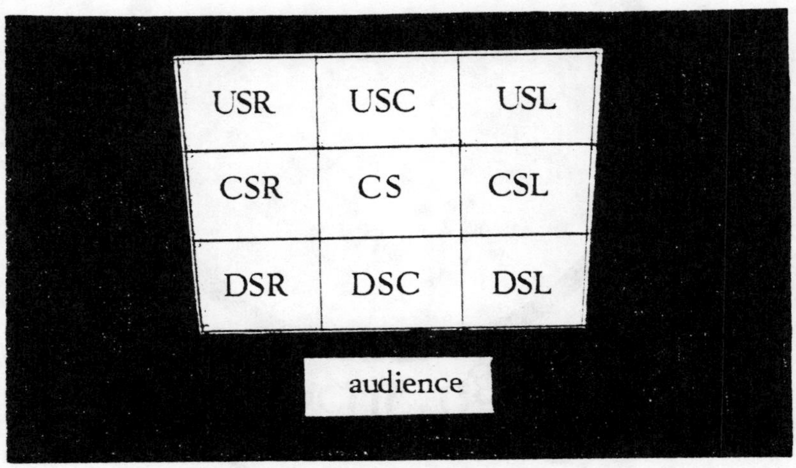

Illustration 1-2

Familiarize yourself with all of the areas and begin to learn the jargon. Theatre has a special language all its own. Learning the language helps you to understand the game and the players.

In this course you will learn the elements of set design, set construction, and lighting. Perhaps you will have an opportunity to design and build a set for a school play. Fashioning raw materials of wood and muslin into a setting for a play is one of the most satisfying theatre experiences. Hammering, measuring, sawing, and painting are just some of the skills you will acquire. The use and development of these skills will open a whole new world of creating. Hanging and focusing lights to set the right atmosphere and mood can transform an ordinary setting into a special place. Through your skills with tools and raw materials, the "actual" space can be enhanced and expanded.

The playing space has another dimension in addition to the actual, physical space - the *imaginative space.* All of you remember what wonderful settings could be created in the "play like" games simply by believing they were real. In Shakespeare's plays a bare stage becomes a castle, a courtyard, or a moor through the power of language and a compelling belief in their reality. Your classroom playing space can become any place you want it to be through use of the imaginative space.

The fourth essential element is *"something to act."* It may be an improvisation, a dramatic work, or prose and poetry. Inherent in the material are ideas and feelings. The skills of the players bring the ideas and feelings to life.

Before the great Greek tragedies of Euripides, Sophocles, and Aeschylus were written, primitive man acted out the drama of everyday life. Routine life for primitive man was a fierce battle with nature. In an attempt to order his life and his destiny, he acted out the real-life happenings of his day. For example, stalking and killing a tiger was presented by the primitive "players" in hopes that through imitation of reality their deadly enemy might be eliminated. This imitation of life gave rise to a conscious imitation of life in written plays.

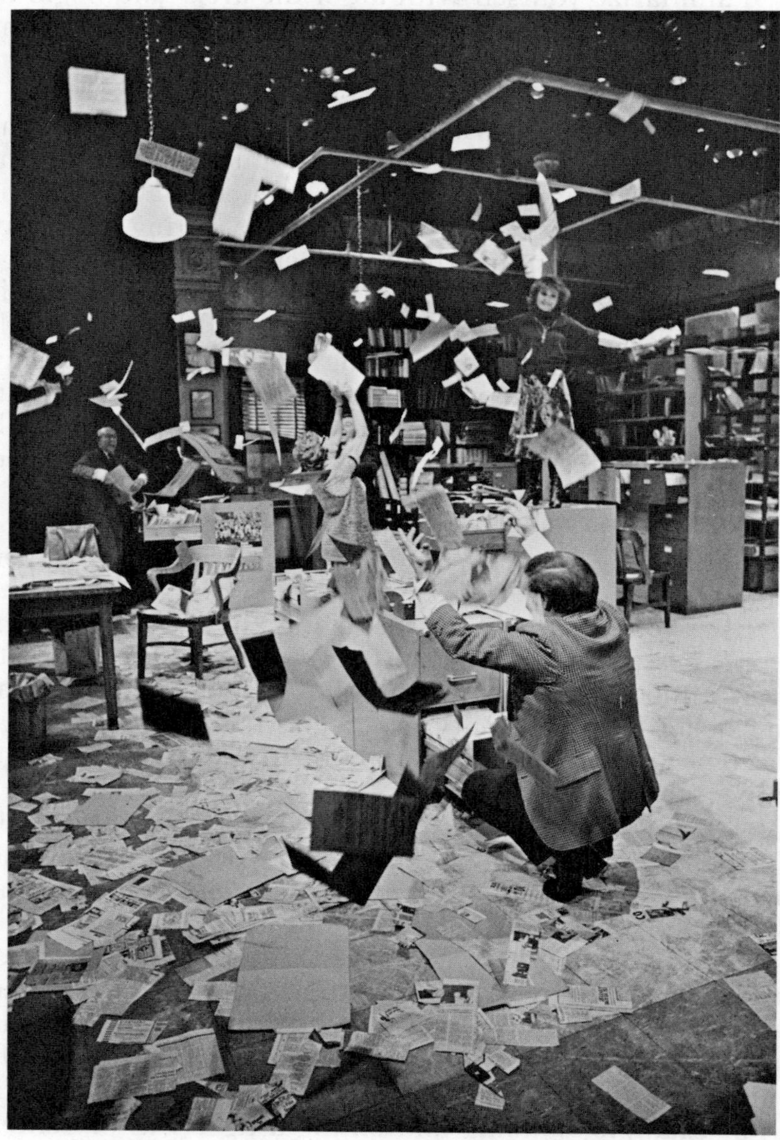

A scene from *Alphabetical Order* by Michael Frayn at Long Wharf Theatre.

The force to act, to create plays, has survived the centuries. Plays exist in many forms and types. You will have opportunities to study plays from the past and the present. You will create improvisational plays, and perhaps you will want to write your own plays. "Something to act," a *play*, will enlarge your vision of the world, increase your understanding of human nature and history, and bring you hours of pleasure.

In this course you will continue to discover the principles, techniques, and skills of theatre as a conscious art form. You must play many parts - performer, audience member, technician, designer, historian, and critic. Each part you play should be imbued with the spirit of adventure that pervades all of theatre.

DISCUSSION QUESTIONS

1. What are the four elements necessary for theatre?
2. Discuss plays you have seen. How is live theatre different from television and movies?
3. What are the two meanings of playing space?
4. How is theatre like playing?
5. What are the areas of the stage?

VOCABULARY

Thespis	cross
improvisation	relaxation
play	concentration
playing space	setting

SUGGESTIONS

- Keep a loose-leaf notebook for this course. Jot down feelings and observations of plays you have seen and will see. In your notebook keep class notes, articles, reviews, and observations of interesting situations and persons.
- See as many live performances as you can.
- Audition for your school plays and/or work backstage.
- Participate actively in all course work.

Chapter 2

Improvisation

In Chapter 1 you learned that four elements are necessary for theatre to occur - an audience, players, a playing space, and a play. Improvisational theatre is a form of theatre embodying all of these elements, but with one unique difference. Improvisational theatre does not require a formal, written play. The play emerges spontaneously through a creative process shared by the actors and the audience.

This creative process is not a modern invention. In the sixteenth century, the popular Italian commedia dell'arte presented performances improvised from plot outlines. Each actor in the company played a "stock" (stereotype) character. The familiar characters of Harlequin and Punch are descendants of stock characters created by the commedia dell'arte. Present-day theatre companies continue this acting tradition in varying forms. Instead of working from a plot outline, modern companies often invite the audience to suggest situations, places, or characters. Then the actors improvise a scene creating dialogue and action as they go along.

The creative process is the most exciting aspect of improvisation. Anything is possible and actors are bound only by the limits of their imaginations. How many times have you watched a movie or television show, and were able to anticipate every plot change? Wasn't the enjoyment diminished because the expectancy was diminished? Often the problem lies with a trite script, but sometimes the fault lies with the actors' inability to react spontaneously to dialogue they have heard many times. Improvisation helps develop the actors' skill in listening and reacting as if they were hearing and speaking the words for the *first time.* If the actors are able to create the impression of the first time with each performance, the audience is more willing to become involved with the reality of each performance. Hal Holbrook, winner of the

Tony Award for his one-man show MARK TWAIN TO-NIGHT!, said "the most important thing is never to give the audience a chance to figure out what you're going to do next: surprise is the one thing you have going for you. . . There's drama in a water pitcher if you use it right."* The ability to create the impression of the first time and the ability to create a reality with the audience can be developed through the process of improvisation. Improvisational theatre is an art in its own right - an *end* in itself; and, after working improvisationally, you may wish to present full performances. Improvisation is also an important *means* for learning acting skills. You will discover the techniques of improvisation through a series of exercises designed to free your imagination, relax your body, increase your powers of concentration and observation, and develop your ability to act and react with spontaneity, belief, and feeling.

Before beginning work on the improvisation exercises, a brief look at some basic guidelines of responsibility, courtesy, and common sense is in order. As you progress through the course, you will add to the list. Remember the guidelines and apply them not only in your classroom, but at public performances as well.

AUDIENCE

1. Be punctual! Latecomers annoy other audience members and are a distraction to the actors.
2. Do not talk during a performance. Save your comments for discussion afterwards.
3. By all means respond to the actors. Laugh, cry, applaud if you are moved to do so.
4. If you are asked to analyze a performance, be sensitive and tactful, but do give your honest opinion based on sound reasons.

*William Goldman, *The Season: A Candid Look at Broadway* (New York: Bantam, 1970), p. 122.

PLAYERS

1. Be punctual!
2. Don't break character during a scene or performance. It reflects lack of concentration and lack of respect.
3. Do not chew gum while performing, for aesthetic and safety reasons.
4. Do not "mug" (overact). It detracts from the performance and makes you appear silly.
5. When you are waiting offstage, do not talk or distract the audience's attention in any way.
6. Do participate enthusiastically and energetically!

Adherence to these basic guidelines smooths the way for positive theatrical activities. Experiencing the invisible link and rapport between actor and audience is one of the most thrilling aspects of theatre. Because of the immediacy of theatre, audience and actors work together to shape a performance. As you practice, participate, and perform you will discover this for yourself.

EXERCISE #1

Creating a Set.

Begin with a bare playing space. Each student adds an imaginary item to the stage. For example, student A unlocks an imaginary door, turns door knob, enters room, closes door, walks across the stage, and exits. Student B opens door A has created, walks into room, finds it stuffy, crosses to DSC, opens window, inhales fresh air, exits. Students C, D, E might add books, lamps, rugs, pets.

Each student must carefully observe what other students have added. Walking through a wall or stepping on a dog breaks the illusion.

Practice this exercise until you can create a variety of places smoothly and believably. Make your actions clear and visible to the audience. No talking. Show rather than tell.

You will quickly discover that details are very important. If a player forgets to turn the doorknob before opening the door or walks through a table instead of around it, it is quite noticeable! The absence of a real set and real props causes the audience to focus primarily on the actors. Thus, concentration on exactly what you and the other players are doing is of the utmost importance. Concentrating and observing intently can help you to relax by focusing your energies on the task at hand instead of worrying about how you appear to the audience.

EXERCISE #2

Using the Set.

In Exercise #1 you created a variety of sets. Now, use any one of those sets to tell a simple story. For example, if a living room set has been created with a wall safe hidden behind a painting, the story might proceed as follows: A stealthy burglar enters the room through a window, shines his flashlight around the room, sees the painting, discovers the safe, steals the contents, and slips quietly out of the room.

Or maybe he trips over a rug and wakes up the family who catch him in the act . . . or . . . the possibilities are endless!

Anyone may begin this exercise by walking onstage and suggesting an action. Other students then join the scene as they are needed.

Practice this exercise until you have created a variety of scenes in a variety of sets.

Do not talk. Show rather than tell. Make your movements and actions clear, visible, and relevant.

Perhaps this is a good place to set down some basic guidelines for improvisation. You've probably already discovered some of these for yourself. Feel free to add your own guidelines to the list.

1. Try to relax. There's no reason to rush or resort to frantic

behavior. The best method of relaxation is to focus your attention on what you are doing.

2. Don't plan! Improvisation should evolve. Your idea for adding an item to the set must fit in with other ideas. For example, if you've planned a zoo set with a gorilla, and you observe that the scene begins in a church, your idea is out of place. Better to wait and let your ideas arise naturally out of the preceding action. "But," you say, "someone has to plan the first action." Again, it is better to take a deep breath and walk onstage without any idea at all. If you can't think of anything while you're onstage, simply exit. Many excellent ideas are lost because players sit back planning and rejecting ideas in their heads instead of spontaneously acting them out.
3. You're an actor, not a playwright. A gesture, a movement, an expression says much more than torrents of words. (Creating speech and dialogue will be explored in later exercises.)
4. Don't try to *be* funny or to *be* tragic. Comedy and tragedy should arise out of the action, not be imposed upon it.
5. Don't be afraid to try. And try again. Sometimes ideas just don't work or aren't clear, but if you don't take risks you won't be rewarded.

EXERCISE #3

Position!

For this exercise you may use a bare stage or two chairs or two stools. All props are imaginary. No talking. Show rather than tell.

Player A creates a position onstage and then freezes that position until Player B enters and *justifies* Player A's position. Player A and B then interact.

For example, Player A may simply sit in a chair facing straight out. Player B enters, crosses upstage of A, ties a cover-up around A, and proceeds to cut A's hair. In other words, B *justifies* A's position. He shows A where he is. A, of course, must be sensitive to B's actions and react accordingly. B's actions must be clear and defined. What are the possibilities? A might be a small boy getting his first haircut, or he might be Samson getting *his* first haircut from Delilah! Add your own possibilities.

Practice this exercise until you can create a variety of justifications for a variety of positions.

Exercise #3 may be expanded to include several people. Make sure, however, that there is only one *focus* on stage at a time. Focus simply means one point of interest. If several scenes are taking place at once the audience becomes confused and the focus is lost. Also, with several people in the scene, concentration and observation skills become even more important.

What possibilities are suggested by the positions of the actors pictured above and on the facing page?

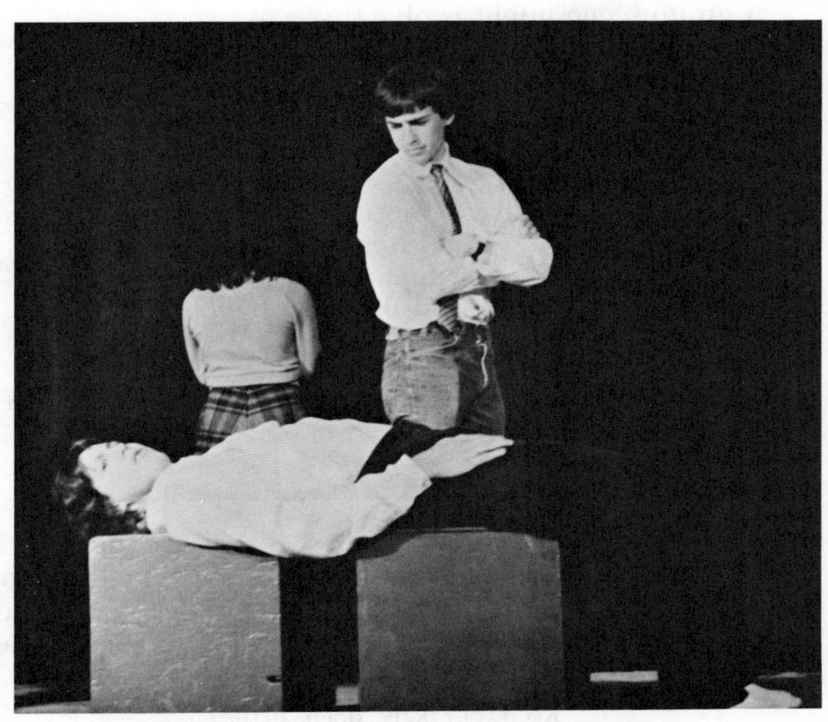

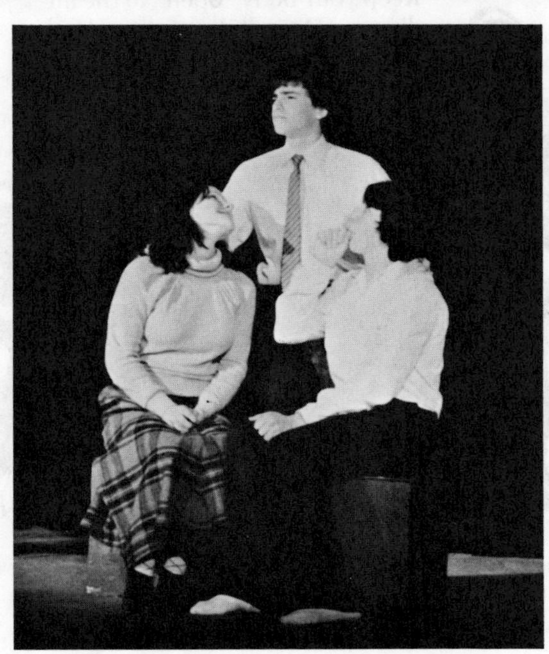

A group scene might evolve this way:

EXERCISE #4

Position! - Group

Player A enters, sits CS, faces out. Player B enters, holding popcorn, sits beside A, proceeds to eat popcorn while watching "screen." (A and B must sense each other's reactions to the movie. Is it funny, sad, romantic?) Player C enters, sits between A and B, chews bubble gum loudly, blows bubbles, bubble gets out of control, bursts! A and B react. How might this scene end? What are the choices? Try acting out different possibilities and then create your own group scenes.

Again, no talking.

As you perform these exercises you can see that position onstage is very important. Effective stage position illuminates and suggest relationships, but an improper stage position can detract from a scene. Some basic position guidelines are as follows.

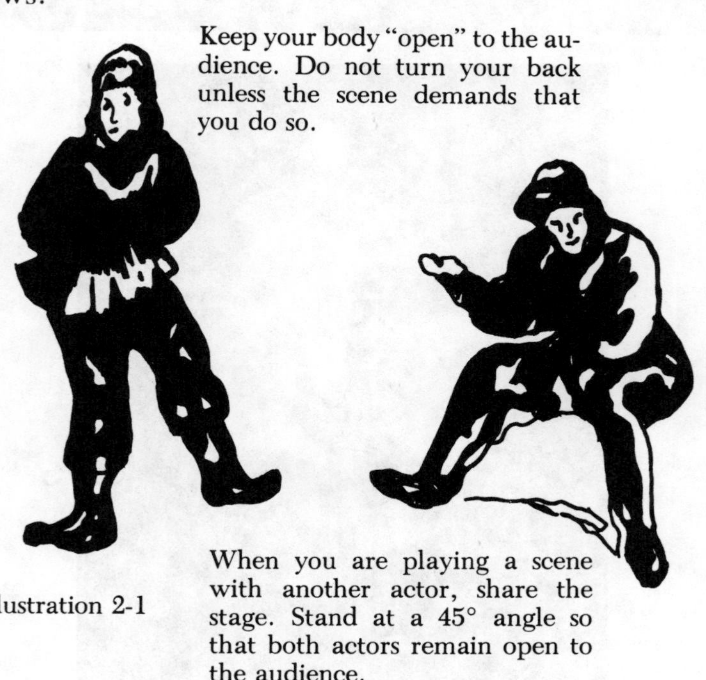

Keep your body "open" to the audience. Do not turn your back unless the scene demands that you do so.

When you are playing a scene with another actor, share the stage. Stand at a 45° angle so that both actors remain open to the audience.

Illustration 2-1

Do not "upstage" or take attention away from another actor.

As you can see from the diagram, A moved upstage of B forcing B to give his back to the audience.

Illustration 2-2

Do not block yourself behind another actor, or behind furniture.

Illustration 2-3

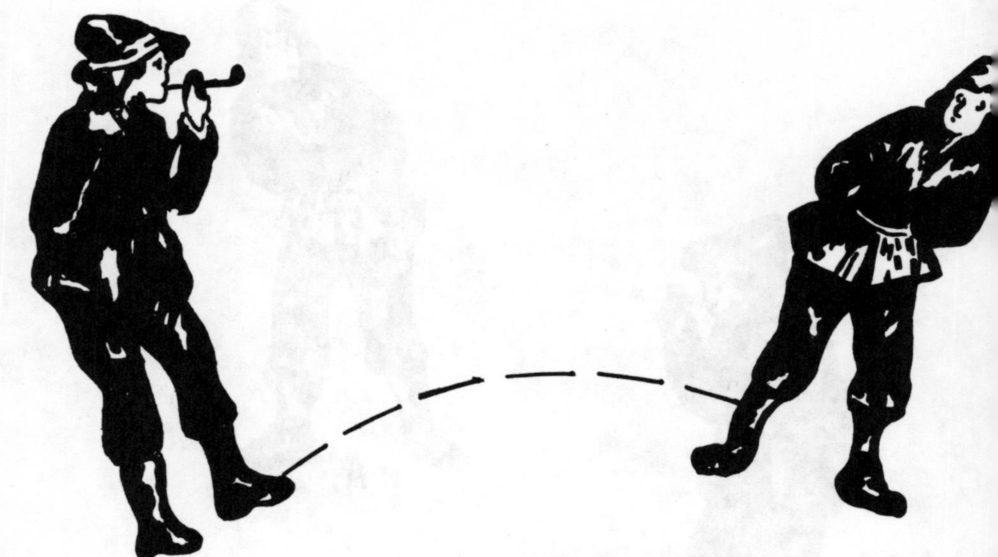

Illustration 2-4

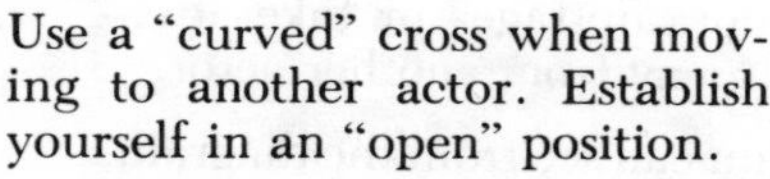

Use a "curved" cross when moving to another actor. Establish yourself in an "open" position.

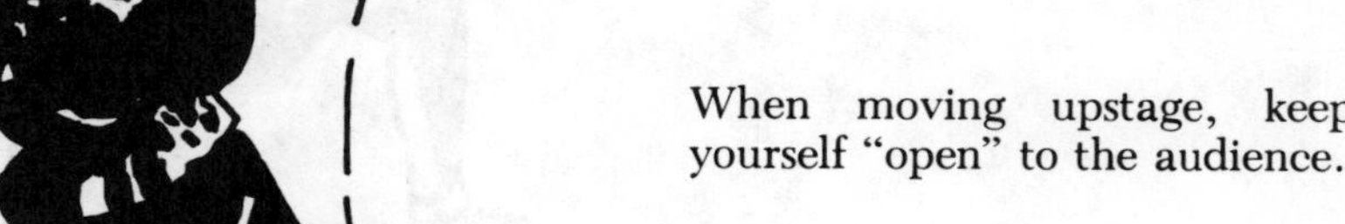

When moving upstage, keep yourself "open" to the audience.

Illustration 2-5

In the preceding scenes you have exercised concentration and observation skills to help you become more relaxed. The following exercises are designed not only to continue developing basic techniques of relaxation, concentration, and observation, but they will also help to develop your relationships to props, words, and other players. The result of these exercises will be to develop scenes and performances in which you are able to incorporate all the techniques that you have learned.

EXERCISE #5

Relating to Props - Group.

For this exercise you may use any medium-sized object such as a rolled-up sweater or even a book. Take turns using the prop in a variety of ways. *Endow* the prop with the appropriate qualities by using all of your senses - sight, smell, taste, touch, and sound.

Use the object as if it were:

- a glass jar with a tarantula inside
- a sleepy puppy
- a witches' bubbling cauldron
- a cactus
- a fifty-pound barbell
- a box of chocolates
- an ice cream cone
- an antique, hand-crocheted shawl
- a jack-in-the-box
- a fidgety, "wet," baby
- a fishing pole with a worm on the hook
- a ticking bomb
- a bee hive
- a mirror
- add your own

After practicing with the prop, you may expand the exercise by creating a scene around the prop. Add a reason for the action. Perhaps you are a seven-year old in a classroom who accidentally drops her science project - a jar with a tarantula inside! The jar breaks, the tarantula escapes, and the other students and the teacher react. What are the choices? How will the scene develop?

Again, no talking. Show rather than tell.

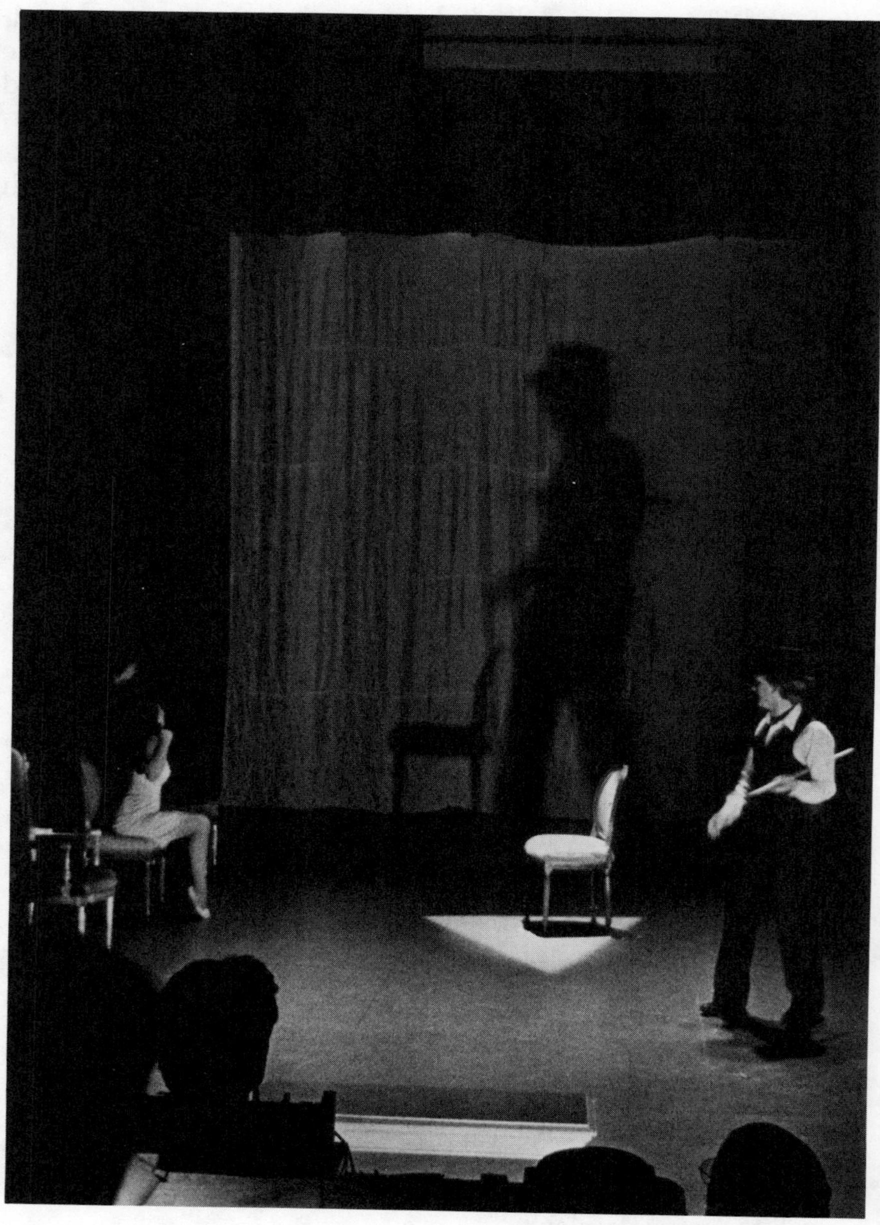

A scene from "The Lost Reflection" in the Hartford Stage Company work-in-progress, *The Hoffmann Project*. The company worked improvisationally to create theatre pieces based on the tales of E. T. A. Hoffmann.

EXERCISE #6

Relating to Props - Imagination!

Divide into groups - three to five in a group. Your teacher will give each group a prop, perhaps a stick. Your group will improvise a scene centered around the prop. Through your actions transform the prop into any number of items. A stick could become an old man's cane, a scepter, a telescope, an oar, etc.

You may begin by placing the prop onstage, or one person may carry it onstage, but your point of interest must be the prop.

Again, no talking. Make your actions clear, visible, and relevant. Let your imagination flow!

(This exercise may be repeated as many times as desired with a variety of simple objects. Remember, your *use* of the object determines its nature.)

Language adds another dimension to improvisation, but it does not take the place of clear, strong action. Use words sparingly in improvisation. Speak only if words are necessary to convey your meaning or feeling. Words mean what you want them to mean. A simple "hello" may have multiple meanings depending on how you say it and what thoughts are behind it. "Hello" might mean "Good morning, I had a wonderful breakfast, and I'm planning a day at the beach!" *or* it might mean "I don't want to talk to anyone. I couldn't sleep last night, and I didn't finish my homework."

EXERCISE #7

Relating to Words. Dialogue.

Choose a partner. In this exercise one of you will ask "How are you?" The other will reply "I'm fine." Think of a reason for the dialogue. For example, one player may be an indifferent doctor examining an irate patient. Or they might be friends meeting after a five-year separation.

Perform the scene. Try to convey with your voice and body who you are and what the situation is.

Bertha Bumiller (standing) lectures her son Jody Bumiller (Jaston Williams) in a scene from GREATER TUNA by Ed Howard, Joe Sears, and Jaston Williams. The play premiered in Austin, Texas, in September, 1981; opened in New York at Circle in the Square Downtown in 1982; and since then has been seen in theatres around the country.

The two actors in GREATER TUNA play all the characters who inhabit or visit the town of Tuna or the Greater Tuna area, including the long-suffering housewife, Bertha Bumiller, and her three problem children; lovable but dog-poisoning Aunt Pearl; self-righteous Vera Carp; and the two "good old boy" radio announcers Thurston and Arlie.

In creating the play the three writers (who also functioned as actors and director) used improvisational techniques to shape the script. Several exercises are outlined below which were used by the GREATER TUNA company for writing and acting work.

RADIO

Line up 10 people onstage. The audience gives each onstage actor a type of radio station - FM, easy listening, country and western - or "Afghanistan New Wave" - "French News." Another actor "conducts" the scene, turns the dial, and turns the actors "on." (You might try taping this exercise and using the material to build scenes.)

NEWSPAPER

Select a story or photo in a newspaper. Build an improvisation scene around the story or write a short scene about the story. (The GREATER TUNA company used their daily newspaper for story ideas and improvisations. For example, one of the scenes in the play concerns the efforts of the "Smut-Snatchers" squad to remove words from the dictionary - an effort duplicated by a real life censorship squad which was detailed in the newspaper.)

CARTOON

Select a cartoon or comic strip. Using the lines given in the cartoon, continue the scene or build an entirely new one.

CHARACTER

Select an interesting "character" from your family or friends. Imagine that character in different situations. For example, your Uncle Fred appearing on the evening news. Jot down Fred's mannerisms, voice type, etc. Write out or improvise the scene.

EXERCISE #8

Relating to Words. "Yes" and "No"

Choose a partner. Think of a situation in which only the words "yes" and "no" will be used. Again, meaning depends on the way you say the words.

For example:
- a boy and girl at a movie
- a surgeon and a nurse
- a song-and-dance routine
- a dentist and a patient
- a telephone solicitor and customer

Keep in mind the following guidelines when you are speaking in a scene.

- Project your voice so that you can be heard.
- Speak clearly and distinctly so that you can be understood.
- Think before you speak.
- Listen to other actors and react accordingly.

In all the improvisation exercises thus far you have been working with other students. Physical relationships, props, and words determined how you would interact with other players. Character, or *who* you are, also determines relationships.

EXERCISE #9

Relationships

Coach - Player	Policeman - Criminal
Teacher - Student	Director - Actor
Employer - Employee	Lawyer - Client
Parent - Child	Clerk - Customer
Husband - Wife	Sergeant - Private

With a partner choose a pair of characters. Plan a situation in which the characters are in conflict. Each character should have a specific reason for his or her behavior. For example, the director wants the actor to play a scene for comedy because the director wants the play to be popular and make a lot of money. The actor, who wants to play the scene seriously, has visions of winning the Tony for best dramatic actor. How is the conflict resolved?

Obviously, dialogue is required. The scene should not be repetitious. If one approach doesn't work, try another. The scene might end with one character giving in to the will of the other.

Improvisation can be great fun, but it requires discipline. As you practice and perform improvisationally, you will discover the joy of "playing." Try to retain that joy and spontaneity when you move into acting with a written script.

QUESTIONS FOR REVIEW AND DISCUSSION

1. How is improvisational theatre different from conventional theatre?
2. What are the rules of courtesy for players and audience?
3. What is meant by the phrase the "first time"?
4. What are five guidelines to keep in mind when you are performing improvisationally?
5. Do you think improvisational theatre is closer to "real life" than conventional theatre? Why?
6. Analyze what made the scenes that you performed successful or unsuccessful.

VOCABULARY

improvise
commedia dell'arte
upstaging
justification
curved cross
stock character
blocking yourself
endow
mugging
focus
open

SUGGESTIONS

- Form your own improvisation company.
- Keep a file of unusual situations or characters to use in developing scene material.
- Read plays and improvise the situation *before* the play begins. Or *after* the play ends.

Do a character study of one of the people in the paintings in The Externals chapter or go to a museum and select a painting. Begin with a visual analysis: facial expressions, gestures, posture, eye contact, etc. Write a dialogue between people in the painting based on close observation. Or, introduce your portrait to another portrait. Write out their conversation or improvise a scene between the two.

Chapter 3

Acting

No one knows what motivated Thespis to break away from the chorus. Perhaps he felt a simple, human need to communicate directly with his audience or perhaps he became bored with the sameness of the chorus and decided to "act" independently. At that moment, Thespis engaged his voice, body, emotions, and mind in an effort to create a reality with the audience. Today, many centuries after Thespis, actors continue this acting tradition.

Actors, more than any other artists, depend upon their own resources. While most other artists have paint and canvas, pen and paper, camera and film, actors have only themselves.

Voice, body, mind, and emotions are their instruments, and they must be kept in tune through active study, training, practice, and performance.

Actors have always searched for the appropriate techniques to bring their art to life. Greek actors concentrated on voice training, but emotional truth was also important. The Greek actor, Polus, in his portrayal of Electra, used his dead son's ashes to generate real feeling. Centuries after the Greeks, we find Shakespeare's characters in Elizabethan England discussing acting techniques. Hamlet's speech to the players (HAMLET, Act III, Scene 2) is famous. Shakespeare also parodied bad acting as shown in the following scene from A MIDSUMMER NIGHT'S DREAM.

Enter QUINCE *the carpenter and* SNUG *the joiner and* BOTTOM *the weaver and* FLUTE *the bellows-mender and* SNOUT *the tinker and* STARVELING *the tailor.*

Quin. Is all our company here?

Bot. First, good Peter Quince, say what the play treats on; then read the names of the actors; and so grow to a point.

Quin. Marry, our play is *The most lamentable comedy and most cruel death of Pyramus and Thisby.*

Bot. A very good piece of work, I assure you, and a merry. Now, good Peter Quince, call forth your actors by the scroll. Masters, spread yourselves.

Quin. Answer as I call you. Nick Bottom the weaver.

Bot. Ready. Name what part I am for, and proceed.

Quin. You, Nick Bottom, are set down for Pyramus.

Bot. What is Pyramus? a lover, or a tyrant?

Quin. A lover, that kills himself most gallant for love.

Bot. That will ask some tears in the true performing of it. If I do it, let the audience look to their eyes. I will move storms; . . .

Bottom is interested primarily in the effect his acting will have on the audience.

Quin. Francis Flute the bellows-mender.

Flu. Here, Peter Quince.

Quin. Flute, you must take Thisby on you.

Flu. What is Thisby? a wand'ring knight?

Quin. It is the lady that Pyramus must love.

Flu. Nay, faith; let not me play a woman; I have a beard coming.

Quin. That's all one; you shall play it in a mask, and you may speak as small as you will.

Since women were not allowed to perform on the stage, boy players took the women's roles.

Bot. And I may hide my face, let me play Thisby too. I'll speak in a monstrous little voice, "Thisne! Thisne! Ah, Pyramus, my lover dear! thy Thisby dear, and lady dear!"

Bottom, the consummate "ham," wants to show off his acting skill in the part of Thisby.

Quin. No, no, you must play Pyramus; and, Flute, you Thisby.

Bot. Well, proceed.

Quin. Robin Starveling the tailor.

Star. Here, Peter Quince.

Quin. Robin Starveling, you must play Thisby's mother. Tom Snout the tinker.

Snout. Here, Peter Quince.

Quin. You, Pyramus' father; myself, Thisby's father; Snug the joiner, you the lion's part. And I hope here is a play fitted.

Snug. Have you the lion's part written? Pray you, if it be, give it me, for I am slow of study.

Quin. You may do it extempore, for it is nothing but roaring.

Bot. Let me play the lion too. I will roar, that I will do any man's heart good to hear me. I will roar, that I will make the Duke say, "Let him roar again; let him roar again."

Again, Bottom has lofty visions of his effect on the audience.

Quin. And you should do it too terribly, you would fright the Duchess and the ladies, that they would shrike; and that were enough to hang us all.

Quince naively worries that the "lion" will actually frighten the ladies.

All. That would hang us, every mother's son.

Shakespeare's "fun" at the expense of these rustic players who overact and play for emotional effect instead of emotional truth suggests that Elizabethan actors, at least in Shakespeare's company, were quite adept at natural, believable playing.

Natural, believable playing was the cornerstone of an acting system developed by the Russian actor/director/producer, Constantin Stanislavsky. The system which he outlined in his books MY LIFE IN ART, AN ACTOR PREPARES, and BUILDING A CHARACTER was developed at the Moscow Art Theatre in the early years of this century. The story goes that when Stanislavsky was asked by the American actor, John Barrymore, how he chose his actors, Stanislavsky held up a pin. He then asked Barrymore to leave the room. Stanislavsky hid the pin and asked Barrymore in to find it. Barrymore carefully searched the table top, picking up glasses and plates, and then felt along the top of the tablecloth until he discovered the pin. Stanislavsky applauded and said that Barrymore had passed the test. Pretending to look for the pin, striking poses, and exaggerating is not good acting. Stanislavsky had cleverly illustrated his insistence on internal truth rather than dramatic artifice.

The Stanislavsky system had a profound influence on the American theatre. Lee Strasberg's Actors' Studio in New York taught a technique based on the Stanislavsky system which became known as the "method." The "method" has been criticized because of its strong emphasis on psychology with a lack of emphasis on technical skills of voice and movement. Many fine actors, however, have trained at the Actors' Studio; and the Stanislavsky system has had a great impact on American acting styles.

Theatre artists of the past have experimented, struggled, and used all of their emotional resources to bring their art to life. In your study of acting you will continue this experimentation. Just as the art of performing is active and alive, so must be the study of performance. You will learn to act by *doing*.

Through the study of improvisation you have begun to explore your potential as an actor. In your study of acting you will use a written script and develop a character based on the imagination of the playwright. The concepts of relaxing, concentrating, listening, and reacting which you discovered in Chapter 2 will be expanded and developed in your study of acting. The exercises in this chapter are designed to shape and develop your skills in using your body, voice, emotions, and mind.

You discovered in earlier chapters that a relaxed, comfortable body is essential for ease of movement and flexibility onstage. The relaxation exercise that follows helps release tension, warms up muscles, and promotes flexibility.

EXERCISE #10

RELAXING

1. Stand up and shake out your arms, legs, and hands.
2. Take several deep breaths.

3. Drop your chin to your chest.
4. Roll your head from front to side, to back to front again. Relax your neck muscles as much as possible. Let your jaw drop loose.
5. Relax your shoulder muscles and bend, vertebra by vertebra, until you are in a "rag-doll" position.
6. Keeping your knees slightly bent, and your legs relaxed, gently bounce a few times from the waist.
7. Gradually reverse the procedure until you are in a standing position. You should feel relaxed and comfortable.

Note: Do this exercise slowly. Do not strain.

This exercise is a basic warm-up, but it will not help you to relax onstage if you have not prepared and practiced. Again, the best method of relaxing onstage is to feel confident and know that you have something to do.

Finding exactly what to *do* onstage is the topic of the next exercise. In Act II, Scene 2 of Shakespeare's HAMLET, Hamlet tells the players to

> . . . Suit the action to the word, the word to the action, with this special observance, that you o'erstep not the modesty of nature: for anything so o'erdone is from the purpose of playing, whose end both at the first and now, was and is, to hold as 'twere the mirror up to nature: to show virtue her feature, storm her own image, and the very age and body of the time his form and presence. . .

Implicit in Hamlet's instruction to "hold a mirror up to nature" is a command for the actors to *observe* what is around them and reproduce what they observe with truth. A good actor observes and notes the particularity of people and places - the detail that makes one old man sitting on a park bench unique from all other old men sitting on park benches. Train your eye to see past the stereotypes. The actor's observations are a valuable source for things to do onstage.

A nineteenth-century Hamlet — Sarah Bernhardt

A modern Hamlet — Stacy Keach

EXERCISE #11

Observe one particular person sitting, standing, and walking. What does the movement tell you about the person? Why does the person move in a particular way? Does the movement change as the situation changes? After you have studied your subject in some depth, develop a short scene in which you move as your subject moved. Try to convey with your body the essence of the character you have studied.

Examples: You might observe someone doing a particular job - a janitor cleaning the hall, a secretary answering the phone, a painter painting a house.

Imagine reasons for your subject's actions. Perform the scene. Discuss class reactions. Were you successful in conveying the essence of the character? Why or why not?

From your discussion of observation and movement, you will find that your selection of details to present is extremely important. Your choices give the audience clues to character and shape audience response. Developing these clues to character is the subject of the next two exercises.

EXERCISE #12

CHARACTER/ACTION

Select an interesting picture of a person from a magazine or a newspaper. DO NOT select famous or well-known people. Write a brief biography of the person. Choose several actions that this character might do.

Perform the scene showing through your action *who* the character is. Props and costumes can be helpful, but they are not essential.

Evaluate.

EXERCISE #12A

CHARACTER/ACTION/EMOTION

Using the same character you portrayed in Exercise #12, expand your scene to include the emotional life of the character. If your character is an old woman rocking on a porch, show through your actions the character's feelings. If she is rocking energetically, tapping her foot, and humming to herself, perhaps she's remembering a dance she attended. Recreate in your mind details of that dance and bring the character's thoughts alive through actions. Be sure to use specific thoughts and specific actions.

Perform and evaluate.

Inner feelings, desires, and motivations can only be seen through what the actor *does* and *says* as the character. But, conversely, outer actions are shaped by inner feelings and drives. Some actors prepare for a role with the outer elements of costume and make-up and then develop the inner life of the character. Other actors develop the inner life of the character and work outward while still other actors work on inner and outer elements simultaneously. The point is that there is no one correct way of developing a character, but voice, mind, body, and emotions must all work together to create the desired effect. In some productions the actors become "talking heads." Their voices and heads are energetic and full of life, but their bodies are listless and unresponsive. Hamlet was talking about just this problem when he said

> Suit the action to the word,
> the word to the action.

EXERCISE #13

WORD/ACTION

Find actions that are appropriate to the following phrases. Each actor should imagine a reason or motivation for the words and actions. Believe what you are doing and your audience will believe.

Perform and evaluate.

- Help! Let me out.
- There's a bug on the chair. Don't move. I'll get it.
- I'm really sorry.

- I have only two dollars.
- Why do we have to go now?
- Do you want the lights on or off?
- I'm so tired.
- I have to use the phone now.
- Please, I want to talk with you.
- This seat is reserved.
- Where did she go?
- I don't know how to open this.
- Their house is one block that way, turn right, go up the hill, and it's on your left.
- Don't make me spill this.
- My feet are killing me!
- Let's turn to page 83.
- Hurry up! Let's go!
- You're holding it upside down!
- Larry? Are you in there?

Note: Be wary of stereotyped gestures and poses.

EXERCISE #13A

WORD/ACTION/CHANGE

Using the same phrase that you used in Exercise #13, change your actions and the delivery of the phrase to suggest an entirely new meaning.

Words mean what you want them to mean. Often there is a contrast between what is said and what is *meant*, or between what is said and what is *done*. It is up to the actor to control the meaning.

Perform and evaluate. Discuss the changes made.

In your discussion of Exercises #13 and #13A, analyze the relationship of actions and words. Did the actor perform the action, then say the line? Did the actor say the line and then perform the action? Were the lines and action simultaneous? What difference does it make in terms of the message conveyed? What led you to believe some actors and not believe others? As you become more experienced performers and audience members, you will become very sensitive to the whole question of belief. Some actors are able to shed real tears at will, but often the tears are meaningless because there is no true feeling or belief behind the tears. The tears become a trick. An actor with a beautifully articulated voice, speaking Shakespeare's lines with no thought as to what the words *mean* and with no sense of who the character is and what is felt, turns Shakespeare's poetry into noise. An actor's voice, body, mind, and emotions must form a creative unit to express the playwright's words and characters.

Relaxation, observation, action, and emotion have been the focus of the preceding exercises. You have discovered the importance of suiting the word to the action, and you have learned that words mean what you want them to mean. You have concentrated on your own actions and feelings, but now it is time for you to relate to another person. Before beginning Exercise #14, however, a look at some acting terms and guidelines is in order.

VOCABULARY

ad lib - lines or words that are not written by the playwright, but supplied by the actors as needed. Usually used for crowd scenes.

aside - words spoken to the audience, but supposedly not heard by other characters onstage. Widely used in seventeenth and eighteenth century plays, but infrequently used in modern plays.

blocking - the planned pattern of movement of the actor onstage.

business - any action that a character performs onstage, reading a book, mixing a drink, etc. Business should be appropriate to the character and purposeful. It should tell the audience something about the character.

byplay - conversation, gestures, or actions of characters carried on underneath the main action of the play.

character part - a role in a play very different in type (age, physical appearance, etc.) from the actor playing the part.

climax - highest point of action and feeling.

cover - if a line is forgotten the actors move the play forward without any indication that a line has been missed.

cue - word or action signaling entrances, exits, actions, or lines.

cut-off - interrupt line of character speaking before you. Usually indicated in script by dash line.

delivery - manner of speaking.

dialogue - conversation between two or more persons.

drop - used to indicate a line that is too soft to be heard or a line that is forgotten.

hold - usually to indicate "holding for laughs." Actors wait for laughter to begin to subside before continuing. This is to insure that the audience does not miss any of the lines.

intensity - strength, energy, or force of feeling, action, or voice.

lines - words making up a part in a play.

motivation - a need or a reason that impels a character to act in a certain way.

pace - the movement or rate of progress of the play or scene.

pick up cues - to eliminate lapse of time between cues. Cues may be picked up with gestures and actions as well as words.

pointing - to direct attention through emphasis of word or gesture.

project - make your voice audible to the audience.

stage whisper - a low, hushed tone that indicates a whisper, but is projected and heard by the audience.

straight part - a role in a play very similar in type (age, physical appearance, etc.) to the actor playing the part.

timing - to set the tempo and duration of a performance or line delivery.

volume - the degree of loudness and intensity of sound.

Learn these terms and apply them in your acting. The following guidelines will aid you in performing the acting exercises and in preparing a part.

ACTING GUIDELINES

1. Try to relax both physically and mentally.
2. If you're uncomfortable and don't know what to do with your hands, try working with a prop - a book, a pipe, a glass. Make sure the prop is appropriate to the character and the scene. Don't just clutch the prop - use it.
3. Really *listen* to what the other characters say. Don't anticipate your line or merely wait until it's your turn to speak. Listening is an action.
4. Look at and *see* your acting partner.
5. Make your movements purposeful and motivated. Even confused, wandering movements must be motivated.
6. As a general rule, don't move around while someone else is speaking.
7. Know what you're saying and why. If you mean what you say and do and *believe*, your audience will believe.
8. Don't rush your lines or actions.
9. Share the stage. Make sure that you can be seen and heard.
10. Your delivery should sound as if you are saying the words for the first time.

Keep in mind that acting is a cumulative process. You will not be able to do everything perfectly and remember every technique each time you perform, but you will improve as you practice and as you gain experience. The following exercise gives you experience in performing written lines with a partner.

EXERCISE #14

DIALOGUE

Choose an acting partner. Select one of the following dialogues. With your partner plan a situation in which the dialogue might occur. Punctuation marks have been deleted so that you may add your own punctuation to fit the circumstances. Decide who you are and what motivates you. Interpret your lines - discover the surface meaning and the deeper meaning. Listen and react as if you are hearing and seeing for the "first time."

To review, *write* out the following:

1. a situation in which the dialogue will occur.
2. who you are and what motivates you.
3. the literal, surface meaning of the lines.
4. the deeper, hidden meaning of the lines.

Learn the lines. Practice with your partner. Plan actions to suit the words and perform. Evaluate.

Dialogue X	Dialogue Y	Dialogue Z
A. Is it time	A. Hiya	A. Good morning
B. Yeah	B. Hi	B. Hello
A. Great	A. How are things	A. Have you said anything
B. Isn't it	B. Things	B. No
A. Really	A. Things	A. Good
B. Okay	B. Fine	B. Morning
A. Right	A. Everything	
B. Let's go	B. Everything	
	A. See ya later	

EXERCISE #14A

DIALOGUE/BEFORE/AFTER

With your partner decide where you were and what you were doing before the scene. Decide where you are going and what you will do after the scene. Play the scene again showing where you were and what you were doing before the scene began and show where you are going and what you will be doing after the scene ends.

This is a subtle exercise. Stay away from stereotyped gestures such as rubbing your stomach to indicate that you are hungry and must soon eat. Remember — thinking and concentrating must be paired with words and actions.

Perform and evaluate.

LEARNING THE LINES

Ask any beginning theatre student what he or she fears most about acting and inevitably the reply will be "Learning the lines!" Ask any advanced theatre student what the *easiest* part of acting is and the reply will be "Learning the lines!"

Advanced students know that the real work of acting can be accomplished only when they learn the lines so well that they "forget" them. When the actors "forget" the lines, they seem to occur spontaneously as the actors go through the thought processes of the characters. Too often inexperienced actors wait until the performance or dress rehearsal to have their lines learned completely. When this happens, the performance is not creative and not acting. The actor is continually trying to remember the lines instead of concentrating on the character and the action of the play. When lines are learned completely, the actor can experiment with delivery, meaning, and relationships. Movement and gesture can be integrated with thoughts and feelings. Although learning lines requires discipline, desire, and solid effort, the following techniques can help speed the process.

1. Read the entire play several times to see how your character fits into the action.
2. Before learning the lines, know what you are saying and why. If you don't know what a word means, or if you're uncertain about how to pronounce it, use the dictionary.
3. Do not learn line by line or by rote. Learn groups of lines at the same time and then move on to the next group. With each group of lines be able to paraphrase what is being said.

4. Say your lines aloud. Speaking the lines seems to reinforce memory.
5. Use a piece of paper to conceal *your* lines, but reveal your cue line. Say your line, move the paper to check yourself, read your cue making sure that your next line is concealed and proceed down the page.
6. Have a friend cue you when you have the lines almost learned.
7. *Listen* to your cue. Often your line is a response to a question or reply to a statement. If you know what is being said to you, your reply makes sense.
8. Think about what you're saying. Understanding the thought processes of your character instead of memorizing makes remembering much simpler.
9. Get away from your script as soon as possible. Call for a line if you need it, but do not use your script as a crutch.
10. Set aside at least twenty or thirty minutes at one time to work on lines. The time varies, of course, according to the size of your part.

CREATING A CHARACTER

Creating a character who lives through you, but is not you, is one of the joys and mysteries of theatre. How does this creation come about? As a child you "played like" you were someone else, and you really didn't think much about how you did it. As an actor you draw on this childlike ability to believe and imagine, but you also use your intellectual, physical, and emotional resources to bring a character to life. The playwright provides the script and the characters, the director adds interpretation and guidance, and the actor breathes life into the character.

Characters live in plays. To discover who a character is, you must explore the character in the context of the play. There are many different techniques used in this discovery, but a straight-forward approach seems to work best. Your experience in creating an improvised character will be very useful in your development of a particular character from a play.

CHARACTER DEVELOPMENT

1. Read the play several times. Note the time and place. If the play is not a modern one, researching the period may be very helpful.
2. Carefully read the playwright's description of your character.
3. Note the actions and personal habits of your character.
4. Note what your character says about himself or herself. Also note how your character speaks. A character who uses complete sentences is different from a character who uses few words.
5. Do the actions and speech of the character mesh? Or does the character say one thing and do another?
6. How does your character act towards the others? How do the other characters describe and act towards your character?
7. What is the emotional make-up of your character? Is it generally cheerful and enthusiastic or sad and morose? Are these emotions shaped by changing circumstances?
8. What does the play tell you about your character's life before the play begins?
9. Does your character change during the course of the play? Is it a physical, mental, or emotional change?
10. What seems to motivate your character? Does he or she have a specific aim or goal to achieve?

Obviously, the play cannot tell you everything there is to know about your character. The gaps of information and detail must be filled in by the actor. The details that the actor selects must fit the playwright's concept of the character. Often an actor must supply a background - the events and actions that lead to the entrance of the character onstage. Many of these details are added and refined in rehearsals, but a good actor or actress prepares the part thoughtfully and doesn't expect the director to contribute every aspect of characterization.

The following exercises are designed to give you practice in creating a character.

EXERCISE #15

CHARACTER

In our society people are often defined by what they do. Choose an occupation - dentistry, engineering, saleswork, teaching, practicing law, etc. - with which you are familiar. On a piece of paper write down the occupation, select an age or age range (thirty-five to forty), and write a sentence or phrase that your character might say. For example: "We're overbudget on the Harris Proposal. We'll have to narrow the scope of the design."

Divide into groups of three or four. Decide on a place where your characters might logically be together - in an elevator, waiting in line at the bank, in a coffee shop, at a cocktail party, etc.

Perform a short scene in which your characters come together. Evaluate. Did the characters seem one-dimensional? Why?

EXERCISE #15A

CHARACTER

Write a background for your character. Give your character a distinctive walk, gesture, or personal trait. Your observation skills can be very useful here. Try using a prop or costume piece. Decide how your character feels about talking with others - shy, gregarious, loud, etc.

Perform the scene again. What changes were apparent?

EXERCISE #15B

CHARACTER

Continue to develop your character by adding physical, emotional, and mental details. Make sure the details are believable. Don't overdo.

Now - play the scene again, but with another important addition. Give your character *motivation*. For example, if the scene is in an elevator, the engineer might be concentrating on the talk that he or she will deliver in a few minutes. The engineer is trying to read the notes of the talk. The dentist, who is extremely outgoing, wants to tell the engineer about the latest advances in root canal surgery.

Perform and evaluate. How have the characters and the scenes changed?

Rehearsing and performing a one-act play will enable you to put these exercises to the test in a real theatre situation.

REHEARSAL

Rehearsal time, when used effectively, can be very rewarding. At rehearsals the actors explore character relationships, movement, voice techniques, and various interpretations. There is never only one way of presenting a play, but in rehearsals the director and the cast work together to find the appropriate choices for their production. If you are working on a one-act play with other members of your class, set up a rehearsal schedule and rehearsal objectives. Objectives will vary according to the play and the actors, but working from the general to the specific is usually best. The first rehearsal objective might include blocking the overall movement of the play, and later objectives might include timing and polishing delivery and business. Several dress rehearsals simulating the actual performance are necessary before presenting the play in front of an audience.

PERFORMANCE

If your rehearsal time has been productive and well spent, your performance will reflect this. Stage fright is natural and a sign of energy and excitement, but extreme nervousness and genuine fright are often caused by inadequate preparation. The performance is not the time to worry about lines or if the prop is in the right place. Attention to detail *before* the play begins can make your performance experience much happier.

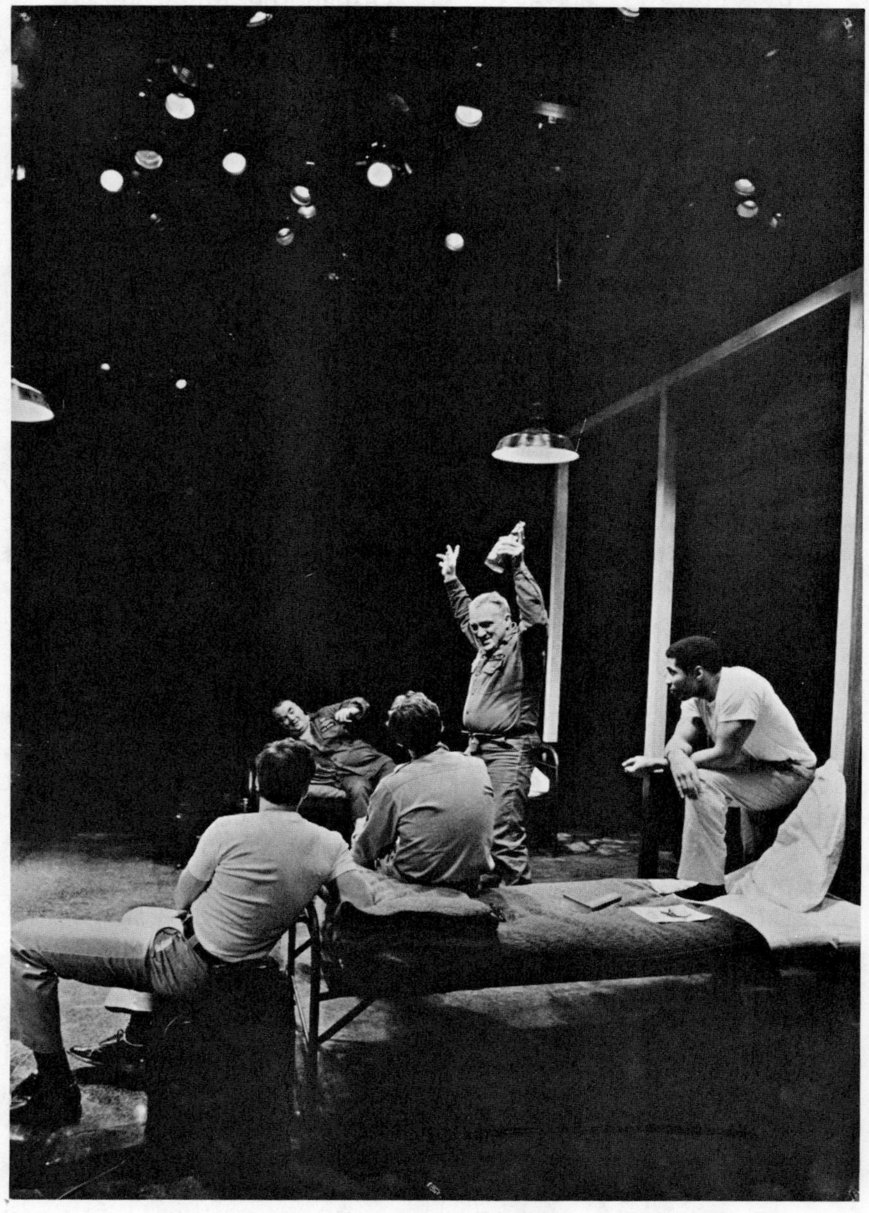

Observe how *focus* is achieved through stage position in the scene above. What relationships and character details are being presented?

If your preparation has been thorough and your performance is going well, be aware of the "How am I doing?" syndrome. This syndrome is asking yourself onstage, while you're supposed to be in character, "How am I doing?" or trying to check your effect as an actor on the audience. If you do this, it means you are breaking concentration and losing sight of your character. Of course, you must retain a realization that you are acting, and you must be aware of any changes or adjustments that you must make as an actor such as raising your voice or altering blocking to clear another actor. If you deliver a line well and the audience laughs appreciatively, don't take time to pat yourself on the back or grin at the response. Breaking the illusion of theatrical reality can have a devastating effect on audience response. If you allow yourself to remain open to the audience's response, you will note that rushed lines and actions delivered by ill-prepared actors make an audience restless and inattentive, but a well-timed, believable scene or play presented by confident actors will have quite the opposite effect.

In acting there is no substitute for hard work and a willingness to share yourself with an audience. All the hard work, however, is amply rewarded by the sheer joy of performance and the celebration of life that theatre and acting affirm. As an actor you will experience the feelings that all actors have in common, even the misguided Bottom, that acting is profoundly human, richly generous, and life enhancing.

QUESTIONS FOR REVIEW AND DISCUSSION

1. What aspects of acting does Shakespeare parody in the scene from A MIDSUMMER NIGHT'S DREAM?
2. How can observation enhance your acting ability?
3. Why is it important to know where a character has been before he or she steps onstage?
4. How is speaking written lines different from improvising your own lines?
5. What are some useful techniques to aid you in learning lines? Do you have any personal techniques that you use?
6. List the steps in creating a character.

VOCABULARY

See pages 39–41.

SUGGESTIONS

- Read and report on AN ACTOR PREPARES or BUILDING A CHARACTER by Constantin Stanislavsky.
- See a play and analyze the actors' techniques in character portrayal.
- Act in school plays, assemblies, scenes for English class, etc. The best training is to get in front of an audience and learn by doing.
- Invite a professional actor to talk to your class about the acting profession
- First, read the "Costume" section of chapter 6. Then, keep a Clothing Journal for one week. Note down each day what you wore (color, specific garments) and then describe how you felt on each day, and how others reacted to what you wore. Are you more comfortable in certain clothes and certain colors? How does clothing (costuming) influence the way you act and feel?

Chapter 4.

Oral Interpretation

Bard, wandering minstrel, troubadour, and storyteller are a few of the names for people who shaped the tradition of oral communication and interpretation. This tradition not only provided artistic enjoyment, but it also was a way of recording historical events, legends, and personal heritage. Before the advent of the printing press and before writing was widely known and used, people, through word of mouth, kept their heritage alive from one generation to the next. Today, we have no real need for this type of history — except in some cultures — but we do have a desire for such communication and interpretation.

Oral interpretation is a very special form of communication. It is the art of bringing literature to life through the medium of an interpreter. Although vocal interpretation is a performing art, an interpreter is not an actor. Unlike the actor who represents, the interpreter suggests. Unlike the reader who conveys only information, the sense of the material, the interpreter not only conveys the sense, but the sensibility of the literature as well.

From this definition we see that oral interpretation has three requirements:

1) an interpreter who analyzes the
2) literature - stories, poems, letters, biographies, essays, song lyrics, newspaper articles, plays, etc.

and conveys it to an

3) audience

Literature consists of words which convey mental pictures or images, express ideas, and represent emotions. The interpreters analyze the literature, discover its meaning, and through their interpretation convey its ideas, images, and emotions to the audience. The audience experiences the literature and responds to it. The response is communicated back to the interpreters who use the response to enrich their presentation of the literature.

The interpreter is fortunate in that this communication process is a part of our culture. Listening to stories and telling stories is a part of our daily life. Even the "You'll never believe what happened to me on the way to school. . . !" story is a performance. The speaker suggests characters, images, and emotions with voice and body. Effective storytelling or effective oral interpretation depends to a great extent upon the interpreter's desire to communicate. The interpreter must want to share the literature or story with the audience. The interpreter must care about the material and care enough to present it clearly. The following exercises illustrate the communication process and the problem of clarity. In Exercise 16, an improvised story has been substituted for the literature, but the process remains the same.

EXERCISE #16

STORYTELLING

Sit in a circle on the floor or form your chairs in a circle. Appoint a leader. The leader chooses a person to begin the story using one of the sentences listed below or any other sentence. The first person adds to the sentence, thus beginning a story. At some moment - usually a crucial one - the leader points to another person who continues the story. Continue until everyone has had a chance to participate, including the leader.

Listen closely so that you may pick up the threads of the story at any moment. Try to hold the attention of the audience not only with the plot of the story, but with your voice and body as well.

Sample Beginning Sentences:

1. You know what a coward he is especially when it's dark. And believe me, it was the blackest night . . .
2. Now don't let the fact that she was eighty-four fool you . . .

3. Talk about stupid things! I remember, I was just a little kid . . .
4. Normally there isn't any crime in our area so . . .

EXERCISE #17

WHISPER

Form a circle. The teacher or group leader begins by writing down one or two sentences which are not shown to anyone else. The leader then whispers the sentences in the ear of the person on the left. The person on the left then whispers the sentences to the person on his or her left, and so on around the circle. The person at the end says the sentences aloud then reads the original sentences which the leader wrote down. Are the sentences the same? If they're not, what does this mean in terms of effective communication?

Many factors come between the interpreter and the audience making the message unclear or garbled. Weak projection, slurred words, monotone delivery, speech patterns, distracting body movements, no eye contact, outside noise, a hot or cold room, or inattentive, whispering audience members are just some of the factors that can inhibit effective oral communication and interpretation. In this chapter you will work on correcting some of the problems you have, and you will improve your positive qualities. Keep in mind that you have been communicating ever since you were born. You are not learning a completely new skill. You are merely refining, polishing, and extending the skills you already have.

From the moment of birth,you have been actively using your voice and breathing quite nicely. When you need to speak or to have enough breath to speak, somehow you manage. Breathing and speaking for oral interpretation, however, require conscious control. The voice is the interpreter's greatest physical asset. If not used properly, however, the voice can be the interpreter's greatest liability. "Dija gi tha? Ya know wha ah mean? Les' go on!" Sloppy, slurred speech detracts from the presentation of the literature and impairs the communication process. After a sincere desire to communicate, the most important requirement for oral interpretation is a clear, flexible voice. The following exercise gives you practice in forming consonants - the chief villains of sloppy speaking.

EXERCISE #18

CLARITY

Practice saying the following sentences. Make sure words are clear and distinct. Practice a few times overdoing the distinctness, then practice using a natural delivery.

If you find you have difficulty with a particular consonant such as "hissing s's" or "l's," practice will help remedy the problem.

(B) Bungling bugler Bob bugled backward before Back Bay's boring battle.

(C) Curious cats cause countless catastrophes.

(D) Did Dave and Doug drink drams or drops during dinner?

(F) Four fat, frightened fish floundered frantically from five fast fishermen.

(G) "Good grief," groaned Greta, "George gargled glucose gleefully!"

(H) Hordes of hapless hippies hurried hysterically home.

(J) Jerry and Joan judiciously joined Judge Jacobs' jury.

(K) King Karl's kind kiss kindled kinship in Katherine's Korean kin.

(L) Lovely Lily Langtry laughed liltingly and liberally at Lieutenant Larry's lilliputian limbs.

(M) Miniature, militant moles madly manufactured massive, mysterious molecules.

(N) Ninety nomads nibbled narrow noodles nightly.

(P) Plump Patricia pounced on poor Paul's porridge.

(Q) Quaint Quigley quickly questioned the Queen's quarrelsome quartet.

(R) "Reasonable Roger recited random riddles," roared Rosa.

(S) Six, sick snakes slithered silently across the slippery slope.

(T) Twenty, two-ton toy tanks trundled timidly through the tiny, Transylvanian town.

(V) Various, vocal vagrants vacillated vainly.

(W) While Wanda Worm wiggled weakly west, Walter Worm waited wanly.

(Y) Young, yoked yaks from yonder Yucatan yodelled at Yorkshire's yellow-bellied yeoman.

(Z) Zounds! Zillions of zany zeppelins zigzagged zealously over Zululand's zesty zebras.

Correct *articulation*, clear and distinct formation of words, must also include correct *pronunciation*. If you find that you do not know how to pronounce a word, look it up in the dictionary. But good speaking is not just clear articulation and correct pronunciations. Proper *phrasing* and *emphasis* are necessary to make words meaningful. A phrase is a group of words that makes up one thought. Phrasing, then, is breaking a piece of literature into thoughts. You discover how to phrase and how to emphasize by discovering meaning. Look at Exercise #18 again. If all words in each sentence were said with the same force, emphasized equally, the sentences would be unclear. Some words are more important than others and deserve more emphasis. For example, the sentence

Curious cats cause countless catastrophes.

Try emphasizing every word with the same degree of loudness and force. Now, say the sentence emphasizing the underlined words.

Curious <u>cats</u> <u>cause</u> countless <u>catastrophes</u>.

What does the sentence mean? Say the sentence again only this time emphasize these underlined words.

<u>Curious</u> cats <u>cause</u> <u>countless</u> catastrophes.

There is a shift of meaning as the emphasis on words shifts. As an interpreter you manipulate meaning by manipulating your voice to suggest a particular interpretation. Underlining emphasized words is a visual aid to help you interpret the selection correctly. The interpreter also uses a slash mark (/) to indicate where the thought changes. For example,

Curious cats cause countless catastrophes/unlike dogs who are devoted, domestic darlings.

Vary phrasing and emphasis in the following sentence to change the meaning.

Woman without her man is nothing.

The sentence may be read as: Woman without her man (pause) is nothing; or as: Woman, without her, man is nothing.

The meaning then depends upon the interpreter's ability to use the voice with flexibility to achieve the proper effect. Someone who speaks in a monotone is someone who speaks constantly with the same pitch. In other words, the highness or lowness of the voice does not vary. Inflecting the voice is necessary to indicate subtleties of meaning. Inflection is changing the pitch of the voice on a sound. You may have a rising inflection ↗, a falling inflection ↘, or a curved inflection ∼. Rate, or the speed at which you speak, also affects meaning. It takes *time* to say whole words clearly and with meaning. Your audience also needs time to absorb the words and their meanings. Practice the following inflection exercise and experiment with different rates.

↗Question	↘Statement	∼ Sarcasm or irony
Really?	Really.	Really.
Really? May we go?	Really. I don't want to leave.	Really, you look great. (Means just the opposite.)

The same pitch combined with unvaried emphasis and identical volume can be quite monotonous, and the meaning of the selection is lost.

The following exercise gives you practice in phrasing, rate, emphasis, volume, pitch, and inflection.

EXERCISE #19

SHOTT-KNOTT

Read the following selection. Lightly pencil in where thought groups change or where you would pause to make the meaning clear. Use a slash (/) line. Lightly underline the words you should emphasize.

The meaning is only made clear in this selection by careful phrasing, subtle emphasis, and inflection. You may have to practice several times before you succeed.

Present to the class. Evaluate. Was the meaning communicated?

THE SHOTT-KNOTT MURDER MYSTERY.

Ned Knott was shot
and Sam Shott was not.
So it is better to be Shott
than Knott.

Some say Knott
was not shot.
But Shott says
he shot Knott.
Either the shot Shott shot at Knott
was not shot,
or Knott was shot.

If the shot Shott shot shot Knott,
Knott was shot.
But if the shot Shott shot shot Shott,
then Shott was shot,
not Knott.

However, the shot Shott shot shot not Shott -
but Knott.

Effective interpretation not only requires a sincere desire to communicate; a clear, flexible voice with proper articulation, pronounciation, phrasing, emphasis, and pitch; but interpretation also requires an ability to "see" and experience the images present in literature. This "seeing" which involves all the senses is essential to the interpreter's craft. An interpreter who "sees" knows that words are symbols for the richness

Energy, vitality, a willingness to communicate, and "seeing" the images of literature are conveyed by these interpreters.

and complexities of life - its sights, scents, sounds, and textures. The interpreter should allow the voice and body to respond to the images in literature. The response will be communicated to the audience and the audience will experience the richness of the literature. Just as the audience believes an actor who *believes*, the audience is able to *see* what the interpreter *sees*. Use the next exercise to practice your response to images.

EXERCISE #20

IMAGE/RESPONSE

Say the following phrases aloud. Try to picture the image evoked by each phrase. Allow your voice and body to respond to the image. Try to convey your response to the audience.

Note the onomatopoetic words - the sound of the word imitates the meaning.

Present and evaluate.

a. deep-fried to a crispy, golden brown
b. the bees buzzed over the fragrant flowers
c. a hot, scratchy wool sweater
d. the screech of fingernails scraping across a blackboard
e. clean, crisp cotton sheets
f. fresh, cool rains and rich soil
g. ice clinking in a frosty glass
h. tight, stiff leather shoes
i. sparks flying from a crackling wood fire
j. a long, cool shower after a sizzling summer day
k. a juicy, grilled hotdog covered with melted cheese and bacon
l. the snake hissed at the fat, green toad

Another block to clear speaking and effective communication is the speech pattern. This problem is most evident in rhyming poetry and is called a "sing-song" pattern, but it also occurs in prose. An interpreter is said to have a speech pattern when rate (relative slowness or speed of speech), volume, pitch, and emphasis follow the same pattern throughout the selection regardless of *meaning*. Since meaning is essential to effective interpretation, an understanding of the process of determining meaning is necessary. The process requires a step-by-step progression, but when used faithfully the discovery of meaning is clarified. Just as there are many different ways of interpreting a character there are also many different interpretations of literature. *Your* interpretation when based on the foundation of the literature is just as valid as that of anyone else.

Analysis Process - Discovery of Meaning

1. Read the title and the selection aloud. Experience the material sensuously. Allow yourself to "feel" the words. What is your immediate emotional response to the literature?
2. Again, read the selection aloud. What is being said? Is there a story? a description? a character or characters?
3. Look at the selection again. Are there key words or recurring images? What feelings are expressed? What is the predominant mood or feeling of the selection? Does the author have a particular attitude toward the material?
4. Does your emotional response to the material coincide with your intellectual response? If the responses are quite different, another look at the material is in order.
5. Paraphrase (restate in your own words) the selection. Check your paraphrase with the material.
6. Read the selection aloud. Divide into thought groups with a slash line, and underline emphasized words.
7. Practice the selection. Listen to yourself and have others listen to you. Integrate your emotional and intellectual responses with your voice and body.
8. Present and evaluate. Was the meaning of the selection clear? Was the "feeling" of the selection conveyed?

The following exercise will give you practice with the problems of meaning and speech pattern.

EXERCISE #21

SPEECH PATTERN

Practice the following selections until you are able to convey the meaning and feeling of the piece without a "sing-song" delivery.

Use the process above to determine the sound of the piece

and its sense and sensibility. Lightly pencil in slash lines for phrasing and underline for emphasis.

Present and evaluate.

a. Once upon a midnight dreary, while
I pondered, weak
and weary,
Over many a quaint and curious volume of forgotten
lore -
While I nodded, nearly napping, suddenly there came
a tapping,
As of someone gently rapping, rapping at my
chamber door.
" 'Tis some visitor," I muttered, "tapping at my
chamber door -
Only this and nothing more."

"The Raven"
Edgar Allen Poe

b. Sunset and evening star,
And one clear call for me!
And may there be no moaning of the bar,
When I put out to sea.

"Crossing the Bar"
Alfred, Lord Tennyson

c. It is an ancient Mariner
And he stoppeth one of three,
- "By thy long gray beard and glittering eye,
Now wherefore stopp'st thou me?
The Bridegroom's doors are opened wide,
And I am next of kin;
The guests are met, the feast is set:
May'st hear the merry din."

"The Rime of the Ancient Mariner"
Samuel Taylor Coleridge

d. There was an old man with a beard,
Who said: "It's just as I feared -
Two owls and a Hen
Four larks and a Wren
Have all built their nest in my beard."

Book of Nonsense
Edmund Lear

Understanding your material and your medium involves several levels of interpretation.

1) Physical

   A clear, flexible voice with knowledge of vocal techniques such as volume, articulation, pronunciation, pitch, phrasing, emphasis, rate, inflection, and a responsive body.

2) Emotional

   A genuine desire to communicate, and an openness to the sensibility of the material, and a willingness to respond freely to the sense images.

3) Intellectual

   An analytical ability to understand the sense of the material, the plot, the literal and figurative meaning of the words, and the ideas presented.

All of these levels must be present for effective interpretation and communication to occur. The physical level can be developed by practice and training. Good vocal habits must be a part of your life outside of class as well as inside. The emotional level is more elusive. The base of your emotional understanding will be formed by allowing yourself to experience the literature and by genuinely wanting to communicate. The intellectual level can be developed through study and work on skills. Proper balance of these three levels is extremely important. Different literature will require different balances; the emotional might be more important in some selections, the intellectual in others, and a flexible voice in still others. The interpreter must find the appropriate balance for each selection.

Before practicing what you have learned, some guidelines for oral presentation must be established.

GUIDELINES FOR ORAL PRESENTATION

1. Choose material that interests you and which you want to share.
2. Analyze the material using the steps provided in this chapter.
3. Practice the material. If possible, use a tape recorder. Practice in front of your family and friends.
4. Type or clearly print your selection either on note cards or paper. If paper, back the paper with stiff cardboard so that it will not flutter. Make two copies. Keep one at school and one at home.
5. Prepare a brief introduction to the selection. In your introduction you set the mood for the presentation. Make sure your introduction is appropriate. DO NOT MEMORIZE the introduction. *Know* what you are going to say and speak directly and simply to the audience.
6. When you are called to present the selection, walk to the appointed place with good posture, look at your audience, introduce the selection, pause, and then begin the selection. A pause and perhaps a shift in body position is necessary to signal the transition between introduction and presentation.
7. If you stand during the performance, or if you are seated on a stool, use good posture. Good posture is important not only in terms of proper breathing, but also aesthetically.
8. Hold your selection approximately at chest level. It should be low enough not to obscure your face and high enough to be seen without lowering your head and obscuring your expression. And, of course, the selection should not be held stiffly. It moves with you in response to the demands of the presentation.
9. Do not make any distracting physical gestures, e.g., playing with your hair, standing on one leg, etc. Because you are the primary focus, any physical movement becomes extremely heightened. By all means, allow yourself to

relate to the material, but any movement should be appropriate. "Suit the action to the word, the word to the action."

10. Make eye contact with your audience during the presentation. Your primary purpose is to share the selection with them. Your copy of the material should be a guide only. Remember, you're an interpreter, not a reader. More time should be spent looking at the audience than looking at the paper.
11. When you finish, pause, and then walk to your chair.

EXERCISE #22

PRACTICE SELECTION

Choose one of the following selections. Interpret the selection using all three levels of understanding - the physical, the emotional, and the intellectual.

See the images. If you are interpreting the lines from a play, suggest the character - do not try to become the character.

Copy and back the selection with stiff paper. Practice.

Present and evaluate.

a. During the whole of a dull, dark, and soundless day in the autumn of the year, when the clouds hung oppressively low in the heavens, I had been passing alone on horseback, through a singularly dreary tract of country; and at length found myself, as the shades of the evening drew on, within view of the melancholy House of Usher.

"The Fall of the House of Usher"
Edgar Allan Poe

b. Five years have passed; five summers with
the length of five long winters! and again
I hear these waters, rolling from their
Mountain springs with a soft inland
Murmer. Once again do
I behold these steep and lofty cliffs,
That on a wild secluded scene impress
Thoughts of more deep seclusion; and connect
The landscape with the quiet of the sky.

"Lines"
William Wordsworth

c. The whole forest was peopled with frightened sounds - the creaking of the trees, the howling of wild beasts, and the yell of Indians; while sometimes the wind tolled like a distant church bell, and sometimes gave a broad roar around the traveller, as if all Nature were laughing him to scorn.

"Young Goodman Brown"
Nathaniel Hawthorne

d. They were men. They crept upon their hands and knees. They used their hands only, dragging their legs. They used their knees only, their arms hanging idly at their sides. They strove to rise to their feet, but fell prone in the attempt. They did nothing naturally and nothing alike, save only to advance foot by foot in the same direction. They came by dozens and by hundreds; as far on either hand as one could see in the deepening gloom they extended and the black wood behind them appeared to be inexhaustible.

"Chickamauga"
Ambrose Bierce

e. Whoever has made a voyage up the Hudson must remember the Kaatskill Mountains. They are a dismembered branch of the great Appalachian family, and are seen away to the west of the river, swelling up to a noble height, and lording it over the surrounding country. Every change of season, every change of weather, indeed every hour of the day, produces some change in the magical hues and shapes of the mountains, and they are regarded by all the good wives, far and near, as perfect barometers.

"Rip Van Winkle"
Washington Irving

f. No one who had ever seen Catherine Morland in her infancy would have supposed her born to be an heroine. Her situation in life, the character of her father and mother, her own person and disposition were all equally against her. . . . She had a thin awkward figure, a sallow skin without colour, dark lank hair, and strong features; . . . She was fond of all boys' play and greatly preferred cricket, not merely to dolls, but to the more heroic enjoyments of infancy, nursing a dormouse, feeding a canary-bird, or watering a rosebush. . . . She never could learn or understand anything before she was taught, and sometimes not even then, for she was often inattentive, and occasionally stupid.

"Northanger Abbey"
Jane Austen

g. They sailed to the western seas, they did -
To a land all covered with trees:
And they bought an owl, and a useful cart,
And a pound of rice, and a cranberry tart,
And a hive of silvery bees;
And they bought a pig, and some green jackdaws,
And a lovely monkey with lollipop paws,
And seventeen bags of edelweiss tea,
And forty bottles of rin-bo-ree,
And no end of Stilton cheese.

"The Jumblies"
Lewis Carroll

h. The sea is calm tonight.
The tide is full, the moon lies fair
Upon the straits; - on the French coast the light
Gleams and is gone; the cliffs of England stand
Glimmering and vast out in the tranquil bay.

"Dover Beach"
Matthew Arnold

i. Come, my friends,
'Tis not too late to seek a newer world:
Push off and sitting well in order smite
The sounding furrows; for my purpose holds
To sail beyond the sunset, and the baths
Of all the western stars until I die.

"Ulysses"
Alfred, Lord Tennyson

j. Prospero: Our revels now are ended. These our actors
(as I foretold you) were all spirits, and
Are melted into air, into thin air,
And like the baseless fabric of this vision,
The cloud-capp'd towers, the gorgeous palaces,
The solemn temples, the great globe itself,
Yea, all which it inherit, shall dissolve,

And like this insubstantial pageant faded
Leave not a rack behind. We are such stuff
As dreams are made on; and our little life
Is rounded with a sleep.

The Tempest
William Shakespeare

You are ready now to prepare and present selections of your own choice. When choosing material for oral interpretation find something that you want to share. Select material that is appropriate for your audience. In your search for material, look for literature with emotional power, vivid images, interesting characters, exciting ideas, and vital language.

Often material has to be "cut" to fit into a time limit. Cuts should be made only after you have analyzed the material. Mark all the parts that are essential to the selection, and then "cut out" all the other parts. Read the material through to make sure it flows smoothly and coherently. Several revisions may be necessary before you achieve a "cutting" which retains the integrity of the whole.

Some suggested presentations are as follows:

1) poem, story, essay, etc. by one author
2) several poems of one author
3) several poems of different authors centered around a theme
4) combinations of literature - poems, stories, essays, letters, newspaper articles, etc. centered around a theme. For example: anti-war
   prejudice
   love
   friendship
   nature
   (Focus the theme on one aspect such as "loss of love" or "preservation of natural beauty")
5) combinations of literature focusing on a particular mood or feeling. For example: melancholy
   joy
   anger

6) different material focused on a particular person or event. Use newspaper articles, biographies, histories, essays, poems, etc. For example:

Vietnam War
Women's Movement
Abraham Lincoln

(Again, focus on one aspect)

Use your imagination to develop compelling interpretation presentations.

The art of making literature come alive in all its richness and complexity is one of the most satisfying experiences for interpreter and audience. You will become a part of the oral tradition - bard, wandering minstrel, troubadour, story teller, interpreter - and realize the joy of sharing a common experience.

QUESTIONS FOR REVIEW AND DISCUSSION

1. Discuss how oral interpretation is different from acting. How is it similar?
2. What are the requirements of oral interpretation?
3. What is meant by the term "seeing" the words?
4. What are the three levels of understanding?
5. Why is it important to analyze the selection before presenting it? What is the sequence of steps in analyzing a selection?

VOCABULARY

oral interpretation	phrasing	inflection
articulation	emphasis	speech pattern
pronunciation	pitch	onomatopoetic
	rate	

SUGGESTIONS

- Listen to recordings of poets reading their own work. Evaluate. Record your interpretations of the work and compare the two.
- Present material written by English classes or the creative writing club.
- Present children's stories to the kindergarten and first-grade students.

Chapter 5

Reader's Theatre

Reader's Theatre, a part of the oral tradition that fostered bards, troubadours, and storytellers, is a combination of oral interpretation and theatre. It is a performing art involving two or more interpreters sharing literature with an audience.

Although the name "Reader's" Theatre suggests a limited image of a group reading, the scope of Reader's Theatre is virtually limitless embracing all kinds of literature and a variety of performance techniques. In Reader's Theatre, as in Oral Interpretation, interpreters present literature using both voice and body to make the material come alive for an audience. Unlike the actor in conventional theatre, the interpreter does not become the character, but suggests the character through vocal and physical techniques. Reader's Theatre fills a need not met by oral interpretation or theatre by providing a means of sharing material other than plays, furnishing opportunities for group creativity as opposed to the individual performance in oral interpretation, and Reader's Theatre provides a unique experience for the audience.

Although original scripts for Reader's Theatre are written and performed, most Reader's Theatre scripts are adapted from novels, short stories, poems, biographies, essays, letters, magazines, newspaper articles, speeches, plays, and history. Because of the richness and variety of material available for Reader's Theatre presentations, the techniques used for performing scripts are also rich and varied. Each script has its own special challenges and needs. There are, however, a few basic principles which apply to most Reader's Theatre performances. Leslie Irene Coger and Melvin White, in their READER'S THEATRE HANDBOOK, have been instrumental in shaping understanding of this medium and its principles. The principles are not rigid, but may be adapted as the requirements of the material change.

BASIC PRINCIPLES

1. The primary objective of Reader's Theatre is to share literature with an audience.
2. Reader's Theatre is primarily presentational, not representational. Interpreters present characters, ideas, and actions through vocal and physical suggestion instead of representing them as in a play. The interpreter "sees" the images and conveys this vision to the audience.
3. Interpreters often play several parts in one performance. One or several narrators may be used to speak directly to the audience and make transitions.
4. Movement is usually limited; the amount of movement depends upon the material. For example, a children's story may require more movement than a poem by Robert Frost.
5. Often settings, properties, costumes, and make-up are suggested or imagined, but their use depends upon the requirements of the literature. Emphasis should remain on the literature rather than on secondary elements. If costumes serve the literature and make the experience richer, then costumes should be used.
6. Lighting, sound, and music all may be used to enhance a performance.
7. Interpreters may interact directly with each other onstage as in a play; or they may present the material while facing out to the audience and "placing" the other characters out in the audience instead of onstage. (Ill. 5-1)

   The interpreters in #1 are using onstage focus. They are making direct eye contact. In #2 the interpreters are still relating, but the focus and point of contact have been shifted to offstage. In #3 the interpreters are using a combination of onstage and offstage focus. Often it is best to maintain one focus throughout the presentation. However, if one interpreter is playing both a character and a narrator, the interpreter may use onstage focus as the character and offstage focus as the narrator. In this way,

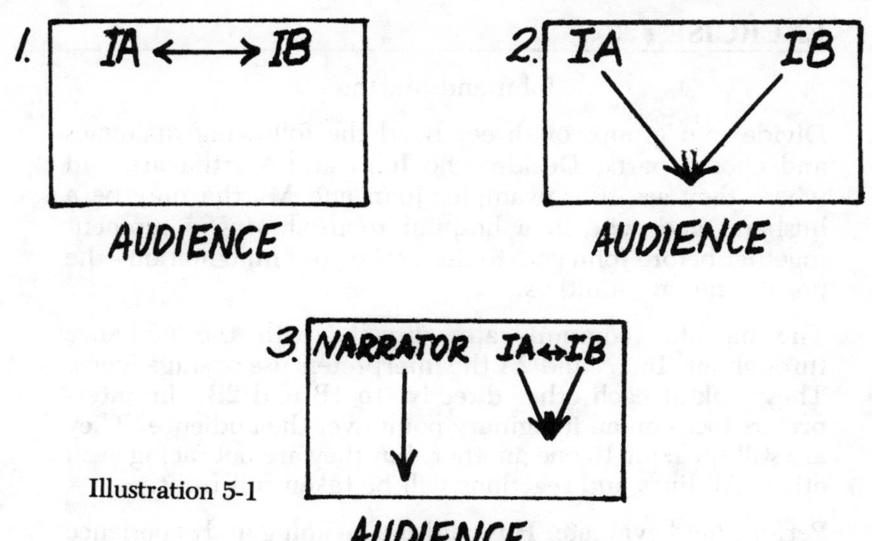

Illustration 5-1

the audience will see that there are clearly two distinct characters.

8. Scripts may be carried by interpreters, or the interpreters may work without scripts. Lines must be learned, however, as scripts are only a guide. If scripts are used, they should become an integral part of the performance. (Note Alice's use of the script in "Alice's Jabberwocky" on page 75 ff.). Scripts convey an authority to the interpreter and a feeling that the literature is concretely present, but again, the use of scripts depends upon the requirements of the literature. Scripts should be backed with stiff paper, kept in folders or books, or prepared in an attractive manner. Crumpled, stapled sheets of paper are distracting and unattractive.

Offstage and onstage focus techniques and voice flexibility are explored in the following exercise. In this exercise you will be able to draw upon your acting skills.

EXERCISE #23

"John and Martha"

Divide into groups of three. Read the following dialogues and choose parts. Decide who John and Martha are and where they are. For example, John and Martha may be a husband and wife in a hospital room sharing a moment together before John goes to sleep. Use your imagination - the possibilities are limitless.

The narrator communicates directly with the audience throughout. In 1A and 2A the interpreters use onstage focus. They look at each other directly. In 1B and 2B, the interpreters focus on an imaginary point over the audience. They are still speaking to one another, but they are not facing each other. All lines and reactions will be taken full front.

Perform and evaluate. How did the meaning and experience of the dialogue change when the focus was changed? Was it difficult to maintain concentration on an imaginary point in space? Were you able to use your voice and body to suggest subtle alterations of moods? Did you listen and react? What other acting skills were you able to employ? How might you improve?

1A - Onstage Focus

Narrator: She whispered
She: John
Narrator: He murmured
He: Martha
Narrator: She breathed
She: John
Narrator: He moaned
He: Martha
Narrator: She rasped
She: John
Narrator: He croaked
He: Martha

1B - Offstage Focus

Use the same dialogue as 1A, but switch to offstage focus. Martha and John are still speaking to one another, but their physical position has shifted.

2A - Onstage Focus

Narrator: She said
She: Reginald
Narrator: He replied

2B - Offstage Focus.

Same as above.

He: Margaret
Narrator: She questioned
She: Reginald
Narrator: He answered
He: Margaret
Narrator: She shouted
She: Reginald
Narrator: He echoed
He: Margaret

Even a simple dialogue can be exciting and entertaining if you present the material dynamically and vividly. But all of us like to tell and hear stories. The following exercise will enable you to continue to use your acting skills in exploring and creating Reader's Theatre.

EXERCISE #24

"Storytelling"

Divide into groups of three to five people. Choose one of the familiar stories listed below or make up an original story. Your challenge is to "tell" the story in the most effective, dramatic way.

1. Write out a plot outline.
2. Decide on a point-of-view. Will you tell the story from the point-of-view of an omniscient narrator, a character, or a character/narrator? The choice you make will shape how the story is experienced by the audience. For example, "The Three Little Pigs" could be told from the point-of-view of the wolf, the pigs, or a narrator outside the action.
3. Decide on a focus. Will the characters use onstage or offstage focus? Keep in mind that if the characters use a combination of focus the effect might be confusing to the audience. The narrator, of course, addresses the audience directly.
4. Cast the narrator and characters. Improvise dialogue. One interpreter may play several parts by changing voice and physical characteristics.
5. Practice a few times. Work out stage positions and movement which reflect the "feeling" of the story.

6. Present and evaluate. Did the interpreters genuinely want to share the story? Was the focus clear? Were the interpreters energetic? Did the story flow smoothly with the narrator making transitions?

SUGGESTED STORIES: "Three Little Pigs"
"Little Red Riding Hood"
"Hansel and Gretel"
"Rumplestiltskin"

Feel free to change the stories or update them.

The preceding exercises introduce the basic techniques of Reader's Theatre. As you discovered, many of the techniques and skills you learned in improvisation, acting, and oral interpretation provide a basis for performing Reader's Theatre. However, performing is just one aspect of the process. Adapting and compiling your own scripts,which you can then perform,is one of the most exciting features of Reader's Theatre.

Selecting suitable literature is the first step in the process of creating your own adaptation. All literary sources are available, but certain material works especially well. Find material that excites you and which is appropriate for your audience. Literature rich in interesting characters, lively language, emotional and intellectual power, and vivid images makes for compelling Reader's Theatre. The most important requirement, however, is that *you* find the material interesting and enjoyable. If you enjoy the material, the chances are good that your audience will enjoy the presentation as well.

The second step in creating your own Reader's Theatre presentation is adapting the material. The literature must be analyzed and understood completely. Use the analysis process provided in Chapter 4, Oral Interpretation. After analyzing the material,you will be ready to make decisions concerning point-of-view, focus, narrators, and characters. The needs of the literature often dictate these decisions, but if you are compiling a script from several sources,you must form decisions based on your analysis and understanding of the material. "Cutting" the material to fit your theme requires careful thought and planning. It is often not possible because of time limits to present an entire short story, thus you have to "cut" the story for performance. If you are presenting a Reader's Theatre performance around a theme such as "First Love," you may draw material from poetry, novels, songs, and letters to form a complete presentation. Careful selection of materials and transitions must be made so that the presentation flows smoothly. Revisions are often necessary before the final script is ready for performance. Read your script aloud - listen to how it *sounds*, as well as to what it says.

In the following script, adapted from Lewis Carroll's novel ALICE IN WONDERLAND and his poem "Jabberwocky," two literary forms have been joined to form a performance piece for Reader's Theatre. "Jabberwocky" is a nonsense poem, but when the poem is given meaning by the adaptor and the interpreters, it makes sense. As you read the script, note the format used, the staging and vocal directions, and try to visualize the overall effect. All staging and vocal directions are decisions of the person adapting the work. Numbers are used to indicate who is speaking rather than names. Although in "Jabberwocky" each interpreter plays one part only, in some adaptations one interpreter may take several parts, and it is easier simply to use a number to indicate who is to speak. For example, Interpreter #1 - Johnny, the giant, and the worm is much clearer than listing the different characters every time Interpreter #1 speaks. Thus, for the purpose of clarity and consistency, numbers are used to indicate who is to speak.

ALICE'S JABBERWOCKY
by Lewis Carroll

adapted for Reader's Theatre by Helen Sheehy

#1 - Tweedledee type (Narrator)

#2 - Tweedledum type (Narrator)

#3 - Fatherly type or motherly type

#4 - boy, the hero

#5 - Alice

#6 - Humpty Dumpty

Setting: One tall stool up center - Humpty Dumpty seated on it with his back to the audience.

#1 and #2 seated on stools at DSR with backs to each other.

#3 standing CSL slightly upstage of #4 with foot on small stool.

#4 sitting on stool with chin resting on hand.

All except Alice enter and freeze into position.

Alice enters with a large, colorful book. She sits crosslegged DSC facing upstage - back to audience.

#6

#3

#4

#1 & #2 #5

Illustration 5-2

AUDIENCE

(Note: Alice is the only interpreter with a script or book.)

(Alice opens the book and begins to "read." As she "reads" the characters come to life. Her attention shifts from the book to the actions of the characters. Focus will be offstage throughout.)

#1 - (turns head full front, body remains profile - movement should be quick and sharp) (speaks ominously)

'Twas brillig and the slithy toves
Did gyre and gimble in the wabe:

#2 - (turns head full front, body remains profile - movement should be quick and sharp) (speaks ominously)

All mimsy were the borogoves
And the mome raths outgrabe.

(#1 and #2 return heads to profile position. Movement should be timed so that #1 and #2 function almost as one person. The effect should be quick, sharp, and comic. This pattern continues throughout the performance.)

#3 - (as if giving fatherly advice) Beware the Jabberwock my son! The jaws that bite, the claws that catch! Beware the jubjub bird, and shun the frumious bandersnatch!

#4 - (during Father's advice, the son looks very bored, yawns)
And as in uffish thought he stood,

#1 - (turns head out) The Jabberwock, with eyes of flame, came

#1-#2 - (#2 turns head out) whiffling

#2 - through the tulgey wood and

#1-#2 - burbled

#1 - as it came! (both turn heads back to profile)

#4 - (he has been observing the progress of the Jabberwock, readies himself, crosses a few steps to center to meet the imaginary Jabberwock) One, two! One, two! (acts out dispatching the monster with a sword)

#1 - (turns head out) and through

#2 - (turns head out) and through

#1 - the vorpal blade went

#2 - snicker

#1 - snack!

#2 - He left it dead, and with its head

#1 - He went

#1-#2 - Galumphing back. (both turn heads back to profile)
(boy crosses back to original position)

#3 - And hast thou slain the Jabberwock? Come to my arms, my beamish boy! Oh, frabjous day! Callooh! Callay!

#1-#2 - (both turn heads out) He chortled in his joy. (turn heads back)

#4 - (very pleased with himself) Twas brillig, and the slithy toves did gyre and gimble in the wabe. All mimsy were the borogoves, and the mome raths outgrabe. (#3 and #4 turn back together, facing upstage)

(Humpty Dumpty turns around, facing out, with eyes closed)

(Alice closes book, sees Humpty Dumpty, rises, crosses to him, and looks him over)

#5 - (with wonder) And how exactly like an egg he is!

#1 - (turns head out) Alice said aloud

#2 - (turns head out) standing with her hands ready to catch him,

#1 - for she was every moment expecting him to fall. (#1 and #2 turn heads back to profile)

#6 - (opening his right eye) It's very provoking

#1-#2 - (turn heads out) said Humpty Dumpty

#1 - after a long silence

#2 - looking away from Alice as he spoke. (#1 and #2 return to profile)

#6 - (opening his left eye) to be called an egg - very!

#5 - I said you *looked* like an egg, Sir. And some eggs are very pretty.

#1 - (turns head out) She added

#2 - (turns head out) hoping to turn her remark into a sort of compliment. (#1 and #2 return to profile)

#6 - Some people

#2 - (turns head out) said Humpty Dumpty

#1 - (turns head out) looking away from her as usual (#1 and #2 return to profile)

#6 - have no more sense than a baby! Don't just stand there

#2 - (turns head out) said Humpty Dumpty

#1 - (turns head out) looking at her for the first time (#1 and #2 return to profile)

#6 - (looks sharply at Alice) tell me your name and your business!

#5 - My name is Alice, but -

#6 - It's a stupid enough name. What does it mean?

#5 - Must a name mean something?

#6 - Of course, it must. My name means the shape I am - and a good handsome shape it is too. With a name like yours you might be any shape almost.

#5 - You seem very clever at explaining words, Sir.

#1-#2 - (turn heads out) said Alice (#1 and #2 return to profile)

#5 - Would you kindly tell me the meaning of the poem, "Jabberwocky"?

#6 - Sure, let's hear it.

#1-#2 - (turn heads out) said Humpty Dumpty. (#1 and #2 return to profile)

#6 - I can explain all the poems that ever were invented. And a good many that haven't been invented just yet.

#1 - (turns head out) This sounded very helpful

#2 - (turns head out) so Alice repeated the first verse.

(Alice opens book to check the poem and as she does #3 and #4 turn around, and 1, 2, 3, 4, 5 all say together:)

Twas brillig and the slithy toves,
Did gyre and gimble in the wabe:
All mimsy were the borogoves,
And the mome raths out -

(#3 and #4 resume position with backs to audience - #1 and #2 return to profile)

#6 - (during the poem, Humpty Dumpty seems very confused, but attempts to cover his lack of knowledge with bravado) (cuts them off sharply) That's enough to begin with. There are plenty of hard words there. (searching for something to say as Alice watches him intently) "Brillig" means four o'clock in the afternoon - the time when you begin broiling things for dinner.

#5 - That'll do very well

#1-#2 - (turns head out) said Alice. (#1 and #2 return to profile)

#5 - and "slithy"?

#6 - (again, searching for an answer) Well, slithy means lithe and slimy. "Lithe" is the same as "active." You see, it's like a portmanteau - there are two meanings packed up into one word. (very pleased with himself)

#5 - I see it now. And what are toves?

#6 - (beginning to enjoy himself) Well, toves are something like badgers - they're something like lizards, and they're something like corkscrews!

#5 - They must be very curious creatures.

#6 - They are that.

#1-#2 - (turn heads out) said Humpty Dumpty. (#1 and #2 return to profile)

#6 - (inspired by Alice's faith in him) Also they make their nest under sundials - also they live on cheese.

#5 - And what's to gyre and to gimble?

#6 - (very confident now) To gyre is to go round and round like a gyroscope. To gimble is to make holes like a gimlet.

#5 - (excited) and the wabe is the grass plot around the sun dial, I suppose!

#1-#2 - (turn heads out) said Alice

#2 - surprised at her own ingenuity. (#1 and #2 return to profile)

#6 - Of course it is. It's called wabe you know, because it goes a long way before it, and a long way behind it -

#5 - And a long way on each side of it!

#6 - Exactly so. Well then, mimsy is flimsy and miserable.

#1-#2 - (turn heads out) There's another portmanteau for you. (#1 and #2 return to profile)

#6 - And a borogove is a thin shabby looking bird with its feathers sticking out all round - something like a live mop.

#5 - And then "mome raths"? (Humpty glares at her, she adds beseechingly) If it's not too much trouble.

#6 - Well, a rath is a sort of green pig; but mome I'm not certain about. I think it's short for "from home" - meaning that they lost their way home, you know.

#5 - And what does "outgrabe" mean?

#6 - Well, "outgribbling" is something between bellowing and whistling, with a kind of sneeze in the middle; however, you'll hear it done, maybe, down in the wood yonder - and once you've heard it you'll be *quite* content. Who's been repeating all that hard stuff to you.

#5 - Repeating to me? Oh no (she opens book)

#1-#2 - (turn heads out) said Alice

#5 - I read it in a book. (all characters face out and freeze as Alice closes book)

As you can see "Alice's Jabberwocky" is a humorous presentation involving unusual characters. This type of presentation requires a lively, sometimes exaggerated style of interpretation. Quick cue pick-up and energy are essential.

The following script adapted from Mark Twain's anti-war poem "The War Prayer" is a sharp shift in tone and style. All references to staging, use of scripts, focus, props, costumes, make-up, and other production elements have been omitted. After you read and analyze "The War Prayer," answer the following questions.

1. The staging or placement of the interpreters should reflect the theme and style of the material. With this in mind, how would you stage "The War Prayer"? Should there be movement? Use a diagram to indicate interpreter placement and movement.
2. Would you use costumes, make-up, or props? Explain.

An energetic cast, colorful costumes, inventive set pieces, and innovative staging make for exciting Reader's Theatre.

3. Would the interpreters use scripts? Why or why not?
4. Would you use offstage or onstage focus? or a combination of both? Explain your choices.
5. Other media such as music, slides, and recordings are often used in Reader's Theatre presentations. Do you visualize other media being used? Why or why not?

THE WAR PRAYER

by Mark Twain

adapted for voices
by Helen Sheehy

Voice #1 - Man
Voice #2 - Woman
Voice #3 - Man
Voice #4 - Woman
Voice #5 - Man
Voice #6 - Stranger

1 It was a time of great and exulting excitement.

2 The country was up in arms, the war was on, in every breast burned the holy fire of patriotism;

3 the drums were beating,

4 the bands playing,

5 the toy pistols popping,

2 the bunched firecrackers hissing and spluttering:

3 on every hand and far down the receding and fading spread of roofs and balconies

4 a fluttering wilderness of flags flashed in the sun:

1 daily the young volunteers marched down the wide avenue

5 gay and fine in their new uniforms,

2 the proud fathers and mothers

4 and sisters and sweethearts cheering them with voices
3 choked with happy emotion as they swung by:
1 nightly the packed mass meetings listened, panting, to patriot oratory which stirred the deepest deeps of their hearts
5 and which they interrupted at briefest intervals with cyclones of applause,
2 the tears running down their cheeks the while:
4 in the churches the pastors preached devotion to flag and country and invoked the God of Battles,
3 beseeching His aid in our good cause in outpouring of fervid eloquence which moved every listener.
1 It was indeed a glad and gracious time, and the half-dozen rash spirits that ventured to disapprove of the war and cast a doubt upon its righteousness straightaway got such a stern and angry warning
2 that for their personal safety's sake they quickly shrank out of sight and offended no more in that way.
1 Sunday morning came -
2 next day the battalions would leave for the front:
3 the church was filled
4 the volunteers were there,
5 their young faces alight with martial dreams -
3 visions of the stern advance,
2 the gathering momentum, the rushing charge,
5 the flashing sabers,
2 the flight of the foe, the tumult, the enveloping smoke, the fierce pursuit, the surrender! -
1 then home from the war,
3 bronzed heroes, welcomed, adored, submerged in golden seas of glory!
4 with the volunteers sat their dear ones,
1 proud, happy, and envied by the neighbors and friends who had no sons and brothers to send forth to the field of honor.

5 there to win for the flag or failing,

3 die the noblest of deaths.

1 the service proceeded

2 a war chapter from the Old Testament was read: the first prayer was said:

4 it was followed by an organ burst that shook the building.

3 and with one impulse the house rose.

5 with glowing eyes and beating hearts, and poured out that tremendous invocation -

ALL God the all-terrible!
Thou who ordainest.
Thunder thy clarion
and lightning thy sword!

1 Then came the "long" prayer.

2 None could remember the like of it for passionate pleading and moving and beautiful language.

5 The burden of its supplication was that an ever-merciful and benignant Father of us all would watch over our noble young soldiers and aid, comfort, and encourage them in their patriotic works;

4 bless them and shield them in the day of battle and the hour of peril,

2 bear them in His mighty hand, make them strong and confident,

3 invincible in the bloody onset:

5 help them to crush the foe

4 grant to them and to their flag and country imperishable honor and glory -

1 An aged stranger entered and moved with slow and noiseless step up the main aisle,

2 his eyes fixed upon the minister

3 his long body clothed in a robe that reached to his feet, his head bare,

4 his white hair descending in a frothy cataract to his shoulders

5 his seamy face unnaturally pale

2 pale even to ghastliness.

3 With all eyes following him and wondering, he made his silent way, without pausing, he ascended to the preacher's side and stood there waiting.

2 With shut lids the preacher unconscious of his presence, continued his moving prayer, and at last finished it with the words, uttered in fervent appeal:

1 Bless our arms, grant us the victory. O Lord our God, Father and Protector of our land and flag!

3 The stranger touched his arm, motioned him to step aside - which the startled minister did - and took his place.

5 During some moments he surveyed the spellbound audience with solemn eyes in which burned an uncanny light, then in a deep voice he said:

6 I come from the Throne - bearing a message from Almighty God!

4 The words smote the house with a shock! If the stranger perceived it he gave no attention.

6 He has heard the prayer of his servant your shepherd and will grant it if such shall be your desire after I, His messenger shall have explained to you its import - You have heard your servant's prayer - the uttered part of it. I am commissioned of God to put into words the other part of it - that part which the pastor, and also you in your hearts, fervently prayed silently. He commandeth me to put it into words.

O Lord our Father, our young patriots, idols of our hearts, go forth to battle - be Thou near them! With them in spirit we also go forth from the sweet peace of our beloved firesides to smite the foe.

O Lord our God help us to tear their soldiers to bloody shreds with our shells: help us to cover their smiling fields with the pale forms of their patriot dead: help us to drown the thunder of the guns with the shrieks of their wounded writhing in pain: help us to lay waste their humble homes with a hurricane of fire: help us to wring the hearts of their unoffending widows with unavailing grief: help us to turn them out roofless with their little children to wander unfriended the wastes of their desolated land in rags and hunger and thirst, sports of the sun flames of summer and the icy winds of winter, broken in spirit, worn with travail, imploring Thee for the refuge of the grave and denied it - for our sakes who adore Thee, Lord, blast their hopes, blight their lives, protract their bitter pilgrimage, make heavy their steps, water their way with their tears, stain the white snow with the blood of their wounded feet!

We ask it in the spirit of love, of Him Who is the source of love, and Who is the ever-faithful refuge and friend of all that are sore beset and seek His aid with humble and contrite hearts.

Ye have prayed it, if ye still desire it, speak! The messenger of the Most High waits.

1 It was believed afterward that the man was a lunatic, because there was no sense in what he said.

Performing or adapting a script for Reader's Theatre involves many complex choices. The only way to know if the choices you made were good ones is to see your ideas become reality in a performance. As a class exercise, you might select two distinct interpretations of "The War Prayer" and perform each interpretation. Perhaps one group has decided to emphasize the ironic elements - another group might heighten the tragic effects of the poem. The staging, focus, and production elements of costumes, music, and sound should all be chosen to illuminate the group's particular interpretation of the poem. The point is that there is no *one* way of performing material. There are as many different methods of presentation as there are people performing and adapting the material. The choices that you make must be true to the literature. Again, the primary objective of Reader's Theatre is to share a literary experience with an audience and to create, as Leslie Irene Coger describes it, "Theatre of the Mind."

QUESTIONS FOR REVIEW AND DISCUSSION

1. Explain the difference between Reader's Theatre and Oral Interpretation.
2. Discuss the differences and similarities of Reader's Theatre and conventional theatre.
3. Discuss ideas for compiling Reader's Theatre scripts centered around a theme, a mood, an event, a person, an author. What other possibilities are there?
4. What improvisation and acting skills are used in Reader's Theatre?
5. Discuss the basic principles of Reader's Theatre.

VOCABULARY

onstage focus
offstage focus
adaptation
point-of-view
"Theatre of the Mind"

SUGGESTIONS

- Compile a Reader's Theatre script and present it to English classes or other student groups.
- Keep a notebook of newspaper articles, interesting stories or jokes, and ideas for Reader's Theatre presentations.
- Read Edgar Lee Master's SPOON RIVER ANTHOLOGY and compare it to the adaptation made for the stage by Charles Aidman.

Part II.

PRODUCTION SKILLS

Chapter 6

The Externals

Make-up
Hairstyle
Costume

The way we appear has a profound effect upon our relationship with others and on our self concept. Make-up, hairstyle, and costume may reveal personality, attitude, and emotions. On the other hand, these externals can often conceal who we really are. In this dual role of revealing and concealing, external appearance is a rich source for theatre arts. The actor uses externals to portray the character; the director and designer use externals to set the play in time and to reveal their concept of the play. Aside from the very practical use of externals, they contribute an aesthetic element to theatrical production. Artistically designed externals can transform a humdrum theatrical production into a unified, harmonious work of art.

Unity of concept is the key to a successful theatrical production. Externals must serve the production and the character, not overpower them. If after you see a production all you remember is the leading lady's perfectly coiffed hair, then something is out of balance. The actor, designer, and director must work together to make careful choices. The right collar, or hairstyle, or lipstick can serve to reveal a character as much as a perfectly delivered line.

If unity of concept is the key, then how is this unity achieved? Careful script analysis and character interpretation are the first steps in determining what image to present. The actor works closely with the director and designers, but every actor should be able to apply make-up, arrange hair, and determine the appropriate costume for the character.

Before the externals can be created, the actor and designer, in collaboration with the director, must mutually determine the character's traits by asking the following questions about the character.

Age?
Temperament?
Personal habits?
Physical details? Include practical considerations such as pockets mentioned in script, beard, etc.
Family background?
Relationship to others?
Changes or growth - physical, mental, or emotional?
Economic status?
Social class?
State of health?
Nationality?
Race?
Place in time?
Environment?

The theme and style of the play must be determined and discussed. The actors should be aware of these decisions, so that they may make the appropriate choices regarding the externals.

To illustrate how a character's externals are determined by the factors listed above, ask *yourself* the same questions. Perhaps you have inherited red hair from your father; a bout with the flu might have left you thin and drawn; and your relationship to your classmates is demonstrated by your similar attire of jeans and sneakers. Think about all the different externals you use in the various environments of your life. As you begin to realize the complex role that externals play in your own life, you can appreciate the variety and profusion of choices that you have available when you portray a character.

After you have carefully answered all the questions above, you should know a great deal about the character you will portray. However, the decisions that the director makes regarding the concept of the production will affect the choices that you have. For example, the director might set Shakespeare's TAMING OF THE SHREW in the present, using contemporary costumes, make-up, and hairstyles. The actor then has living research materials available. If the Elizabethan period is chosen, the actor must use books, paintings, and drawings to research the character's externals. When por-

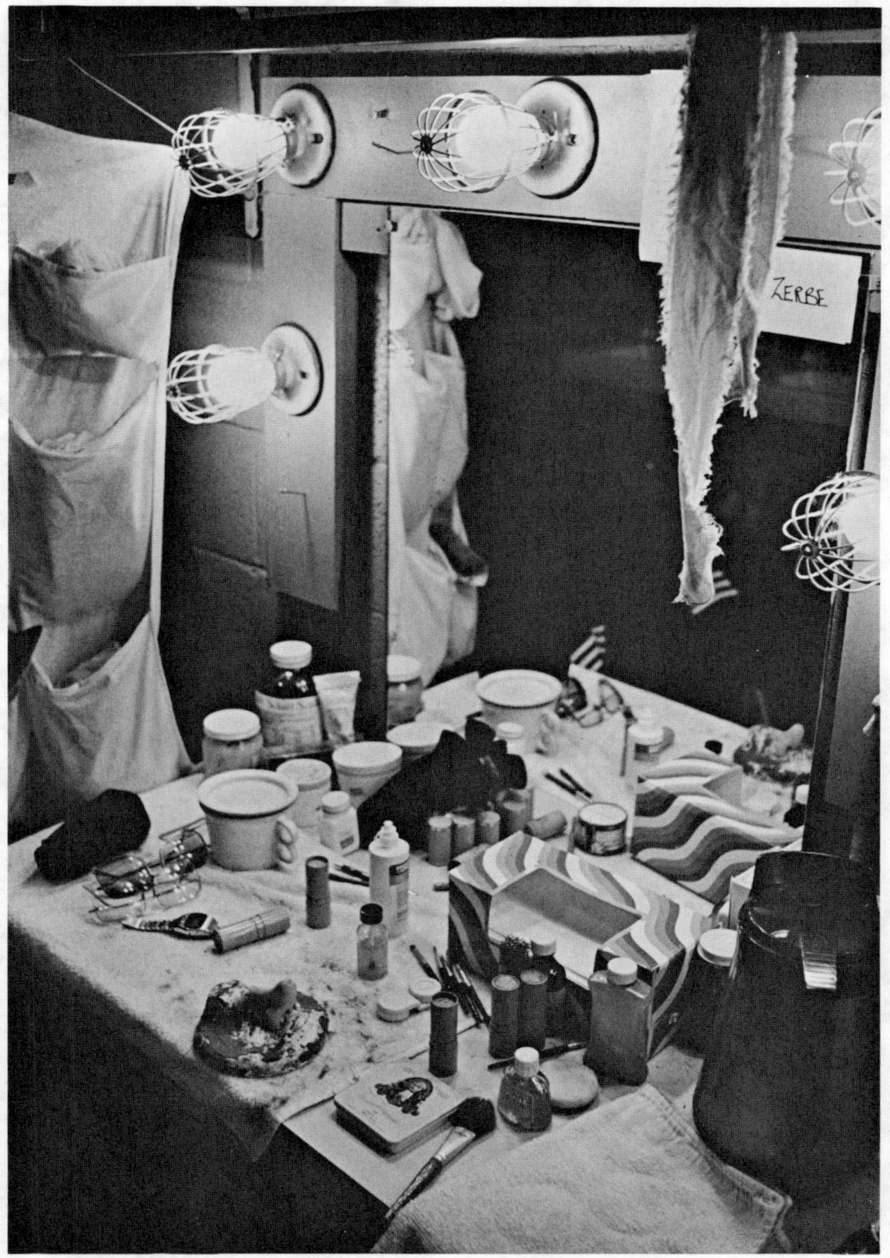

Make-up mirror and make-up for actor Anthony Zerbe in Long Wharf Theatre's production of *Cyrano de Bergerac*.

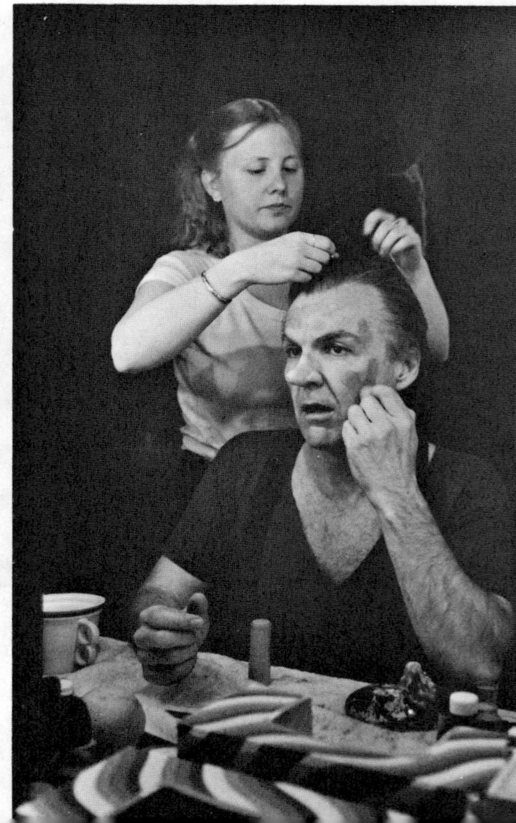

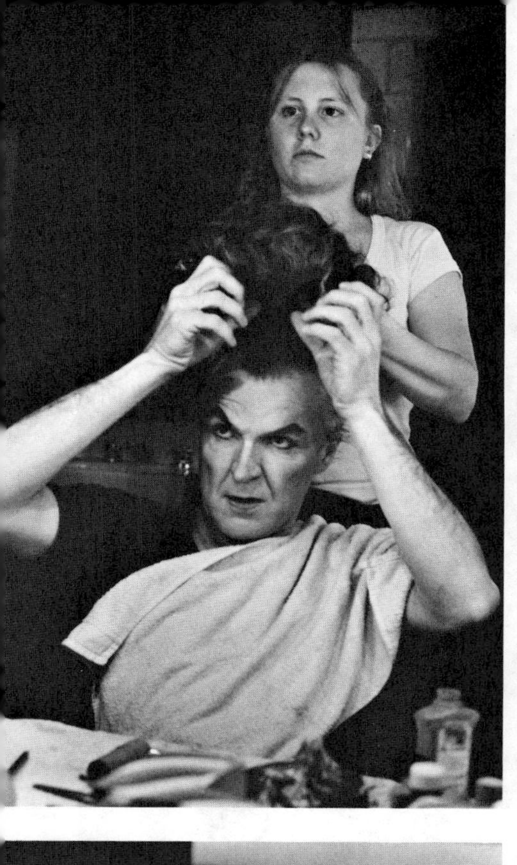

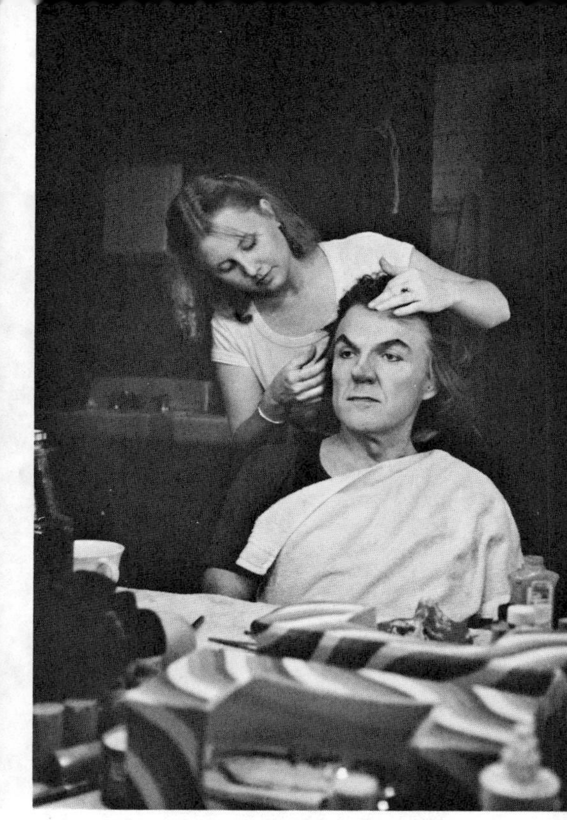

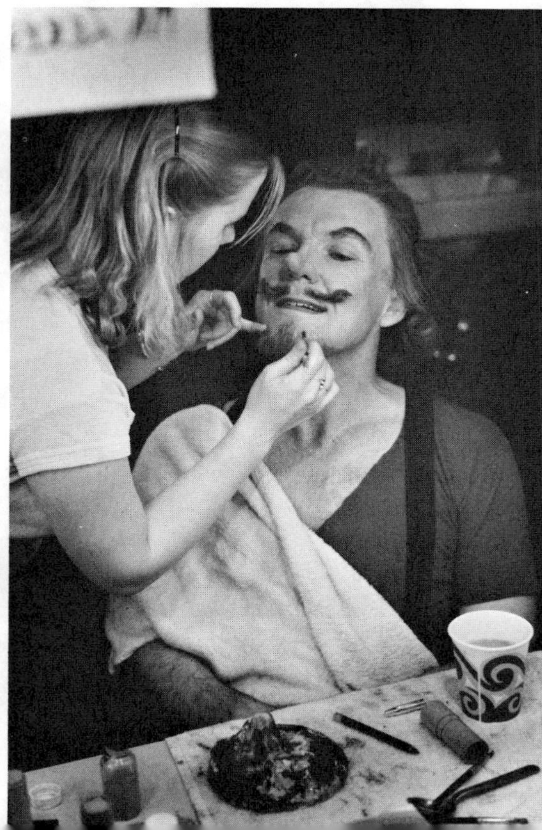

With the assistance of Jan Shoebridge, Anthony Zerbe transforms into the dashing, romantic Cyrano of Rostand's *Cyrano de Bergerac*.

traying characters from a particular period in history, it is important to remember that the purpose is to reveal the character as flesh and blood, not as a mannequin in a museum. This challenge - to make the character come alive, externally and internally - is the goal of every actor.

Stage make-up, hair styling, and costuming will be discussed separately in the following pages. However, it cannot be over-emphasized that these externals all share in serving the characterization and the production. All elements must harmonize if the effect is to be aesthetically convincing and balanced.

Practical exercises are offered in the belief that experience is, indeed, the best teacher. With this thought in mind, the fun and excitement of physical transformation can begin.

STAGE MAKE-UP

Primitive societies realized the importance of make-up in ritual. Fierce masks, animal skins, body and face paint helped shape the primitive's view of the world. The ancient Greeks used painted masks as makeup, for practical as well as aesthetic reasons, in the performance of plays. The masks enabled three actors to play many parts, possibly served as a megaphone to project the voice, and utilized an exaggeration of expression allowing features to be clearly seen from a great distance. Elaborate wigs were worn by the eighteenth century actor, and make-up supplies for the actor in the early 1900's consisted of burnt cork, chalk, and carmine. In fact, every period of theatrical history has been enriched by the use of make-up.

Make-up can be invaluable in helping the actor look the part. Make-up can enhance and change the features, reflect a play's theme and style, and counter the effects of a large theatre and strong lighting.

The first principle of make-up is *observation* - not only of others, but of yourself. Before you can make yourself up as an eighty-year-old or a thirteen-year-old, you must have some idea of the external characteristics of an eighty-year-old person or a teen-ager. Since everyone ages differently and even identical twins have distinguishing features, each make-up will be different depending upon the character to be portrayed and the actor playing the part. Observation of many types of people can aid you in designing and applying make-up. Your own face, however, is the stage on which the drama of make-up is played. Therefore, a thorough understanding of your own features and physical characteristics is essential for the successful use of make-up. There is no *one* way of applying or designing make-up. Techniques must be modified to suit each actor and each character. Make-up application can be learned only through experimentation and practice.

EXERCISE #25

Observe yourself in a mirror. Study your face as if you are seeing it for the first time.

Examine each feature. Is your forehead broad? narrow? Are your eyes large? deep set? Is your nose straight? long? turned up? Is your mouth large? small? Are your lips full? thin? Is your jaw rounded? square? Is your complexion pale? tanned? dark? All one shade or many shades?

Run your fingers over your face. Feel the bones underneath. Are your cheekbones sharply defined? Is your skin smooth? rough?

Study your face in different lighting. Overhead lighting, straight-on lighting, and side lighting all create different effects of light and shadow. What are these effects?

Write your observations down. Then ask your friends or family to describe your face. Compare the observations.

The second principle of make-up is *analysis*. Before you begin to apply make-up, you must analyze several factors:

1) size of theatre
2) lighting
3) type of play
4) character

Make-up must be stronger if your theatre is large; a smaller space requires a more subtle effect. Lighting colors will affect make-up color; therefore, all make-up should be tested under the lights that will be used. A realistic play will require the character to look natural, but a symbolic play might require exaggeration of make-up. Even if you are playing a character very similar to yourself, some modifications in your own features may be necessary.

The first technique to be explored will be basic application of make-up for a character very similar to yourself. You have observed and become aware of your own features. Proper use of make-up can correct weaknesses and enhance your appearance. Small eyes can be made to look larger; a long nose shortened; and skin tone can be evened. The make-up application steps are offered not as hard and fast rules, but as guidelines. As you practice with make-up, you can begin to experiment with techniques that work for you.

Make-up materials vary widely in expense and type. Many companies offer complete make-up kits. The choices can be confusing. However, with a few basic materials — many available in your local drug store or a make-up supply house — you can create a variety of effects.

MAKE-UP KIT

A large fishing tackle box with a lock works quite nicely for make-up storage, and is easy to carry.

MATERIALS

BASE	- Pancake Liquid Creme Stick	(several shades including white, pink, olive, and tan)

LINERS - Blue, Brown, Grey, White, Black (many other colors are available, but these are basics.)

EYEBROW PENCILS - Dark Brown, Medium Brown, Black

BRUSHES - several sizes for lips, wrinkles, and eye shadowing and lining.

ROUGE - (Female)	Medium Red (Male)	Rust
(Dry and creme)	Pink	Liver Brown tones
	Peach	Bronze

MASCARA - Black and white
LIPSTICK - Clear red and bronze or rusts for boys
TRANSLUCENT POWDER
POWDER PUFF
SPONGES - natural silk or polyurethane foam
COTTON BALLS
COLD CREAM AND/OR MAKE-UP REMOVER
HAIR WHITENER
TOOTHBRUSH
KLEENEX
PAPER TOWELS
SOAP
MIRROR
BOBBY PINS, ELASTICS
COVER-UP (such as an old shirt to protect clothing)

NOTE: If you have sensitive skin, or even if you don't, it's a good idea to test a small amount of the make-up on your skin. If the skin reddens or reacts in any way, do not use the make-up. No special hypo-allergenic theatrical make-up is available, but applying a thin film of make-up remover to the skin before applying make-up helps protect the skin.

BASIC MAKE-UP

STEP #1 Wear a cover-up of some sort. An old shirt will do nicely. Secure your hair with bobby pins or elastics.

Never apply make-up in costume. Spillage of materials can ruin a costume.

STEP #2 Clean your face with cold cream or soap and water. Splash with cold water to close pores. If your skin is very dry, apply a thin layer of moisturizer.

STEP #3 BASE. Bases are the foundation for the rest of the make-up. They come in various types - pancake (applied with a sponge), liquid, and creme stick. The base evens out the skin tone, adds color to skin that would be washed out by strong lighting, and covers slight imperfections.

Base is generally applied in a tone one shade darker than your natural color. You may have to mix several shades to achieve the effect you want. The use of a base is not always mandatory. If your skin has a natural glowing color and does not wash out (pale) under lights, you may only need to enhance your eyes, cheekbones, and lips.

Apply the base sparingly in a thin layer. Blend into the hairline and under the jaw into the neck. You do not want a sharp line of demarcation.

STEP #4 SHADOWING AND HIGHLIGHTING makes the face appear less "flat" and also can conceal defects and highlight features. For shadows, use a foundation color 3-4 shades darker than your base. White is generally used for highlighting.

Illustration 6-1

Remember - highlights bring out features; shadows cause them to recede. They must follow the natural contour of your face. Never place a shadow on top of a bone where a natural highlight would appear. The placement of highlights and shadows depends upon the desired effect. For example, to make the nose appear longer and thinner, shadow the sides and highlight the center. Shadowing the center and highlighting the sides will have the opposite effect. Shadow the hollow under the cheekbones and highlight the cheekbones for emphasis.

Always carefully blend highlights and shadows.

Note: For a very subtle effect useful when performing within ten feet or less of the audience, apply dry cake shadow *under* a pancake base. In other words, shadow and highlight, then apply the pancake base.

STEP #5 EYES. Your eyes are your primary means of expression; thus, you will want them to appear larger. Shadow the upper lid with brown liner or a liner to complement your costume or eye colors. Brown, by contrast, helps bring out the white of your eyes. Highlight may be added between the shadow and the eyebrow.

Line the eyes with a brown pencil or brown liner applied with a brush. Black pencil or liner gives a hard look. Make the line as close to the lash line as possible. Liquid liner may be used if you have a steady hand, but it tends to be messy.

Illustration 6-2

Mascara may be applied with a brush or mascara wand. Apply several thin coats, not one thick coat. Make sure lashes are separated not clumped together. For thicker lashes, lightly powder after first coat.

To coat the lower lashes with a minimum of smearing, use a matchbook cover or a small piece of stiff paper. Hold the paper under the lashes and stroke the mascara on, using the paper as a shield.

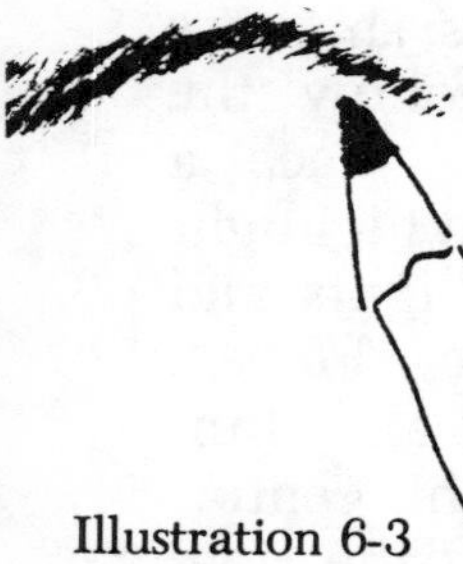

Lash lengthener or "feather lash" may be applied to the eyelashes after the first coat of mascara. The mascara should be moist. The lash lengthener builds and extends the lashes. The effect is similar to false eyelashes and more comfortable.

If false eyelashes are used, the lining of the upper lid is usually omitted. For a natural appearance, false eyelashes must be trimmed. Outsize lashes are available for exaggerated characters.

Illustration 6-3

STEP #6 EYEBROWS. Emphasize and define eyebrows with a pencil. Use short, feathery strokes to simulate natural hair growth.

STEP #7 LIPS. If you have determined that your lips are the proper shape for your character, apply a small amount of lipstick to your finger and apply. If your lips are too full, extend the base over the lips and draw in a new lip line with a brush coated with lipstick. A red pencil may also be used. You may also draw in a fuller lip line if needed.

If your character has a natural, "unmade-up" appearance, just a touch of color is needed. The lips should not fade into the face, however. Test the effect under lights.

STEP #8 ROUGE. Apply cream rouge or dry rouge to cheeks for a healthy glow. Place on the highest part of your cheekbones and blend. Cheek color should appear natural, not like two bright spots of color.

STEP #9 Make-up hands, shoulders, arms, and any exposed part of the body. Again, the effect should be natural; for example, there should be no sharp color difference when the hands are brought to the face.

STEP #10 POWDER. To set the make-up and avoid smudging, lightly puff on translucent powder. Brush off excess. Touch up cheek color with dry rouge if necessary.

STEP #11 Check the make-up under stage lights. Make-up must *always* be tested under the lighting which will be used. Colors may fade or change and features may be lost under strong lighting.

STEP #12 REMOVING MAKE-UP. Never leave the theatre without first removing your make-up. You must not break the theatrical illusion which has been created. Remove make-up with soap and water or cold cream or make-up remover. Finish with a cold splash of water and a moisturizer if your skin is dry.

AGE MAKE-UP

Often high school students are required to portray elderly people. The temptation is to slather on layers of make-up to compensate for the youth of the actor. Avoid this temptation! Age can be represented through careful observation of older people, proper gestures, walk, and mannerisms; and thorough belief and understanding of the character. Do not depend on stereotypes. All elderly people do not walk slowly and have trembling hands. They have unique characteristics just as younger people do. After observation and analysis, make-up can help you look the part. However, a good detailed make-up is no substitute for good acting. The make-up must become an integral part of the character, not a painted facade.

The following steps are guides, and may be modified for each individual need.

STEP #1 Wear a cover-up to protect your clothing.

STEP #2 Clean face. Splash with cold water to close pores.

STEP #3 Apply base. Color is important - very pale, or pink, or grayish pallor or many other combinations depending upon the character. You may have to mix several shades to achieve the effect you desire.

Apply to face, neck, hands, and any other exposed area.

STEP #4 SHADOW AND HIGHLIGHT. Use a darker foundation color to shadow or use liners. Use white to highlight. Shadows may be placed:

in the eye sockets
under the eyes
below the cheekbones
in the temple hollows
under the chin
in the throat indentations

Look at Ill. #6-5 and Ill. #6-6 and note the difference between thin old age and heavy old age. For thin characters a triangular shading is used. For heavy characters use curved, rounded shading.

Carefully blend highlights and shadows.

STEP #5 Wrinkles are simply depressions in the skin. They appear dark because no light falls in the depression.

To draw on wrinkles use your own natural lines as a guide. However, if your own lines are short or broken, or you simply don't have any lines (as yet!), "wrinkle" your face to find the lines. Keep the wrinkle lines clearly separated and use only a few lines. Many lines together tend to project as a dark smudge.

Each wrinkle has a highlight on top of the line where the light would naturally fall. Blend these two lines carefully.

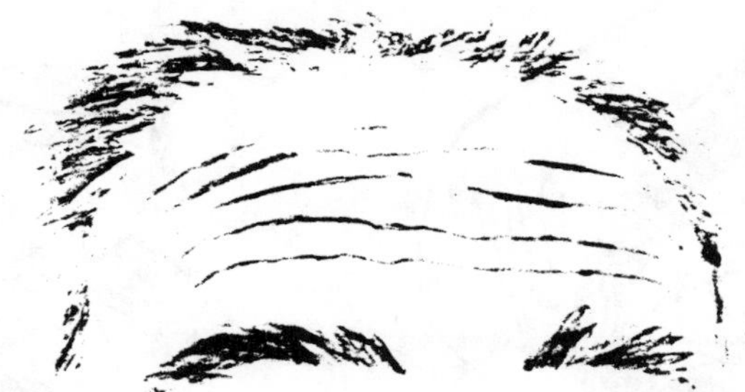

Illustration 6-4

You may use a liner pencil or a brush and liner to draw on the wrinkles. Use brown, or maroon, or grey, but avoid black as it's too harsh.

STEP #6 If cheek color is desired, apply rouge to cheeks and blend. A touch of rouge to the lips is often all that is necessary after the wrinkles have been applied.

STEP #7 Whiten eyebrows and eyelashes with white mascara or hair whitener applied with a toothbrush. To make eyebrows appear bushier, brush them opposite to the way they grow and apply white mascara or hair whitener. White liner or white base may also be used for this effect.

STEP #8 To dull eyes and make them appear tired, apply a *fine* red line (sparingly!) very close to the lower lash line. A red liner may be used. Apply with a brush.

STEP #9 Set make-up with translucent powder.

STEP #10 Test make-up under stage lights.

STEP #11 Remove make-up.

An additional step in achieving a natural age make-up is texturing the skin. Texturing may be accomplished in various ways.

1) Apply fine criss-cross lines with a sharp liner pencil on the face over the base and the rest of the make-up.
2) Cut a small piece of sponge, dip in darker or lighter base

than the base that was used, and lightly touch on the face to give a "stipple" or mottled effect.

Illustration 6-5

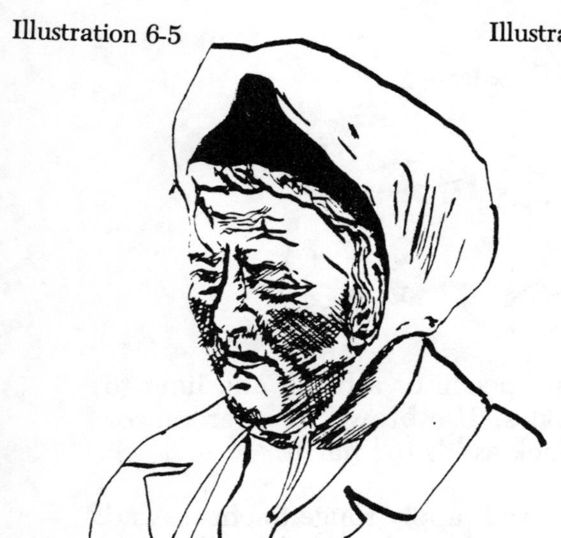

Heavy old age. Curved, rounded shading is used.

Illustration 6-6

Thin old age. Note the use of triangular shading. Wrinkles appear on forehead, around eyes, "smile" lines, lips, chin, and neck.

To complete the age make-up, age hands by shadowing the depressions and highlighting the tendons.

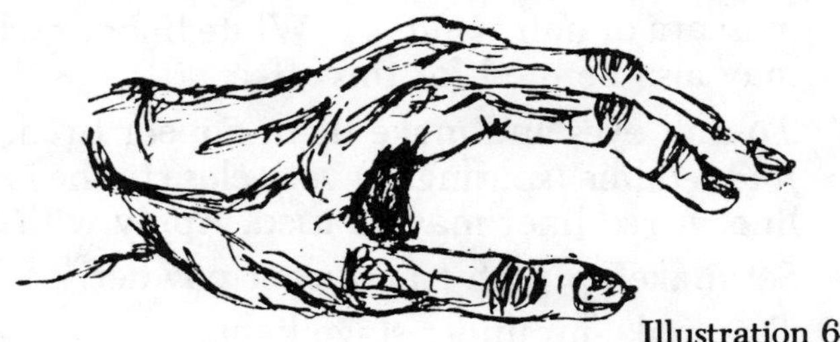

Illustration 6-7

Modifications of the previous two make-up techniques, basic and age, can be used for almost any character. For example, if you're playing a middle-aged character, wrinkles on the forehead, smile lines, and "crows feet" along with an appropriate costume and the proper hairstyle can suggest middle-age. In all your make-up applications keep in mind the following principles:

1) Observation - "See" your own face and observe the faces of others.
2) Analysis - Keep in mind the size of the theatre, the lighting, the type of play, and the character.
3) Application -
    a. Apply make-up sparingly - your goal is to look as your character would look, not "made-up."
    b. Shadow areas that you want to recede; highlight areas that you want to stand out.
    c. Blend highlights and shadows, cheek color, wrinkle lines, and base. There should be no sharp lines of demarcation visible to the audience.
    d. Use your own facial structure as a guide; do not paint on a false face that does not work with your expressions. You must be able to use the make-up and integrate it into your character.

With a few additional materials, many other make-up effects can be created. The materials include:

crepe hair
spirit gum
spirit gum remover
nose putty
collodion (flexible and non-flexible)
liquid latex
stage blood
bald pate
rubber mask grease.

Beards

Crepe hair, which is actually made of wool, is an inexpensive way to make beards, moustaches, and eyebrows. Since crepe hair does not reflect light as natural hair does, choose a shade lighter than your hair color. Also, to achieve a natural effect, several shades of crepe hair are usually blended. Notice that real beards are often lighter at the top and darker at the bottom, and moustaches and beards are usually several different shades.

Straighten crepe hair by unbraiding it and pressing it with a steam iron between two towels. If a wavy or curly look is desired, omit the straightening.

BUILDING A BEARD

STEP #1 Plan the shape you want your beard to be. You might draw the beard on paper, or draw the shape on your face with a lining pencil.

STEP #2 Clean and dry your face. Use an astringent to remove any oil.

STEP #3 Cut the crepe hair — on the bias — longer than you want the beard to be. You will trim the beard after it is fastened. Blend the hair until you have the mixture of shades that you want.

STEP #4 Apply to your face a layer of spirit gum in the desired shape. Allow the spirit gum to become tacky and then apply a second coat. If you want to re-use the beard a few times, the spirit gum should hold. However, liquid latex adhesive may be used instead of spirit gum if you will be re-using the beard many times. Paint the liquid latex on in several layers. (NOTE: GIRLS SHOULD NOT USE LIQUID LATEX TO SECURE BEARDS. WHEN THE BEARD IS REMOVED FROM THE FACE, THE LIQUID LATEX ADHESIVE TENDS TO PULL OUT THE SMALL, FINE HAIRS ON THE FACE. IN A FEW MONTHS THESE HAIRS MIGHT GROW IN AS STUBBLE. NOT AN ATTRACTIVE PROSPECT!)

STEP #5 Apply the crepe hair in sections beginning underneath the chin, then the front of the chin, sides, and top.

STEP #6 Press the *ends* of the crepe hair firmly into the adhesive. Hold for a moment.

STEP #7 After all layers have been applied, check for bare spots. Fill in as needed. Comb out any loose hairs. Notice, however, that real beards often have bare or sparsely covered areas.

STEP #8 Trim the beard with scissors into the desired shape.

STEP #9 To remove, gently pull up one end and carefully pull off. Lightly powder the back of the beard so that it doesn't stick to itself. To re-apply the beard, paint a layer of spirit gum on the top and ends *only* for a more natural appearance.

STEP #10 Remove spirit gum with spirit gum remover.

To give the appearance of "5:00 shadow" or stubble, two methods may be used. A quick method is to use a "stipple" sponge or cut a small piece of a regular sponge and dip the sponge lightly into grey, dark blue, or black liner, and touch to the face. You may also cut tiny pieces of crepe hair and apply them with a sponge. Use liquid latex or beard stubble adhesive as spirit gum tends to be shiny under lights.

If the actor has curly hair or hair with a lot of body, real hair which has been saved from the last hair cut may be used to build a very realistic beard, moustache, or sideburns. Treat the real hair in the same manner as crepe hair.

Moustaches

The hair in moustaches, as in beards, is usually many different shades. Blend the crepe hair until you get the shade you want. Either draw on paper, or with lining pencil on your face, the shape you want your moustache to be. Using small tufts of crepe hair, fasten the ends only to the face. You may use spirit gum or liquid latex adhesive. Leave a small bare space above the center of the upper lip for a more natural look. Trim the moustache to the desired shape.

Eyebrows

Eyebrows can be blocked out by covering with a commercial fixative, then adding derma wax or moustache wax, and covering with a base. Or the eyebrows may be blocked out by rubbing with a bar of soap and then covering with a base. A new eyebrow of crepe hair can then be added. Use short stray pieces of crepe hair and apply with spirit gum or liquid latex. Do not use liquid latex unless your own eyebrow is blocked out completely. Again, when the liquid latex is pulled off, your hair tends to come with it.

Three dimensional effects

Noses, chins, and even cheekbones can be changed with the use of nose putty. Although the use of nose putty takes practice, the effect is certainly worth the effort. To use nose putty:

STEP #1 Break off a piece of the putty.

STEP #2 Knead the putty with your hands until it is warm and pliable.

STEP #3 Shape the putty into the desired form.

STEP #4 Fasten it to the face with spirit gum.

STEP #5 Blend the three dimensional piece into the rest of the make-up with base.

If you wish to re-use these pieces, mix nose putty with one part Derma wax in a double boiler until the pieces are softened. This will keep nose putty soft and re-usable.

Missing Teeth

Apply black pencil or black wax to a *dry* tooth.

Black eyes and bruises

Mix black and blue liner to form purple. Add touches of red for broken veins. Add white for puffiness. (Observe pattern of real bruises and the wide variety of colors.)

Scars

Collodion, a mixture of nitrated cellulose and alcohol, which forms a tough, elastic film and is used by doctors to protect wounds, is also used to form "scars." Collodion draws the skin and forms a puckered line which is lighter in color than the surrounding skin. For a built-up scar, use liquid latex or derma wax or nose putty. When latex dries, it can be pushed together to form a deep groove in the skin. Stage blood or red liner may be used to make the scar appear as a wound. Add "stitches" with black liner or a lining pencil.

Stage Blood

Stage blood may also be poured into tiny capsules which can be crushed or bitten open at the appropriate moment. Stage blood in plastic baggies worn under a costume can be torn open to simulate an injury very realistically.

Fantasy Make-up

A variety of fantasy make-ups can be created using a white base and colored liners. Clowns, skeletons, ghosts, spirits, and many other creatures can be produced using white base and colored liners.

Bald Pate

A bald head can be achieved with a flesh-colored bald pate or even a nylon stocking which has been soaped and covered with a base. To attach a bald pate:

STEP #1 Secure hair tightly to your scalp.

STEP #2 Fit the bald pate over your head and attach with spirit gum at the front and then stretch the pate to the back and secure with spirit gum.

STEP #3 Pull the pate tightly over the ears. At the highest point of the ear, cut a slit in the pate. Attach in front of and back of the ear with spirit gum.

STEP #4 To mask the line of demarcation on the forehead use rubber mask grease and powder heavily.

STEP #5 Hair may be attached with spirit gum. Blood veins may be simulated by stippling a red liner lightly on the pate in a vein pattern.

These are just a few of the many effects you can create with make-up. With practice and perseverance, you can become quite adept at creating your own designs.

EXERCISE #26

Find an interesting picture of a "character" (model, elderly man or woman, clown, witch, bag lady, hobo, cowboy, politician) in a newspaper or magazine. Use the picture as a basis to create a make-up. When you finish have someone else compare your results with the picture.

Perhaps you will be able to put your make-up experience to practical use on a school production or class play. If you are in charge of, or a member of a make-up crew, you have several important responsibilities.

MAKE-UP CREW

1. Check all make-up supplies. Replace any that are needed.
2. If you are designing make-up for a cast member, work out the design on paper and then with the actor. Allow plenty of time to experiment and practice.
3. Set out make-up supplies at all dress rehearsals and performances.
4. Be available to assist the actors when needed.
5. Clean all brushes and sponges thoroughly with soap and hot water after each use. Actors with skin problems should use their own sponges and brushes to avoid transmitting bacteria.
6. Store all make-up at the end of each rehearsal and performance.
7. Check the make-up under lights at the rehearsals. Correct any mistakes or tell the actors of any flaws in their make-up.
8. At the close of the production, take inventory of the make-up and note what supplies must be replaced.

Often the make-up members double as hairdressers - usually pressed into service at the last minute! Poorly-styled hair often mars carefully applied make-up and a well-designed costume. Hair is often neglected, when in fact, hair and costume are the two externals which have the most impact. However, with advance planning and a few basic techniques, hair styling need not be a problem.

HAIRSTYLING

Hairstyling requires the same analysis, preparation, and experimentation that good make-up requires. Your hairstyle can dramatically change how you look and how you feel. The first objective of any character's hairstyle is to make the character look as real and as natural as possible. To determine the appropriate hairstyle for a character, you must first answer the character and play analysis questions on page 88. After you have analyzed your character and the play in collaboration with the director, you then begin planning and researching the hairstyle you will use. If your character is from a seventeenth-century comedy such as SCHOOL FOR WIVES by Molière, you must look at paintings, books, or drawings of the period. In your research you will find that full powdered wigs were often worn by both men and women. The effect was quite unnatural, but "real" for the period. You can duplicate the effect with synthetic or crepe hair. Keep in mind that hairstyles are usually stylized in paintings, and you may modify the hairstyle to suit your character. Of course, common folk in any period lacked the means and materials to copy the elegant hairstyles worn by the wealthy classes. If you are playing a common person in a seventeenth-century comedy, you would not imitate the powdered wig hairstyle of the upper classes. Your hair would probably be covered with a cap or simply tied back. Through your research you are attempting to capture the "feel" of a particular time. Hairstyles or other externals do not always have to be historically accurate, but you do have to seize the essence of the period, adapt it to fit your character, and convey its flavor to your audience.

Photographs of paintings are provided to give you a quick survey of hairstyle and costume from the Greeks to the year 1900. Most of the hairstyles can be achieved by using your own hair; or a combination of your own hair plus synthetic hair and crepe hair. The most common hairstyle for women throughout history is hair pulled back into a little bun. If you have short hair, you merely pull your own hair back and pin it and add a crepe hair or synthetic bun. Pony tails can be added in the same way. Hair can be trimmed or cut professionally to fit a particular character. Also both sexes can set and curl the hair to make it more manageable. To change the color of your hair, sprays are available in most drug stores in a variety of colors which can be washed out quite easily. Hair whiteners available from make-up supply houses give a realistic appearance, and the color is easy to control. The hair whitener can be brushed on with a toothbrush. As you work with your hair and achieve the desired effect, avoid spraying it so heavily with hairspray that it becomes an immovable mass. A few stray wisps and softness are quite attractive and much more believable than stiff, artificial-looking hair.

Paul Huntley designed this extremely natural-looking wig for actress Swoosie Kurtz.

An Old Fisherman. Greek. Sculpture-Statues. II B.C.

Tomb Group: Statues of a woman and a girl — IV century B.C.

Sculptures and paintings are a valuable resource for theatre designers. Each period represented — Greek, Medieval, Renaissance, Elizabethan, Cavalier, Eighteenth Century, Empire, Romantic, Nineteenth Century — has a basic line or silhouette and a distinct "feeling."

Profile Portrait of a Young Man. Florentine — 1401-1428.

The Annunciation. Jan van Eyck. Flemish — 1370-1440.

Portrait of a Lady. Rogier van der Weyden. Flemish — 1399/1400-1464.

Portrait of a Youth. Botticelli. Florentine — 1444/45-1510.

Ginevra de Benci. Leonardo da Vinci. Florentine — 1452-1519.

ortrait of a Youth. Filippino ippi. Florentine — 457-1504.

The Earl of Essex. British School XVI century.

Marchesa Brigida Spinola Doria. Peter Paul Rubens. Flemish — 1577-1640.

Portrait of an Officer. Frans Hals. Dutch — 1580-1666.

Queen Henrietta Maria. Sir Anthony van Dyck. Flemish — 1599-1641.

Marquis d'Ossun. Francois-Hubert Drouais. French — 1727-1775.

Miss Mary Heberden. Thomas Gainsborough. British — 1727-1788.

Mrs. Metcalf Bowler. John Singleton Copley. American — 1738-1815.

The Kitchen Maid. Jean-Baptiste-Simeon Chardin. French — 1699-1779.

Portrait of a Young Woman in White. Jacques-Louis David. French — 1748-1825.

Leconte de Lisle. Jean Francois Millet. French — 1814-1875.

Queen Victoria. Franz Zaver Winterhalter. German — 1805-1878.

L'Andalouse, Mother-of-Pearl and Silver Canvas. James McNeill Whistler. American — 1834-1903.

Louis Husson. Thomas Eakins. American — 1844-1916.

Mother and Child. Mary Cassatt. American — 1844-1926.

A few basic materials are necessary for you to achieve the hairstyles of many different periods.

COMB
HAIR AND BOBBY PINS
BRUSH
HAIR SPRAY
COLORED SPRAYS
HAIR WHITENER
ELECTRIC CURLERS/CURLING IRON
REGULAR CURLERS
ELASTICS
SYNTHETIC BRAIDS AND HAIR PIECES
CREPE HAIR (VARIOUS COLORS)

As you can see from the photographs, ribbons, combs, caps, and other trims may be used to keep the coiffure in line and add interest.

To give you experience in working with your own hair, and to illustrate the effect that hairstyle can have on the image you project, the following exercise is offered.

EXERCISE #27

Using a comb/brush or a few bobby pins, change your hairstyle. You might part it in the middle and slick it back with water; or if you usually wear it back, brush it forward; or twist it into a bun at the back; or change the part to a different side. Study the effect in a mirror. Test the effect on your family or classmates. Do you feel different? Do your friends notice a difference?

Hair styling should be worked out carefully and not saved until the last minute when unexpected problems may arise. The proper make-up and hairstyle help the actor look and feel the part, and the actor needs time to experiment with both.

COSTUME

A costume is both anything an actor wears onstage, and a visual representation of the character. Along with the other externals of make-up and hairstyle, the costume makes a visual statement about the character and the theme and style of the play. The statement may be humorous, ironic, tragic,

Illustration 6-8

Horace

Costume designs for Molière's *School for Wives*. What do the costume designs tell you about the characters?

Illustration 6-9

Georgette

romantic, absurd, or fantastical depending upon the choices the director, designer, and actor make. Usually costume choices are made by the designer in collaboration with the director, but actors and students of theatre should be aware of the basic principles governing the choices which are made

The first principle of costuming is *analysis* of the character and the play. (Refer to questions on page 92) Only after the character and the play are thoroughly understood can intelligent choices be made regarding costume.

The second principle governing costume choices is *artistic quality*. Artistic qualities of line, color, and texture must be employed. As you can see from the photographs on pages 115-122 each major period has a basic line or silhouette. Line is the outer contour of the figure. There are many variations of texture and color within the same period, but the line remains reasonably consistent. Line in costume can become a visual representation of the shape or form of the play. Perhaps you are presenting a Greek tragedy. You research the Greek period - fifth century B.C. - and you find that the basic costume line is vertical with soft draping and minimal decoration. Greek tragedy is written cleanly and elegantly with a strong narrative. The costuming then reflects this lean, powerful force. A comedy such as SCHOOL FOR WIVES by Molière has ornate language, puns, and complicated plot twists. In researching the period 1660-1700 in France, you will find that clothing was festooned, beribboned, and ornamented to a dazzling degree. The costumes of the period then reflect the language and feeling of the play. This is not to say costuming always has to be of the period in which the play was written or originally staged. ANTIGONE by Sophocles, written in fifth-century B.C. Greece, is often done in modern evening dress; the women in long gowns and the men in tuxedos. However, the basic costume line remains unchanged and the formal, classic nature of the play is still reflected in the costuming. Shakespeare's plays adapt readily to many different periods and treatments. The line of the costuming must remain true to the form of the play; harmonized and balanced.

Color, the second artistic quality, is important symbolically, emotionally, and historically as well as aesthetically. Certain colors carry traditional overtones - white suggests purity and innocence, red connotes passion, and green often symbolizes youth and freshness. If we see a group of people dressed all in black, our emotional reaction is usually somber.

In certain periods of history only a few colors were widely worn. The Puritans wore black and browns; no bright colors or decorations.

The colors chosen for a production should reflect the spirit and feeling of the play. A light, bouncy musical such as YOU'RE A GOOD MAN, CHARLIE BROWN would be incongruous costumed in subdued tones of brown and black. Clear, bright, primary colors suggest the energy and spirit of fun that pervade the play. Colors not only reflect the overall feeling of a play, but serve to set apart and characterize individuals in a play. For example, David in DAVID AND LISA by James Reach is an emotionally disturbed adolescent who withdraws from others and is extremely rigid and uptight. To set him apart visually, he is costumed in a dark, tailored suit and tie quite unlike the jeans and tee shirts of the other adolescents in the play. His personality is reflected in the straight line and dark tones of his costume.

The third artistic quality, texture, must also be considered. A supple fabric like a soft wool or crepe might be used for the flow and drape of the Grecian costume line, but a heavy, stiff fabric such as brocade is needed for the Elizabethan look. The following exercise will help you become more familiar with the fabrics available for costuming.

EXERCISE #28

Visit a fabric store and get samples of the following fabrics:

cotton - coarse and fine
wool - soft and heavy tweed
crepe
brocade
corduroy
satin
velvet
leather
lace
velour (select as many different colors and
taffeta weights as possible)

broadcloth
gabardine
muslin
chiffon
burlap

Mount and label the fabrics in a notebook. Observe the texture and weight of the fabric. Note that shiny, smooth fabrics reflect light and textured, rough fabrics do not. What does this mean in terms of choosing fabrics for costuming? Observe that different fabrics have a distinct "feel." What emotional qualities do the different fabrics, and textures, and colors suggest? Imagine what type of character might wear each fabric. For example, what kind of person would wear a scratchy wool tweed?

The third principle to consider in costuming is *individuality*, not only of the character, but of the actor playing the character. Every actor has physical limitations or physical attributes which may be masked or enhanced. A short actor may appear taller by wearing a costume with clean, vertical lines and built-up shoes. A thin actor can be padded to appear stocky. Also, the individual aspects of each character should be visually represented through costuming. Variations of color, texture, and detail can set the character apart, but the line of the costume can still set the character in a particular period.

These three principles of *analysis*, *artistic quality*, and *individuality* are the foundation on which the costuming process must be built. The following exercise allows you to put these principles into practice.

EXERCISE #29

Select someone you know well - a teacher, a coach, an uncle or aunt, a fellow student - and observe the person in several different situations and environments. Observe how the person is "costumed" for each situation and environment. If the person is dressed in a uniform, are there personal touches that have been added to make the uniform distinct? Do you see any behavioral changes as the costume changes? What observations can you make about line, color, and texture? Do you see any overall pattern in dress?

Organize all your observations into a paper. Share your observations with the class.

The preceding exercise gives you an opportunity to observe the costuming process that happens around you every day. As mentioned earlier, externals can reveal or conceal who we really are. This same process occurs in plays. For example, Nora in A DOLL'S HOUSE by Henrik Ibsen is perceived by Torvald, her husband, to be his "doll wife" and his "little skylark." In the beginning of the play Nora "flutters and chirps" and dresses herself in colorful, dainty plumage. Her clothing masks her seriousness and her sacrifice which she attempts to conceal from Torvald. As the play progresses and as Nora grows and changes, she sheds her colorful plumage, and at the end of the play her colorful, silly costumes fancied by Torvald have been replaced by a more sober dress which visually reflects Nora's grown up attitude and serious purpose. Nora's external appearance then is a visual representation of her inner struggle.

Since costumes are a visual representation of a play's theme and style and a character's inner self, their selection and design should not be done haphazardly. All of the costumes in a play must fit together. For this reason, it is not a good idea for actors to plan their own costumes. The costume designer in collaboration with the director usually coordinates the entire visual effect.

Several methods are used in obtaining costumes for a play. If the play is set in the present, costumes may be purchased directly from stores; they may be rented from a costume supply house; they may be borrowed or supplied by the actors; they may be donated; they may be found in second hand and surplus stores; or they may be "built" by a costume crew. Buying or renting costumes is generally quite expensive. Rental costumes must be returned and are available only for a short time. Sometimes it is necessary to rent a few special, unusual items. The most rewarding and educational method, however, is to learn to "build" the costumes yourself. This method allows students interested in design to see their creations come to life, and it gives other students an opportunity to learn the basics of sewing and costume construction.

Illustration 6-10

Miranda

Costume sketches for The Tempest.

Illustration 6-11

Caliban

STEPS IN COSTUME DESIGN AND CONSTRUCTION

1. Read and analyze the play. Discuss the concept with the director and other designers. Keep in mind the three principles of costuming. If necessary, research the period.
2. Do a color chart for each act and each character.
3. Consult with the set designer to check compatibility of colors and line.
4. Do sketches of each costume and a costume plot. The costume plot is a chart of all the costumes worn in the production. If you can't sketch, use swatches of fabric cut in the shape of the costume. Consult with the director who must approve the sketches.
5. Measure each actor.
6. Purchase the fabric necessary or remake old costumes or donated clothing.
7. Fit costume on each actor.
8. Do finish work - hems, trimmings, buttons, snaps, etc.

The responsibility of making the costumes may be carried out by a special costume crew or by theatre classes. The prime requirement for anyone constructing costumes is a willingness to learn and experiment. Costumes must be sturdy enough to wear well, but the sewing does not have to have the quality of clothes that will be worn every day and washed many times. A basic sewing kit, a sewing machine, an iron and ironing board, and a few basic patterns are necessary before costume construction can begin.

Sewing Kit

needles
black and white thread
pins
safety pins
yard stick
tape measure
scissors
pinking shears
seam ripper
chalk
thimble
hook and eyes
elastic

MEASUREMENT FORM

Actor's Name ________________ Character ______________

Name of Play ________________ Performance Dates ________

Measurements Taken By ________ Date ________________

Neck __________

Waist __________

Chest or Bust __________

Hips __________

Armseye __________

Underarm to wrist __________

Shoulder to wrist __________

Length from neck to waist (front) __________

(back) __________

hips (front) __________

(back) __________

Inseam __________

Waist to ankle __________

Waist to knee __________

Shoe __________

Shirt __________

Jacket __________

Pants __________

Dress __________

Skirt __________

Illustration 6-12

SAMPLE COLOR PLOT

THE TEMPEST - Act 1, Scene 2

Character	Color
Prospero	dark blue/gold
Miranda	light blue/green/gold
Ariel	silver/white
Ferdinand	gold/red/blue white hose
Caliban	greyish green/brown

If you use colored pencils or pens to indicate the color choices for costumes, you can look at the color plot and see at a glance how the different colors will look together in each act or scene. Or you may use fabric swatches.

SAMPLE COSTUME PLOT

THE TEMPEST — Act I, Scene 2

Character	Act	Scene	Costume Description
Prospero	1	2	dk. blue robe trimmed with gold, wooden staff, "magic" cape
Miranda	1	2	lt. blue/green/gold dress with chiffon underskirt, slippers, stockings
Ariel	1	2	silver and white leotard
Ferdinand	1	2	gold/red cape lined with blue satin, gold doublet, white hose, slippers, sword and leather belt
Caliban	1	2	large greyish/green cloak stained with dirt and caught with briars

With practice, everyone can learn the basics of sewing. If you can read and follow directions, you can operate a sewing machine, cut a pattern, and with some experimentation make your own patterns.

EXERCISE #30

Find an old shirt or an old pair of pants. Carefully take them apart with a seam ripper or a pair of scissors. Observe how the different parts fit together. Look at the seams, the buttons and button holes, the collar, the sleeves, etc. Now, pin all the different parts back together. Repeat the process until you understand how each part fits together. Finish by sewing the parts together permanently.

Once you understand how clothing fits together and how each piece is constructed, you can begin to see, for example, that a sleeve follows a basic pattern which can be lengthened, shortened, widened, or puffed to achieve the effects of different periods. Men's pants can be cut short and wide for Elizabethan puffed breeches or to knee length for the eighteenth century style. One pattern can be adjusted for many different periods and styles.

Shoes, stockings, and accessories are important parts of the overall costume picture. In many cases, simple black slippers or plain black or brown shoes will serve for many periods. Buckles and trim may be added. Shoes may be made out of cloth or leather. In any case, research on the period will reveal what type of footwear was used. Stockings and hose can easily be purchased in a variety of colors and types. Accessories such as handbags, canes, umbrellas, fans, eyeglasses, and pipes can be found in second-hand stores or donated. The use of accessories can add depth and variety to a characterization, but the actor should work with the accessory and use it properly.

Actors should practice moving, sitting, and standing in their costumes. The costumes should be available in advance so that they can become part of the actors' overall characterization. The actors should be as comfortable and as familiar with their costumes as they are with their own clothes.

To gain practical costume experience, sign up for a costume crew or try your hand at designing costumes for actors in a classroom scene. The head of a costume crew is the wardrobe master or mistress. The crew has several important responsibilities.

WARDROBE MASTER/MISTRESS AND WARDROBE CREW

1. Make a master list of all costumes and accessories used by each character. Note costumes used in each act and any changes that must be made. Also note any quick changes that must be rehearsed.
2. Label each costume with the character's name. Use a laundry marker. Labelling costumes helps eliminate confusion over whose costume is whose!
3. Help the actors get in and out of costume.
4. Keep the sewing box with you to make last-minute repairs.
5. Watch rehearsal and make notes of any tears, uneven hems, missing buttons, or other problems.
6. Check all actors before they go onstage to make sure they have *all* of their costume on. Also check for personal jewelry, watches, rings, and necklaces which are out of character. A theatrical illusion set in the sixteenth century might fade when an actor walks onstage with a digital watch. It's a good idea to collect all extraneous jewelry and put it in a safe place until the play or rehearsal is over. An even better idea is to remind each actor to leave jewelry and valuables at home.
7. See that costumes are hung up and stored neatly at the close of each dress rehearsal and performance. Actors should not take costumes home without special permission. Costumes or accessories can easily be forgotten at home. Storing them all together helps avoid panic and last-minute trips home.

8. Keep a file box with file cards of all costumes rented or borrowed. Sample card:

Production ____________________ Dates __________
Costume Description ____________________
____
____
Condition: Exc. ___ Good ___ Fair ___ Poor ___
Borrowed From: ______________ Date: __________
Washed: _________ Cleaned: __ Repaired: __ Other: __
Returned _____ Date: _____ "Thank You" Sent _____
Rented From: ____________ Date: ____________
Returned: _________ Date: _________

In the following exercise, experiment with fabrics and other materials in the creation of your own costume design.

EXERCISE #31

Read and analyze a play which is not contemporary. Research the period of the play. Do a color chart and costume sketches for two characters. With your sketches and chart submit a written justification for your choices. If possible, include fabric swatches.

The externals of make-up, hairstyle, and costume are often the first impression that an audience has of a character. The externals must harmonize with the overall production, be suitable and practical for the actor to use, reflect the theme and style of the play and the character's inner life, and also be aesthetically pleasing. Care and attention to detail are of paramount importance in creating externals just as care and attention to detail are important in creating the internals of a character. The visual power of the externals to reveal and conceal helps to create a unified, harmonious theatre production.

QUESTIONS FOR REVIEW AND DISCUSSION

1. What are the purposes of externals?
2. Explain the steps in applying basic and age make-up.
3. Why is observation important in make-up design and application?
4. What are the three basic principles of costume design?
5. What are the methods used in obtaining costumes for a play?
6. What are the duties of a make-up crew? a wardrobe crew?

VOCABULARY

shadow
highlight
base
crepe hair
color chart
collodion
spirit gum
costume line
costume plot
liquid latex

SUGGESTIONS

- Design costumes for a children's play or Reader's Theatre performance using only long underwear and basic art supplies such as crepe paper, paper bags, pipe cleaners, etc.
- Compile a notebook of interesting and unusual hairstyles, make-up, and clothing clipped from newspapers and magazines.
- Read and report on UNDERWEAR: A HISTORY by Elizabeth Ewing.
- Visit an art gallery and study the portraits and sculpture of different historical periods.
- Research the make-up, hairstyle, and clothing of a particular historical period. Report to the class.

Chapter 7

The Playing Space

Set Design and Construction

Throughout centuries of theatrical history and technological innovation, the playing space remains a place for actors to perform. This place may be an elaborate 3,000-seat theatre or a modest 100-seat basement off-off Broadway. In any theatre, there must be a space for the actors to perform and a space for the audience. These spaces may take many shapes and forms, and the distinction between the audiences' space and the actors' space may be blurred. However, the playing space is not just a physical space; it is an imaginative space limited only by the creativity of the theatre participants.

The use of actual space and imaginative space, as well as techniques of set design and construction will be explored in this chapter. A *set* is the environment for theatrical action. This environment is a conscious creation of the playwright, director, designer, and actors working in collaboration. A set designer may create a detailed authentic living room set, but it is up to the director and actors to use the space imaginatively and expand the actual set to include the imaginary house and surrounding area. The actual space and the imaginative space fuse to create the total theatrical environment.

The playing space is a meaningless void without a set. The set may be created "out of air," as you did in improvisation, or it may be built with solid materials, but in either case the set serves several important purposes.

Primarily, the set:

1) reflects the theme and style of the play
2) places the play in time, period, locale
3) creates atmosphere
4) reveals characters' mental, physical, and emotional state.

These purposes are explored in the following exercise.

Illustration 7-1

Proscenium stage

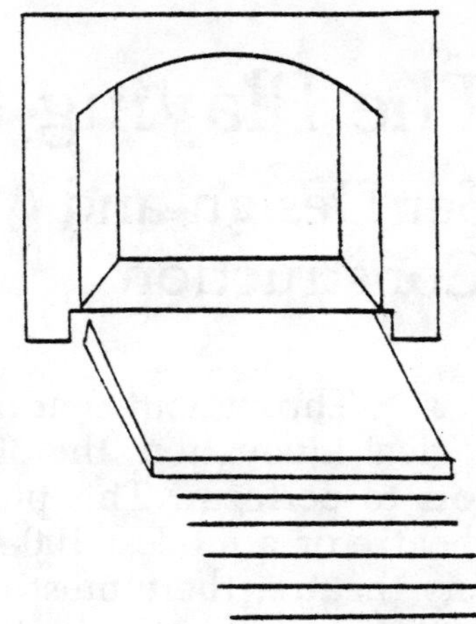

Illustration 7-2

Proscenium stage with thrust

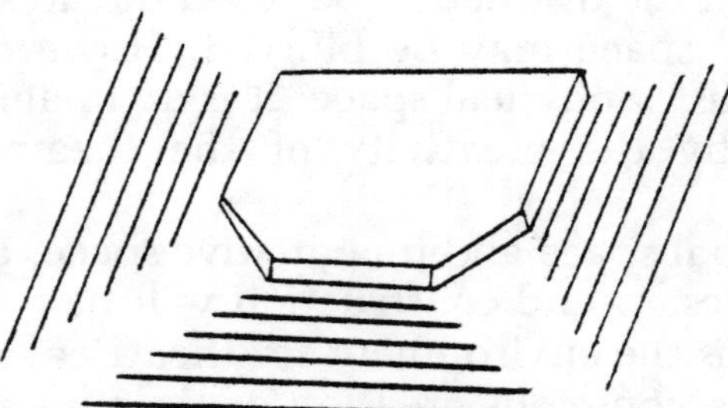

Illustration 7-3

"Open" staging or three-quarter stage

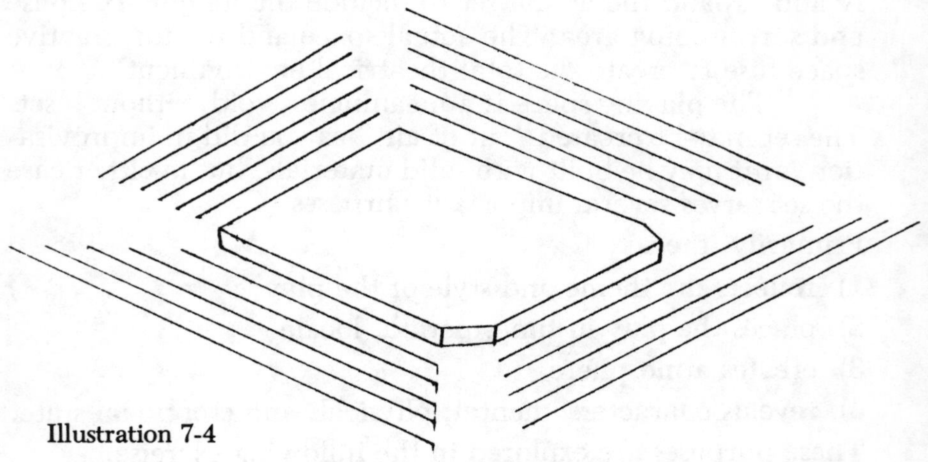

Illustration 7-4

Arena stage or theatre-in-the- round

EXERCISE #31

Describe the appearance of the sets for each of the following situations.

a. a living room after an all-night teen-age party

b. a living room in the year 2100 in New York City at 2:00 in the morning

c. a living room in a deserted, decaying mansion in Transylvania

d. a "typical" living room with a television

In your description indicate color, size, shape, and texture of the objects you use. Also indicate the center of attention in the set, and the "feeling" or theme you wish to convey. For example, to reflect the theme that television controls our lives, the television set in (d) might dwarf all the other furniture. What elements would you show to reveal a "typical" living room?

Share and compare your descriptions with the class.

The range of possibilities for a "living room" set is enormous. The possibilities, of course, depend upon the purposes. The choices made provide the audience with the necessary information, atmosphere, and details. The choices are limited by a few practical considerations, but the limits can provide the incentive for new and creative concepts. The size and type of space available must be analyzed. For example, a fifteen-foot by eight-foot stage cannot comfortably accommodate huge, musical casts. The budget, time to prepare, and staff are also important factors. Before any decisions about the set are made, the theatre group must evaluate the practical considerations of

1) size and type of space available
2) budget
3) time to prepare
4) staff

Before set design can be discussed, the basic terminology must be defined. Learning the language of theatre is essential in order to comprehend theatre set design and construction concepts.

ACTING AREA - the area which the actors use during a performance.

ACT CURTAIN (FRONT CURTAIN) - the curtain which can be opened or closed to reveal or conceal the scene on stage from the audience.

AUDITORIUM (HOUSE) - space in the theatre where the audience is located.

APRON - the part of the stage in front of the curtain line.

ARENA THEATRE - an acting area enclosed on four sides by the audience.

BATTEN - strips of wood or lengths of pipe to which scenery or drops are fastened. Also, refers to 1 × 3 lumber which is used to make scenery.

BORDER - a hard or soft panel attached to a batten. Used to mask the top of the stage.

CONSTRUCTION DRAWINGS - detailed plans for the construction of scenic elements. Includes dimensions and instructions for building.

CURTAIN LINE - the line across the stage which marks the position of the front curtain when it is closed.

CYCLORAMA - a large cloth drop which forms a backing for the set - usually on three sides.

DROP - a large cloth or canvas sheet hung from a batten. May be painted and used for a background.

FLAT - basic unit of scenery made of cloth or canvas stretched over a wooden frame - used to form the walls of a set.

GROUND PLAN (FLOOR PLAN) - a scale drawing showing the layout of the set.

LEG - hard or soft panel which is often attached to a batten. Used to mask offstage areas.

MASKING - a leg or a piece of scenery used to conceal offstage areas from the audience.

MODEL - a scale three-dimensional mock up of a set.

OFFSTAGE - area outside the acting area.

OPEN STAGE - a type of stage which has no permanent barrier such as a proscenium between the stage and the audience.

ORCHESTRA PIT - area between the stage and the audience which is lowered to accommodate an orchestra.

PLATFORM - a portable set unit which is used for an acting area or to vary the levels on a permanent stage.

PRACTICAL - a term used to indicate actual *use* onstage. For example, windows that open and close, lamps that work, are called "practicals."

PROSCENIUM STAGE - the "picture frame" stage which is open to the audience on one side — framed by an arch.

RENDERING - a painting depicting the set designer's conception of the set.

SCRIM - a loosely woven fabric used as a drop. When lighted from the front, it is opaque to the audience; when lighted from the back, it is transparent.

SET - an environment for theatrical action.

> BOX SET - enclosed on three sides by flats,
>
> UNIT SET - made up of several elements which can be combined to form different settings.
>
> INTERIOR SET - suggests an indoor scene.
>
> EXTERIOR SET - suggests an outdoor scene.
>
> FORMAL SET - usually of steps and platforms which lends itself to classic plays. Can suggest many different locales.
>
> SIMULTANEOUS SETS - several sets in place onstage at the same time. Scene shifts accomplished through lighting changes.

SET DESIGNER - the person responsible for creating the physical and aesthetic environment of a production.

SIGHTLINES - the audience's line of vision from seat to stage.

STAGE - acting area.

TEASER - horizontal drop which masks the top of the stage and is used to change the height of the proscenium opening.

THRUST STAGE - a stage which projects into the audience. Usually the audience is on three sides.

TORMENTERS - vertical drops which mask the wing area of the stage and are used to change the width of the stage.

WINGS - the areas to the right and left offstage.

SET DESIGN

The process of set design begins when the play is chosen. The set designer reads the play many times noting theme, style, atmosphere, time period, locale, characters, and practical considerations such as entrances, exits, and movement. Playwrights often indicate the number and type of sets, but each play must be interpreted by a designer and director working with their own needs, desires, and limitations. After the play has been analyzed, the designer confers with the director, and they arrive at a mutual design concept. At this point the designer may research a particular period or locale by looking at paintings and drawings, reading descriptions, or actually visiting a location and examining it. The designer then collects the ideas together into a ground plan which must be approved by the director. Also a model and/or rendering of the design must be approved by the director before actual construction can begin.

Artistic qualities of unity, balance, line, texture, mass, color, and emphasis are utilized by the designer. The set must not only be practical, but it must artistically represent the play. The visual appearance of the set conveys impressions and information to the audience both on a conscious and subconscious level. A set which contains a "hodge-podge" of design elements and does not reflect the theme and style of the play lacks *unity* and is disturbing to an audience. *Balance* in set design is a pleasing harmony of proportion and value. For example, if all the furniture in a set is placed on stage right and stage left is bare, then the stage picture is out of balance. A perfect mirror image of each side is not necessary for proper balance - an important chair can counter balance a large sofa. The line of a set can be straight, curved, jagged, horizontal, vertical, or a combination of any of these. Emotional states can be suggested through line: a curving line can indicate

Illustration 7-5 What impressions are conveyed in this set rendering from *The Ghost Sonata?*

peace and harmony; straight, vertical lines can represent power and majesty; jagged or broken lines can show discord. The *texture* or "feel" of the set also conveys impressions and evokes emotional responses. Textures may be smooth, rough, coarse, shiny, prickly, or soft, but the choice of texture should reflect the feeling of the play. *Mass* is the shape and size of the scenic elements used. The shape and size of the television set in Exercise 31 can convey information and shape an emotional response. If the mass of the television set is exaggerated, dwarfing the other furniture, it then becomes extremely important physically and symbolically. *Color* plays an important symbolic role. If the audience sees a bright, cheery yellow when the curtain rises, they prepare for a pleasant comedy. Dark, somber tones suggest a drama. In a set, as in a painting, there is a point of *emphasis* or weight. If every element has equal weight, the visual effect is uninteresting. Emphasis can be achieved through line, mass, color, texture, or placement on stage. Keep in mind that all of these artistic elements must work in unison to present a visual impression of the play. To summarize, a set should

1) be practical and usable.
2) reflect the theme and style of the play.
3) convey information about the characters, locale, and time period.
4) reveal atmosphere and evoke emotional response.
5) present an aesthetically appealing vision.

A set should also be visible to the audience and constructed with the sightlines of the particular theatre in mind. After the set is constructed and in place, sightlines should be checked from *every* seat in the house to insure that vision is not obstructed.

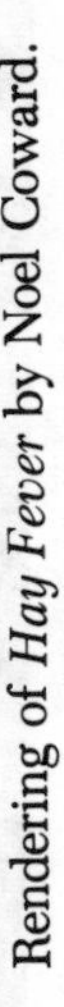

Illustration 7-6 Rendering of *Hay Fever* by Noel Coward.

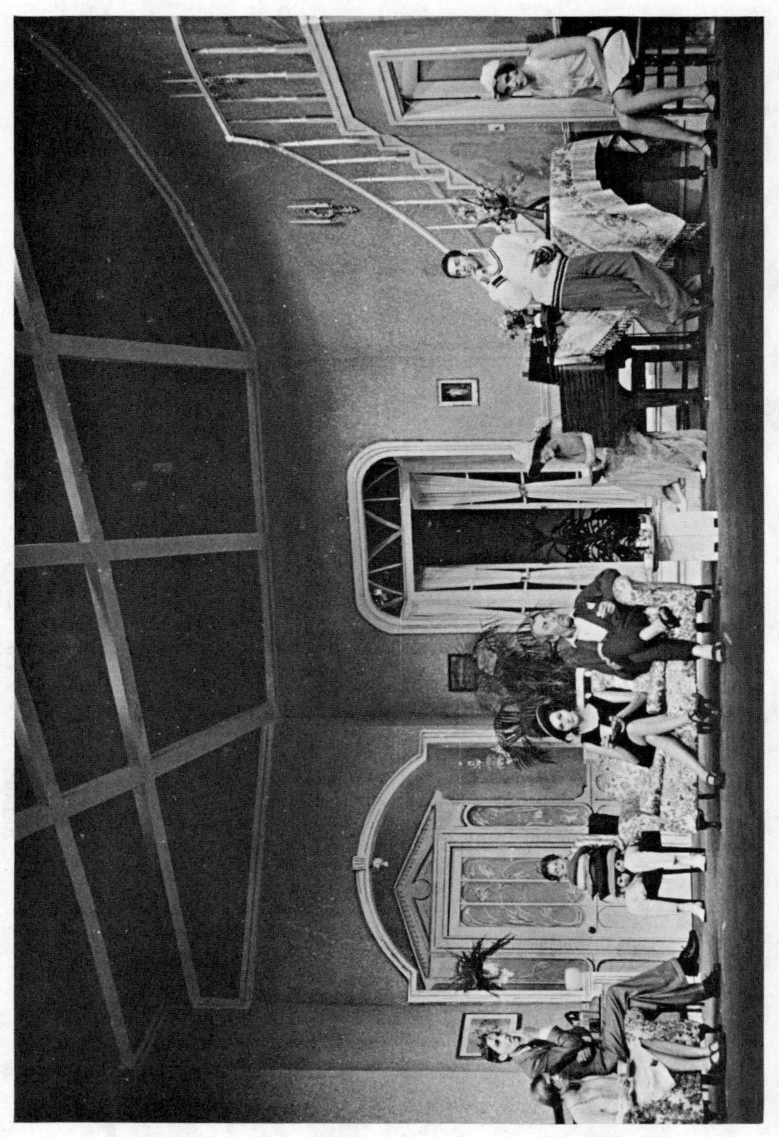

A photograph of the finished set of *Hay Fever*. Compare the finished set with the rendering on page 145.

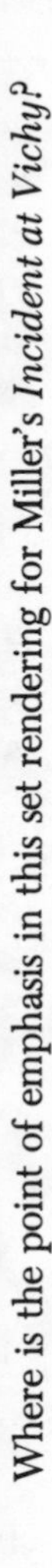

Illustration 7-7 Where is the point of emphasis in this set rendering for Miller's *Incident at Vichy*?

Set Construction

Once the design process and construction drawings are completed, then actual construction of the design can begin. The major scenic elements - flats, platforms, and steps will be discussed in detail. But first, familiarity with common tools and materials and the general working rules is vital for efficient construction of the major scenic elements.

TOOLS

CLAW HAMMER
MATTE KNIFE
CROSS CUT SAW
SCREW DRIVER
PLIERS
WOOD CHISEL
CRESCENT WRENCH
TAPE MEASURE
WRECKING BAR
DRILL
FRAMING SQUARE
COMBINATION SQUARE
STAPLE GUN
ELECTRIC DRILL
SABRE SAW

OTHER MATERIALS TO HAVE ON HAND

PAINT BRUSHES - 5″ to 7″ natural bristle for flat painting
2″ to 4″ all purpose
1″ trim brush
several cheap brushes for glue

PLASTIC OR METAL BUCKETS

YARD STICK

CLINCH PLATE - Metal plate for clinching nails into flats

CLAMPS

PENCILS AND CHALK LINE

MUSLIN OR SCENERY CANVAS (comes in 54″ - 63″ - 72″ - 90″ widths up to 30 feet)

WHITE GLUE

COMMON NAILS - 6D, 8D, and 10D

DOUBLED-HEADED NAILS

WOOD SCREWS

FINISHING NAILS

1¼″ CLOUT NAILS
MACHINE BOLTS, NUTS, AND WASHERS
TIGHT PIN BACK FLAP HINGES
LOOSE PIN BACK FLAP HINGES
BRACE CLEAT
STAGE SCREW
STAGE BRACE
LUMBER

1 × 3 #2 white pine - used for framing flats
2 × 4 - used for legging platforms
1 × 12 #2 white pine - used for framing platforms
¼″ plywood - used for keystones and corner blocks
¾″ plywood - used for platform tops
1 × 2 or 1 × 3 #2 white pine - used for bracing

(Note: Lumber is sold by the board foot. A board foot is 12″ wide, 12″ long, and 1″ thick. 1 × 3 or 1″ × 3″ refers to the thickness and width of the lumber.)

GENERAL RULES

1. Before working on set construction, make sure you are wearing the proper clothes. HARD-SOLED SHOES are a must! Nails can easily penetrate sneakers. Sleeves, shirt tails, and jewelry should not hang loosely.
2. Every tool should be stored in its place when it's not in use. Each tool should be clean and dry when it is put away.
3. Paint cans should be wiped clean and sealed tightly. Brushes must be cleaned thoroughly before storing.
4. Keep work area clean. Cluttered tables and areas invite accidents.
5. Keep visitors away from work area.
6. Don't force a tool. It will do the job better and safer at the speed for which it was designed.
7. Use the appropriate tool for the job.

8. Don't abuse electrical cords. Never carry a tool by the cord or yank the cord to disconnect from outlet.
9. Read the owner's manual carefully before operating any power tools; and get permission from your instructor before operating any power tool.
10. Never leave pieces of wood around that have nails sticking through them. Either pull the nails out or bend them over so that they can't hurt anyone.
11. Measure twice, cut once!
12. Don't rush. Be pleasant and courteous.

The basic unit of scenery, a flat, can be built using the above tools, materials, and rules. A series of flats joined together make up the walls of a set. Flats are easy to construct, inexpensive, and lightweight. They can be painted and repainted. If made well they are durable and will last for years.

Constructing the Framework
Using the following steps, a standard 12′ by 4′ flat can be constructed. The techniques used may be adapted to fit any size flat.

STEP #1 Clear a large working space and assemble the following tools and materials.

1 - 8′ length of 1″ by 3″ #2 white pine
2 - 16′ lengths of 1″ by 3″ #2 white pine
4 - ¼″ plywood cornerblocks
4 - ¼″ plywood keystones
Box of 1¼″ clout nails
Hand saw or power saw
Staple gun and staples
Muslin
Tape measure
Framing square
Combination square
White glue
Matte knife
Pencil

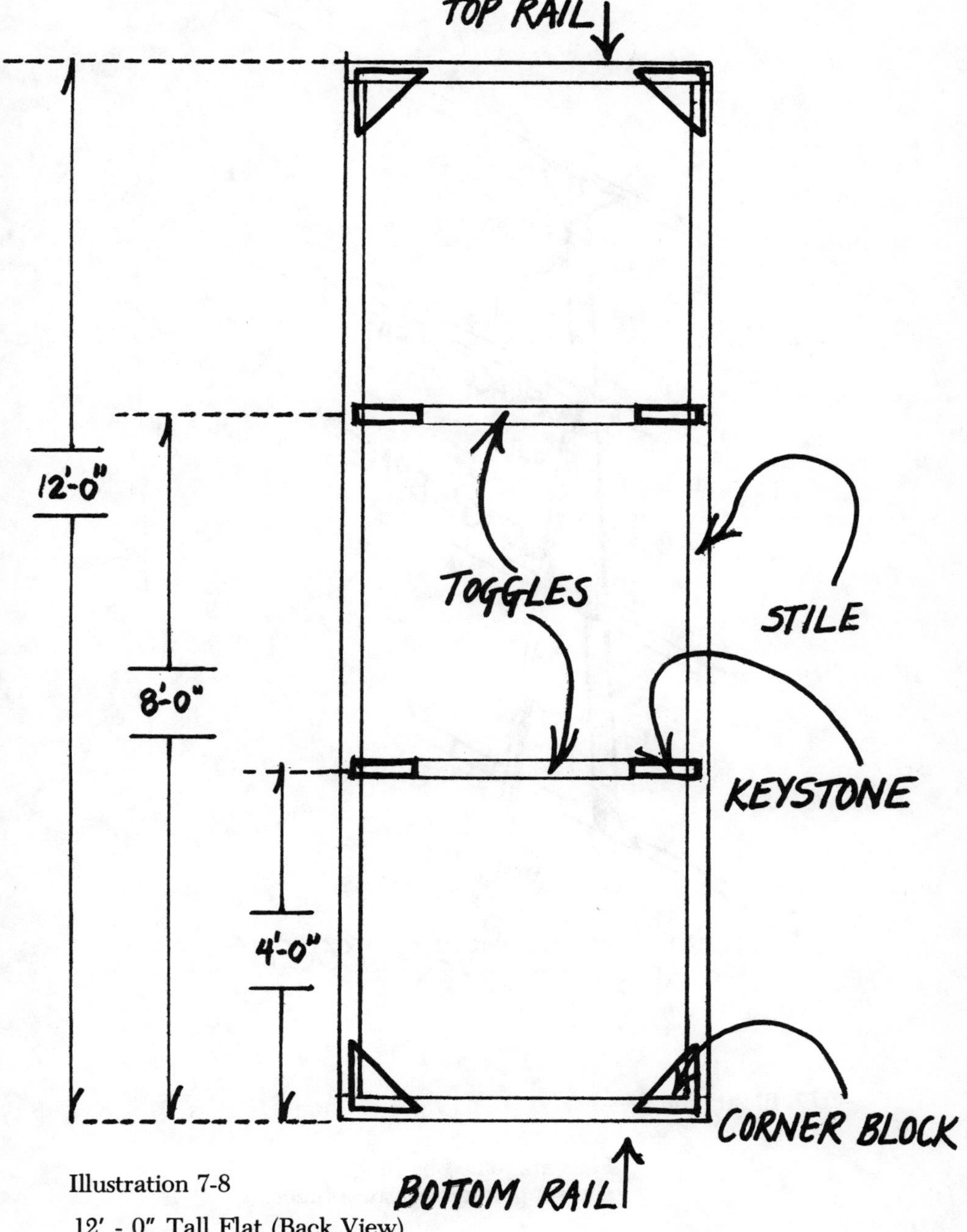

Illustration 7-8

12' - 0" Tall Flat (Back View)
4' Wide

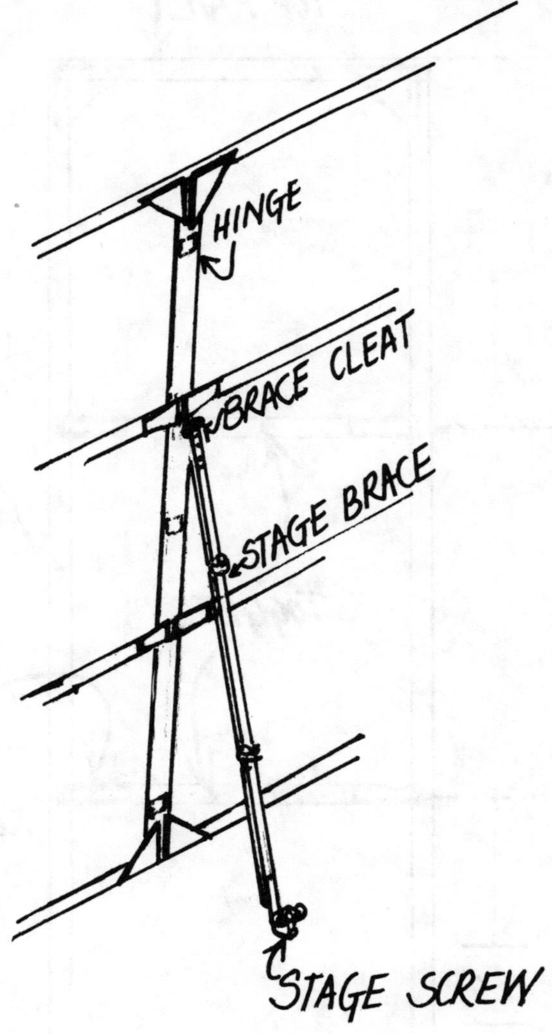

Illustration 7-9

Flats are joined by hinges
and supported by a stage brace.

STEP #2 Measuring and cutting. Look at Illustration 7-8 and note that the stiles fit between the rails, and the toggles fit between the stiles. For a 12 foot flat the side stiles should be cut 12 foot minus 2 rail widths (one width at the top and one at the bottom). The rails are cut the full width of the flat or 4 foot to form the top and bottom of the flat. Before cutting, write out the cutting information on a piece of paper and double check.

For example: **Cutting directions for 12′ by 4′ flat**

Cut 2 lengths of 1″ by 3″ (1 × 3) white pine at 12′ minus 2 rail widths or 11′6½″. Again, note that the width of the 1 × 3 white pine may vary. It is easier and more accurate to use a piece to be used for the rail to mark off the stile measurements.

Cut 2 4′ lengths of 1 × 3 white pine to use as rails.

Cut 2 4′ minus two stile widths (4′-2w) or 3′6½″ for the toggles. The toggles fit between the stiles and again it is more accurate to use a piece to be used for the stiles to mark off the toggle measurement.

Measure the appropriate length, and remember, *measure twice, cut once!* Use a square and mark the cutting line with a pencil, and make the cut with a saw.

STEP #3 Assemble the pieces of the flat frame on a smooth surface (the floor will be fine). The top and bottom rails are placed on the floor and the stiles between them. The two toggles are centered on 4′ and 8′ from the bottom. Placing the toggles in this way provides a support for picture hanging; a window can be cut in the flat, and a chair rail can be added around the bottom.

STEP #4 Use a large framing square to square the corners of the flat. After all corners are square, the cornerblocks and keystones can be attached. The cornerblocks are placed so that the grain of the plywood is

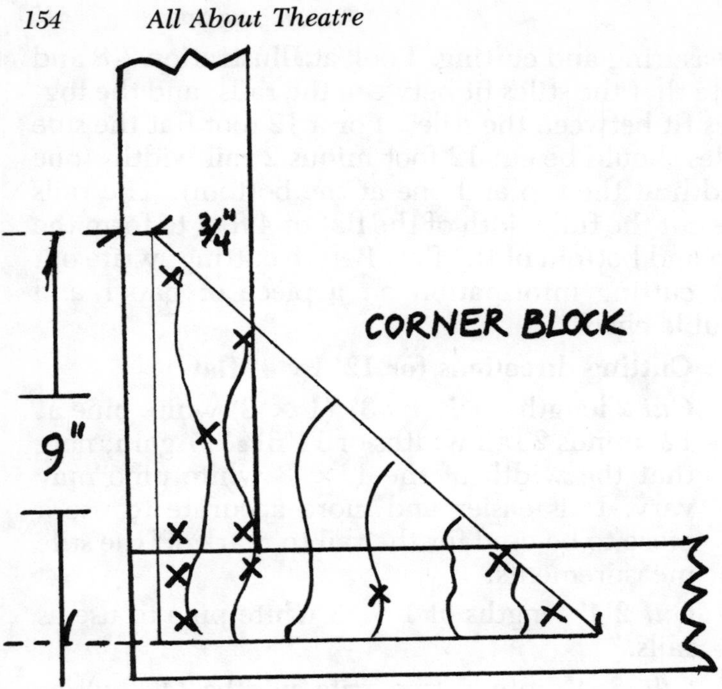

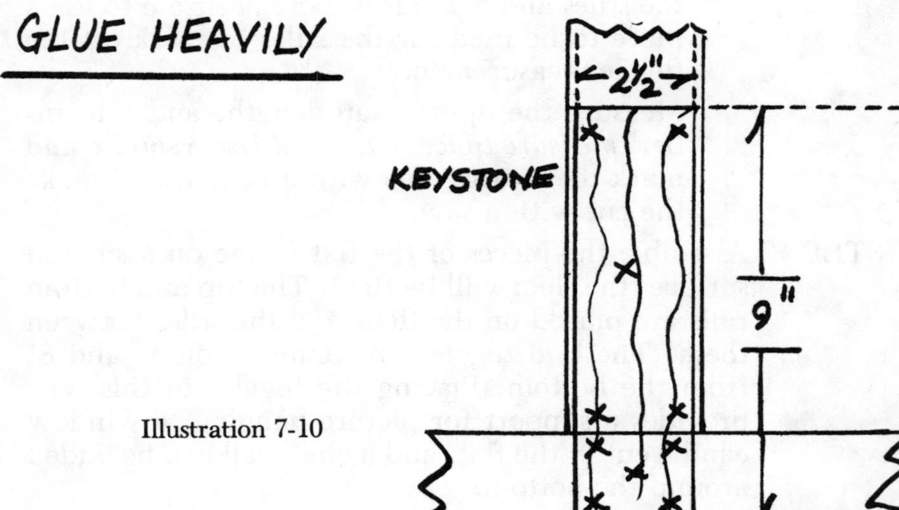

Illustration 7-10

parallel to the side stile or across the joint. This strengthens the joint. If the grain is placed *with* the joint, the joint is easily broken with a little pressure.

STEP #5 Glue the keystones and cornerblocks for extra strength and place ¾" from the edge of the flat. (Use a 1 × 3 thickness to mark the ¾" from the edge.) Nail into place with clout nails in the pattern illustrated. But do not nail all the way through. When all the keystones and cornerblocks have been nailed, place a clinching iron under the corner of the flat and drive the nails in the rest of the way. Since the nails are 1¼" and the flat is 1" (¼" plywood and ¾" pine), the nails will go all the way through, hit the metal clinch plate, and the metal will force the nails to clinch into the surface of the wood.

STEP #6 Before covering the frame, the hardware should be attached. Attach the hinges with wood screws. Place hinges at top, middle, and bottom of flat.

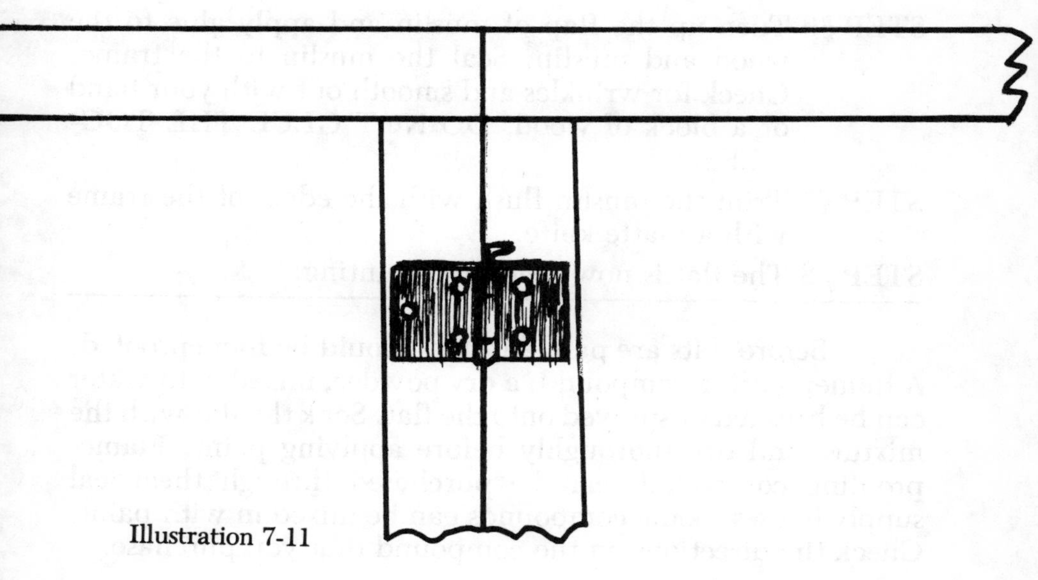

Illustration 7-11

Covering the framework

STEP #1 Cut off a 12′6″ length of 54″ wide unbleached muslin. The extra length and width is necessary for fastening to the frame. Extra cloth will be trimmed later.

STEP #2 Lay the muslin over the *face* of the frame. Take the selvage edge (finished edge) of the length of the muslin and place on the stile up to the edge of the flat. Staple the muslin to the stile starting at the center of the stile and working out. Place the staples 4″-6″ apart and about ½″ from the inside edge.

STEP #3 Pull the muslin to the other stile and staple in the same manner as STEP #2, keeping the material even. The material will shrink when it is painted so it should not be too tightly stretched, but neither should it be slack.

STEP #4 Staple the material to the rails starting at the center and moving out. Keep the material even and taut.

STEP #5 If there is a noticeable sag, remove the staples and start again.

STEP #6 Turn up the flap of muslin and apply glue to the wood and muslin. Seal the muslin to the frame. Check for wrinkles and smooth out with your hand or a block of wood. DO NOT GLUE THE TOGGLES.

STEP #7 Trim the muslin flush with the edges of the frame with a matte knife.

STEP #8 The flat is now ready for painting.

Before flats are painted, they should be flameproofed. A flameproofing compound, a dry powder, mixed with water can be brushed or sprayed onto the flat. Soak the flat with the mixture and dry thoroughly before applying paint. Flameproofing compounds can be purchased through theatrical supply houses. Some compounds can be mixed in with paint. Check the directions on the compound that you purchase.

Painting a Flat

Traditionally, scene paint, a mixture of dry pigment, glue, and water, has been used to paint flats. Although scene powders are relatively inexpensive, for the inexperienced they are difficult to use. The proper mixture of powder, glue, and water can only be determined through trial and error. Scene paint is available with the glue already mixed in which is more convenient. Casein paint and latex paint with glue binders are easy to use, but more expensive than scene paint. Many scenic artists mix casein and latex to achieve a wide variety of colors. The choice of paints depends upon the experience, budget, and needs of the theatre group. The painting process outlined below can be modified to suit your particular needs.

PAINTING A FLAT

STEP #1 Assemble materials:
- 5″-7″ bristle brushes
- Paint
  - (Mix enough to paint all the flats as colors are difficult to match)
- Buckets
- Paint Cloths and Rags to catch and mop up spills.

STEP #2 Lean the flats up against a wall. If this is not possible, lay them on the floor and paint them, but make sure that the paint doesn't puddle on the flat.

STEP #3 A base coat of white or a light color is painted on the muslin to seal the surface. Use a thin coat and cover completely. The back of the flat may also be painted with the base coat to prevent light leakage. Allow to dry thoroughly.

STEP #4 The next coat, the flat coat, is applied using an "X" pattern to distribute the paint into the surface of the muslin. Allow to dry.

STEP #5 The flat must be textured so that it has a more natural, three-dimensional appearance. Several methods are used. The most common method is *spattering* with 2-3 colors. For example, if the flats

Illustration 7-12
X Pattern

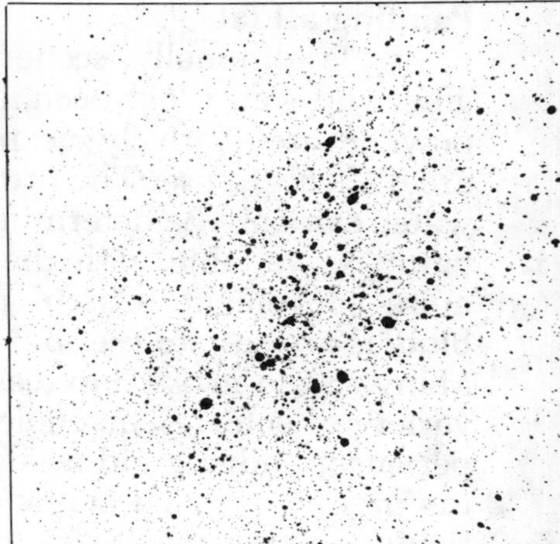

Illustration 7-13
Spattering

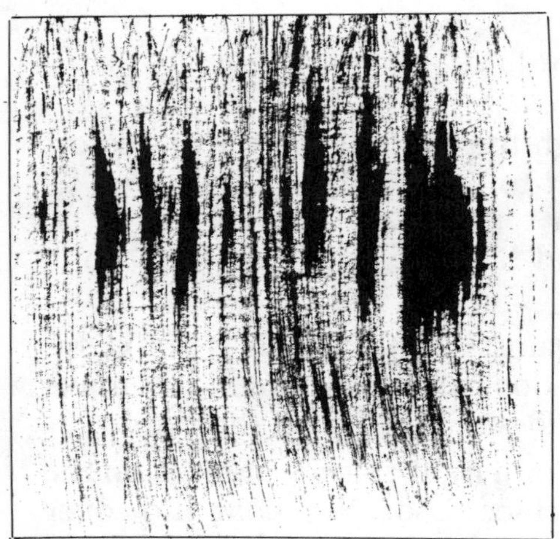

Illustration 7-14
Dry Brushing

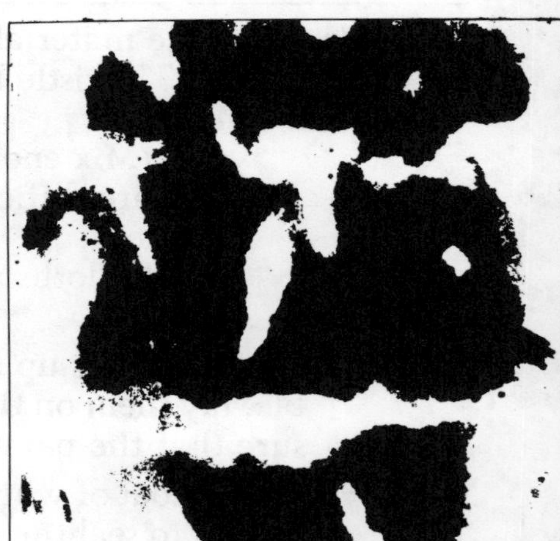

Illustration 7-15
Rag Rolling or Sponging

are brown, spatter with black, rust, and blue. One color should be darker, one lighter, and one complementary. Dip the ends of the brush in the paint, and using your wrist, lightly flip the brush, which flicks spatters of paint onto the muslin. In any case, practice before applying spatter to the muslin. Try to avoid clumps of color; a pattern of fine dots is the desired effect. *Dry brushing* is also used to texture a wood-grain effect. Drag the almost dry brush over the surface of the muslin forming a pattern of lines. A rolled-up rag or sponge dipped in paint and lightly touched to the flat can give a textured appearance. Also, stencils may be used and a wall paper pattern painted on.

STEP #6 After the flats are painted and textured, they are ready to be joined together to form a set.

STEP #7 To mask the space between flats a "Dutchman" is used. A "Dutchman" may be simply a strip of

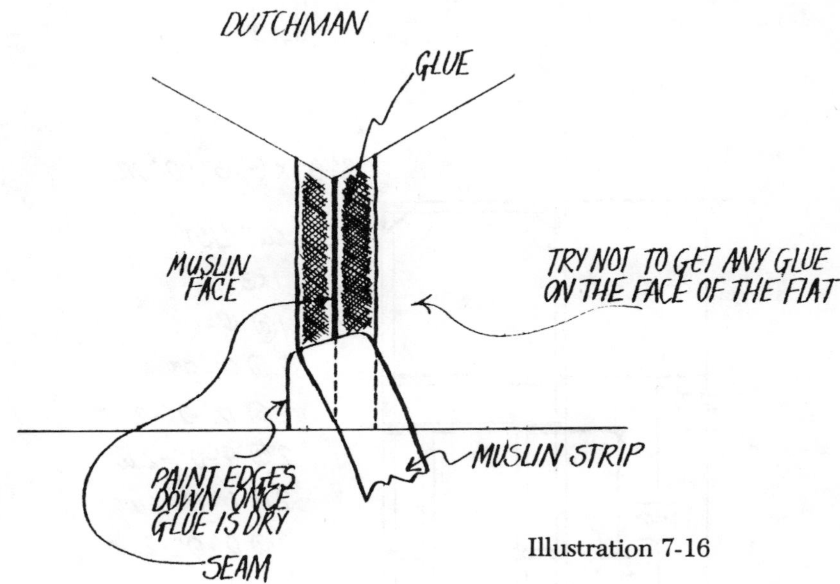

Illustration 7-16

muslin that is glued to the face of the flats and then painted or it may be a special wood strip.

Doors and window frames may be made by adapting the flat construction steps.

DOOR REVEAL

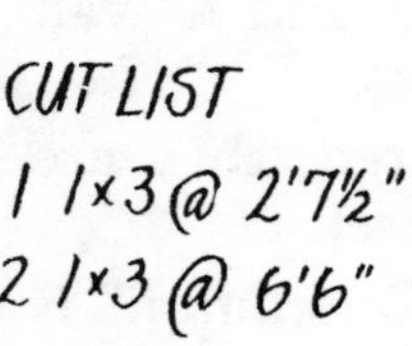

CUT LIST
1 1×3 @ 2'7½"
2 1×3 @ 6'6"

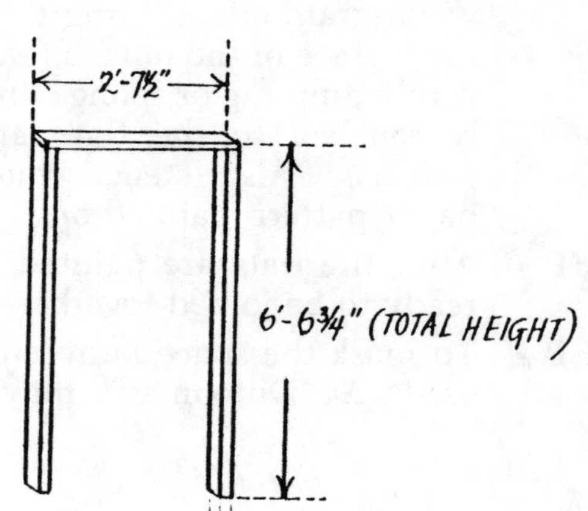

2'-6" × 6'-6" DOOR

CUT LIST
1×3
1@ 4'-0"
2@ 0'-9"
2@ 12'-0"-2w
2@ 4'-0"-2w
2@ 6'-6"-1w
2@ 0'-9"-2w

12'-0"
8'-0"
6'-6"
4'-0"
9" 2'-6" 9"

Illustration 7-17

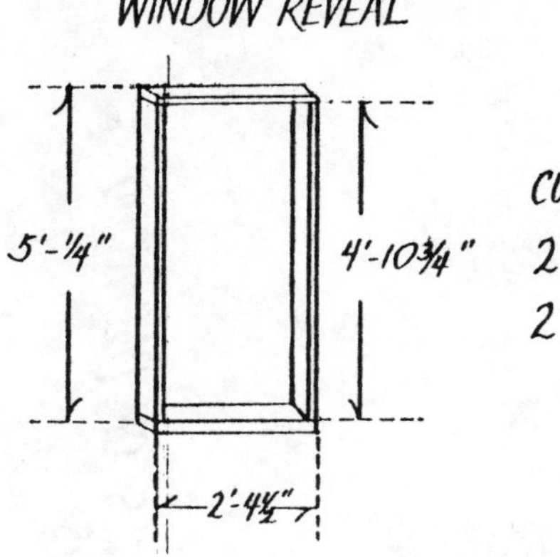

CUT LIST
2 1×3 @ 4'10¾"
2 1×3 @ 2'4½"

WINDOW CENTERED IN THE FLAT

2'-3" × 4'-10¾"

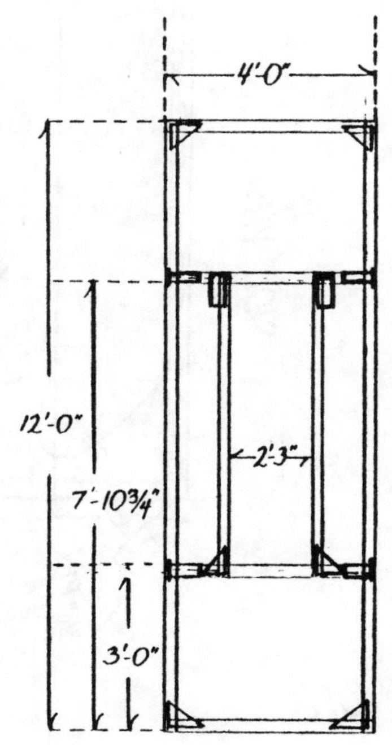

CUT LIST
2 @ 4'-0"
2 @ 12'-0" - 2w
2 @ 4'-0" - 2w
2 @ 4'-10¾"

Illustration 7-18

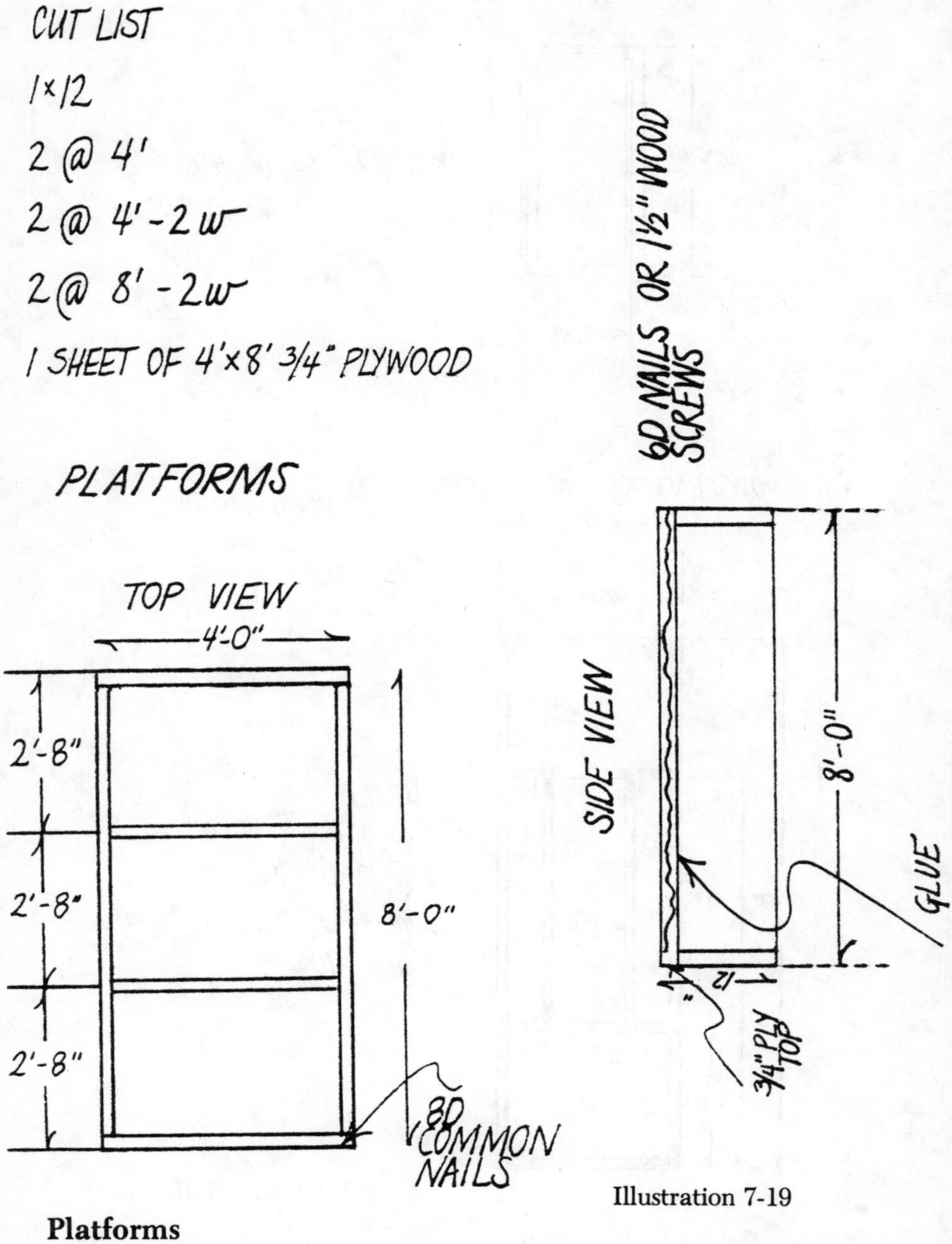

CUT LIST

1×12

2 @ 4'

2 @ 4'-2w

2 @ 8'-2w

1 SHEET OF 4'×8' 3/4" PLYWOOD

PLATFORMS

TOP VIEW

4'-0"

2'-8"

2'-8"

2'-8"

8'-0"

8D COMMON NAILS

SIDE VIEW

6D NAILS OR 1½" WOOD SCREWS

8'-0"

12

3/4" PLY TOP

GLUE

Illustration 7-19

Platforms

One of the most versatile scene units is the platform. It can be raised, lowered, lengthened, slanted, and widened to produce many different effects. The basic platform is made using a sheet of 4 foot by 8 foot three-quarter inch plywood, 1 inch by 12 inch (1 × 12) white pine for framing, and 2 inch by 4 inch (2 × 4's) wood for the legs. Changing the height of the legs changes the height of the platform; several 4 × 8 platforms may be bolted together to form an acting area; or several levels can be achieved using platforms of varying heights.

Step Unit

A step unit must be used with any platform above two feet. A combination of step units and platforms can be used in a variety of ways.

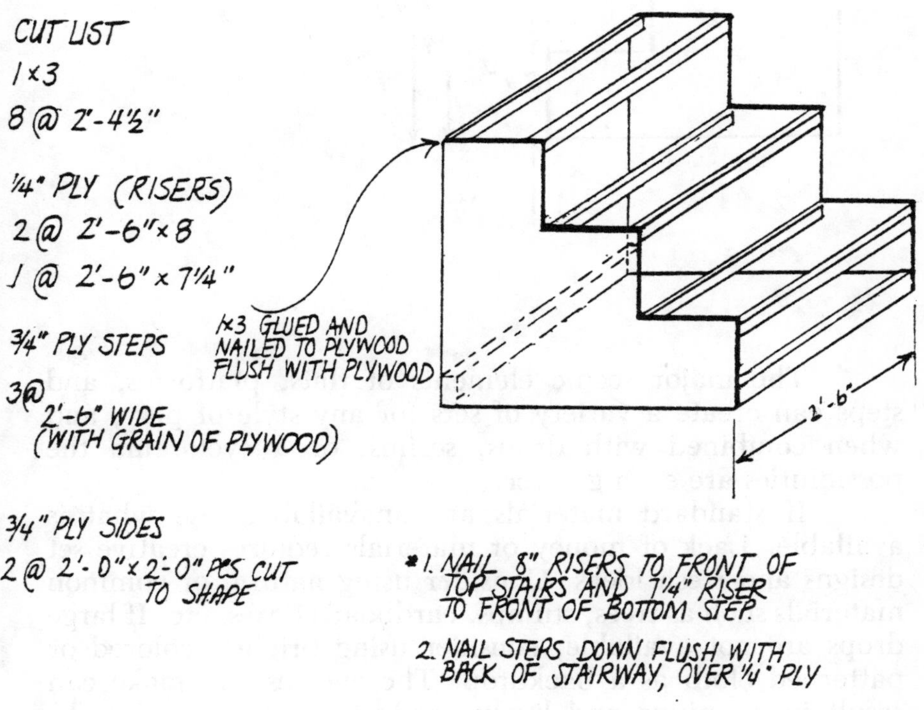

Illustration 7-20

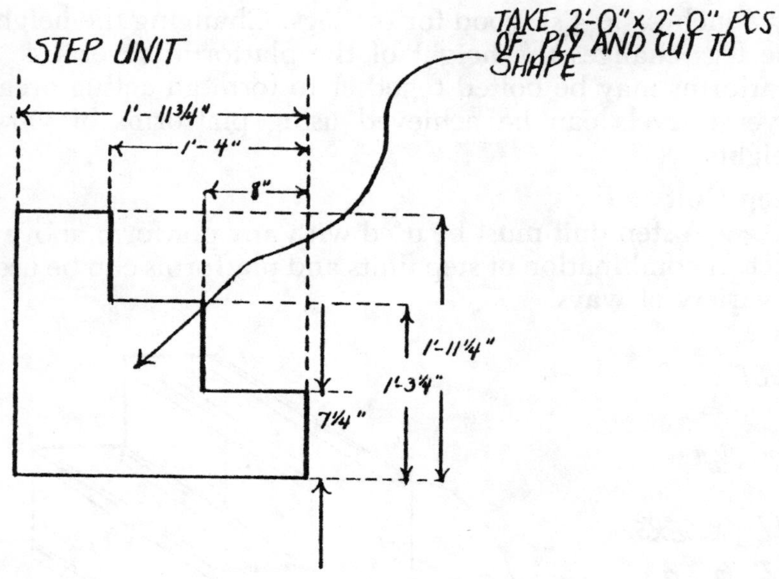

The major scenic elements of flats, platforms, and steps can create a variety of sets for any style of play, and when combined with drops, scrims, or a cyclorama the possibilities are even greater.

If standard materials are unavailable, use what is available. Lack of money or materials requires creative set designs and fresh ideas. Consider using natural or common materials such as trees, stumps, cardboard boxes, etc. If large drops are not available, consider using brightly colored or patterned cloth as a backdrop. The choices you make can result in a unique and lively production. Theatrical techniques are not written in stone, they are as flexible and as imaginative as the individuals in the theatre.

Decorating the set or "dressing" the set with the appropriate furniture, curtains, rugs, and props should be done with care and attention to detail. If a period play is being pro-

Note the detailed set decoration in this scene from *Biography*.

duced, research is essential to capture the "feel" of the period. Again, the set and everything used should reflect the play and the characters. If the set is a home, objects should be chosen to reflect the personality of the person living there. The details of a set, like the details of a character, provide extra dimension and fullness to the production.

EXERCISE #32

Read and analyze a one-act play and design a set. Follow the steps of the design process: either sketch the finished design or build a model. Share with the class. Be able to explain and justify your choices.

Through your use of the physical techniques of set construction and the imaginative use of design, the playing space, an essential element of theatre, can become a total environment; encompassing, revealing, and illuminating the action of the play.

QUESTIONS FOR REVIEW AND DISCUSSION

1. What is a set? What are the purposes of a set?
2. Explain the set design process.
3. What artistic qualities are utilized by the set designer?
4. Discuss the general rules of safety and courtesy in set construction.
5. Outline the process of building a flat - a step unit - a platform.
6. What techniques are used in painting a flat to make it appear three dimensional?
7. Discuss the sets of plays which you have seen. Did the sets reflect the theme and style of the plays? Why or why not?

VOCABULARY

See pages 140–142

"Dutchman"
"dressing" the set
spattering
dry brushing
board foot

SUGGESTIONS

- Research and report on one of the following scenic designers:

  Jo Mielziner, Donald Oenslager, Robert Edmond Jones, Boris Aronson, Mordecai Gorelik, Edward Gordon Craig
- Research the period and build a model of one of the following theatres:

  Shakespeare's Globe, fifth-century B.C. Greek theatre, seventeenth-century French court theatre
- Design and build a set for an improvisational performance or class performance using only "found" materials. Try to use common materials in new ways.

Chapter 8

Stage Lighting

When the house lights are dimmed and the stage lights come up, a powerful creative force is at work. As lighting illuminates, provides atmosphere, and creates environment, the world of the stage "lives." The stage world is shaped by the changing effects of light. The warmth of the sun can give way to a cool moonlit evening. Lighting can symbolize mental illumination or spiritual inspiration. Indeed the physical properties of light - intensity, color, direction, and spread -and its emotional and symbolic qualities unite to form what Adolphe Appia, the Swiss scene and lighting designer, called "living light."

"Living light" which could be controlled and shaped was made possible by electricity. Edison invented the incandescent lamp in 1879, and theatres quickly converted their gas light and limelight systems to electricity. Limelight was a very intense brilliant light produced by heating a piece of limestone with a very hot combination of gases. When used with a curved mirror, the effect was quite dazzling. This is the derivation of the expression "You're in the limelight," which has come to mean being in a very prominent, conspicuous position. Before gas and limelight, theatres were lit by candle light, torches, and natural sunlight. Electricity and modern technology have made it possible to control and shape light to mimic the natural world or to create a new world. Although complete understanding of the process of electricity requires a study of physics, a knowledge of some basic electrical terms is necessary for an understanding of theatre lighting.

Theatre lighting is achieved through the use of lighting instruments with lamps (lightbulbs), dimmers which regulate the flow of current and control the intensity of brightness of the instruments, and cables which carry the electrical power.

All lamps, dimmers, and cables are rated in watts by the manufacturer. *Wattage* is a measuring unit of the amount of electrical energy consumed in a given length of time. For example, a dimmer rated for 2,400 watts can control four lighting instruments with 500 watt lamps. To determine the maximum wattage or capacity of a circuit, multiply the voltage and amperage of the circuit. A 220 volt circuit with 20 ampere cable has a capacity of 4,400 watts. The formula is $W = V \times A$. *Voltage* can be thought of as the force of the electrical current flowing through the circuit. Average household service is 110 volts; 220 volts is the standard for theatre lighting. *Amperage* can be thought of as the speed of the flow of current through the circuit. Electricity creates heat and if a circuit is overloaded, the *fuse*, a protective device will melt and break the electrical circuit. To avoid overloading a circuit, the dimmer wattage load should not be exceeded, so the amperage must be calculated. Watts divided by voltage equals amperage - $W \div V = A$. For example, a load of 4,000 watts on a 220 volt line requires a 20 amp fuse. The cause of the overloading must be found or the fuse will continue to melt and break the circuit. These basic electrical terms - wattage, voltage, amperage, and fuse - are employed in the study of lighting design, principles, and practice.

BASIC LIGHTING EQUIPMENT

Since Edison's invention of the lightbulb, lighting for the theatre has become quite sophisticated. The use of computers, electronics, and miniaturization has revolutionized stage lighting. Almost any lighting effect is possible with this advanced and expensive technology. Effective and artistic lighting can be achieved, however, with basic equipment and an understanding of lighting principles.

FRESNEL

The fresnel light is used to light acting areas from behind the proscenium at distances from 10-18 feet. The beam is soft and fuzzy at the edges which makes it useful for blending with other lights and color toning. 500 watt and 750 watt lamps are generally used.

ELLIPSOIDAL "LEKO"

This "leko" light named for its ellipsoidal shaped lens is used for lighting acting areas. The leko can project a beam from 40 to 60 feet. The light has four shutters which shape the beam in a variety of geometric patterns. These lights are usually hung from balcony fronts, or ceiling ports or battens in front of the proscenium.

BABY LEKO

This small leko is useful for "specials" which must be handled separately. It projects a high intensity sharp edge beam up to 25 feet.

STRIP LIGHTS

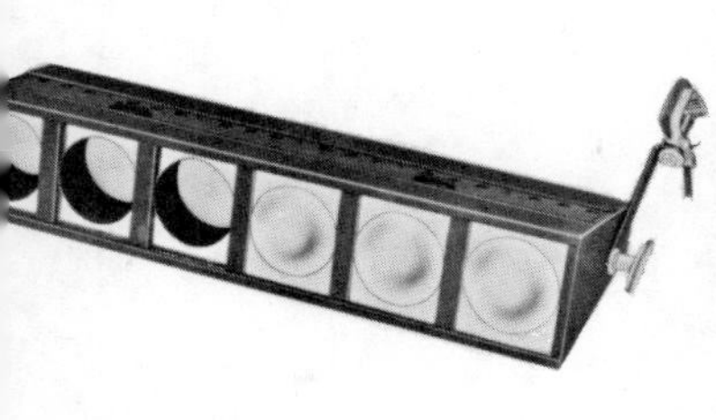

When these lights are used for general illumination and atmosphere behind the proscenium and hung from battens, they are called "border lights." When they are used on the floor of the stage at the proscenium, they are called "footlights." They also may be hung vertically and used as sidelights. The most common use, however, is in lighting cycloramas and backdrops from above or below. The strip lights normally have 3 circuits which control the 3 primary light colors - red, green, and blue.

BEAMLIGHT PROJECTOR

This light projects a soft-edge light beam which is used for intense accent lighting such as shafts of sunlight or moonlight.

FOLLOWSPOT

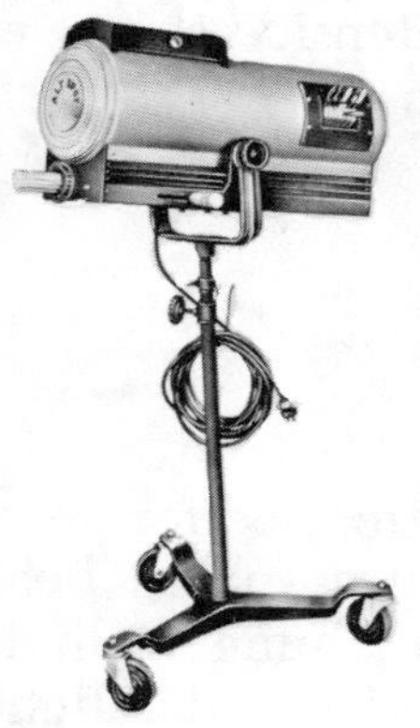

This instrument lights up to a distance of 125 feet. Six colors and framing shutters to adjust the size and color of the beam make this a versatile instrument.

DIMMER MODULE AND CONTROL MODULE

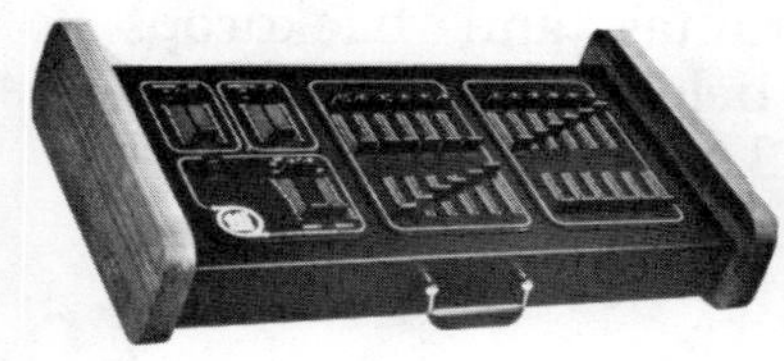

The control box can cover and handle up to twenty-four circuits

BARNDOORS AND TOP HATS

These accessories slip in front of a fresnel to help shape and control the beam.

COLOR MEDIUM OR "GELS" AND GEL FRAMES

Thin sheets of gelatin or plastic in an enormous range of colors are used to give color to light. The sheets are held in place in front of the instrument with a gel frame. Gel colors are loosely divided into two groups - "warms" (amber, straw, pink, red) and "cools" (blues and greens). Because of the tremendous number and variety of colors available, gels are designated by number rather than by name.

C-CLAMP

An adjustable clamp which holds the lighting instrument to the pipe batten.

BOOM AND STAND This heavy iron base and pipe are used as a portable tower for hanging lighting instruments.

LAMPS The type of lamp used depends upon the lighting instrument. 500 watt and 750 watt are usually used. Tungsten halogen lamps or "quartz" lamps are rapidly replacing incandescent lamps in popularity. The halogen lamps last longer, burn cleaner, and produce a more brilliant light.

STAGE CABLE Cable is rated by the manufacturer to take a maximum load of watts and comes in two or three wire.

TWOFERS Two instruments can be "ganged" on one cable with a twofer. The two lighting instruments are plugged into the two female ends of the twofer and the male end is plugged into the cable.

CONNECTORS Two common connectors are the pin and twist-lock. The twist-lock has the advantage of locking securely into place so that it does not come loose. The connection is not made until the connector is "locked" into place which is an additional safety feature. All connectors on lighting instruments, twofers, and cables, should be the same.

LIGHTING APPLICATIONS

Working with the equipment listed above, the lighting designer can begin to plan the lighting. The lighting designer is responsible for the design, focusing, and description of the running of the lights. The designer, in collaboration with the director and the set designer, determines the lighting plan of the production. Like the set designer, the lighting designer begins with the play. The designer reads the play many times noting theme, style, period, locale, time of day and season, characters, and atmosphere. Windows, lamps, chandeliers, candles, and any light source mentioned in the script are carefully noted. Before the lighting designer can complete the design, the set design must be completed. Once the set is in place, lights can be focused and gelled.

The lighting designer has three primary objectives -

1) to provide visibility,
2) create atmosphere, and
3) establish an environment.

Through manipulation of the physical properties of light - intensity, color, direction, and spread or distribution of the light over an area - the designer achieves these three objectives.

Visibility, of course, is the first objective. The audience must be able to see the action of the play without straining. Too much light should be avoided as it wipes out depth and contrasts, and it is also disconcerting for an audience. Highlights and shadows should be used for a realistic effect.

The atmosphere desired depends upon the play. The designer attempts to create an atmosphere which is right for the play. If the play is a warm, cheery comedy in a realistic box set, the lighting should be warm, cheery, and realistic. Thus, the light should seem to come from natural light sources, such as an open window with sunlight streaming in. Atmosphere can be changed by varying the intensity or brightness of the lights and by changing the color of the gels. Dimmers control the intensity from very high to very low with a wide range in between. The direction and spread of the lights can make some areas more important than others. A play such as OUR TOWN by Thornton Wilder, with its many changes from sunrise to midday, from a joyous wedding to a

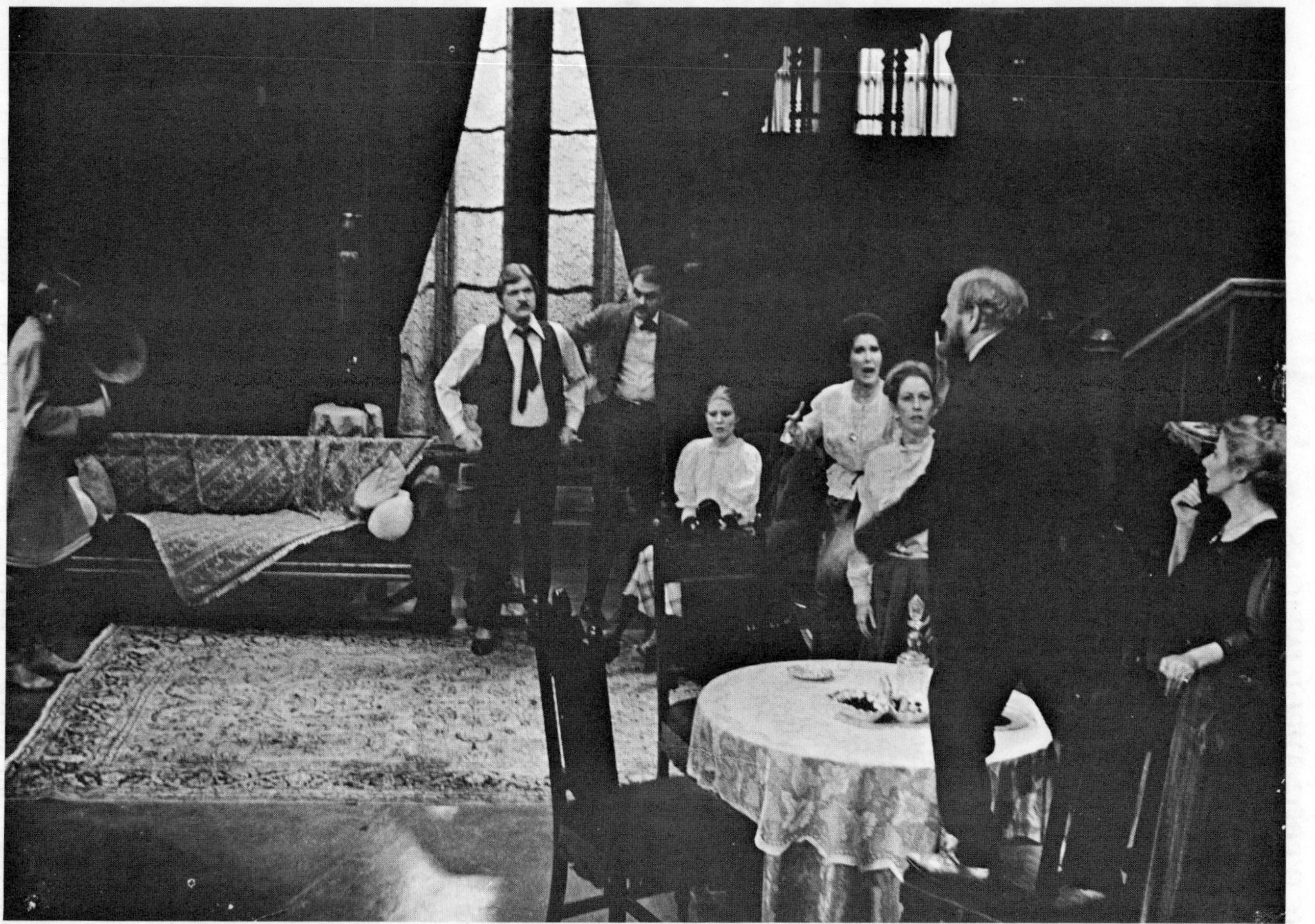

Subtle highlights and shadows are created by lighting designer, Ron Wallace, in this scene from *Yegor Bulychev*.

somber funeral, requires many variations of lighting to create the proper atmosphere.

An environment can be created entirely through lighting and can replace an actual set. Acting areas can be lit separately to suggest different locales. Shakespeare's plays with their rapid scene transitions, different locales, and diverse moods are especially suited to environmental lighting. Shakespeare's THE TEMPEST opens with a violent storm and shipwreck. The atmosphere is dark and tumultuous. The scene can be quite effectively played behind a backlighted scrim which gives a hazy appearance to the action. The next scene can rapidly shift to Prospero's island with a scrim lighted from the front and serving as a backdrop to the action. No set changes are necessary. The magic of light transforms the scene.

The lighting designer is much like an artist who paints a scene except the lighting designer "paints" with light. Like the artist, the lighting designer must be a sensitive observer of the different aspects of light. The following exercise will help you develop your own powers of observation and give you practice in "seeing" light.

EXERCISE #33

Set aside at least thirty minutes to observe one of the following lighting situations. Note the degree of visibility, color, the direction and spread of the light, its intensity, and the source or sources of the light.

a. a sunset or sunrise
b. a living room with a cracking fire in the fireplace and one lamp
c. a business office
d. a classroom (try observing the same room at different times during the day)
e. a city street at night
f. your choice

Write your observations down and share with the class. Include your emotional reactions to the light situation.

To achieve the lighting objectives of visibility, atmosphere, and environment, the designer keeps a few basic lighting principles and terms in mind.

BASIC PRINCIPLES

1. Light sources such as sunlight, moonlight, lamps, etc. should be taken into consideration when planning the lighting.

2. Ellipsoidal lights are normally used to light acting areas.
   Fresnel lights are usually used for general illumination, blending, toning, and creating atmosphere. They may also be used to light upstage acting areas.
   Border lights are used for general illumination and atmosphere.
   Strip lights are generally used to light backdrops, cycloramas, and scenery.
   "Specials" are any lights which create a special effect such as moonlight, sunlight, firelight, or an emphasis light for an actor in a particular scene.

3. Actors and the set should appear three dimensional. Thus, lights are usually operated in pairs - one warm light from the direction of the light source and one cool or diffused light from the other direction. For maximum illumination and dimension, the lights are at 45 degree angles. Straight on lighting tends to wipe out depth and gives a "flat" look. Note: The "warm" and "cool" use of color requires special care in focusing the lights so that parts of the stage and the actors are not lit by one color only. Related gel colors may be used instead of the complementary colors of warms and cools. Some lighting designers do not use colors at all in lighting acting areas. They add color with a "color wash" over the acting area lights. Experiment and discover what method works for you in your particular situation.

4. Gel colors may change the pigment colors of the set. Although the primary colors in light are red, green, and

Note the sunlight streaming through the window and the shadows and highlights in this scene from *Long Day's Journey Into Night*. Lighting designed by Ron Wallace.

blue and the primary colors in pigment are red, blue, and yellow, as a general rule, mixing colored light and colored pigment is the same as mixing two pigments. For example, blue and yellow pigment form green. Blue light on a yellow flat turns the flat green. Light gel colors such as straws and light blues have the least effect on set and costume colors and are the most widely used. However, because of the wide variety of colors, the only way to determine exactly what will happen is to test costumes, make-up, and scenery under lights.

5. White costumes and white paint absorb light color and reflect the color of the light. Off-white or beige has enough color to avoid this effect.
6. The most important acting areas need to have the most light.

7. Avoid over-illumination, especially in a realistic set.
8. Lighting should harmonize and complement the play, not overpower it. Effects, just for the sake of effect(s), are self-indulgent and unaesthetic.
9. Experiment with colors and lighting to achieve the desired effect. If it works, use it!

LIGHTING TERMS

"baby" - a small spotlight usually with a 3½" lens and a 100 to 500 watt lamp.

Backlight - a light which comes from behind the actor.

Blackout - lights turned out suddenly to indicate the end of a scene or act.

Blending - to mix and unite the different beams of light so that the edges become indistinct.

Bring up - to raise the intensity of the light by adjusting the dimmer control.

Circuit - the complete path of an electrical current.

Count - length of time between the beginning and the end of a light cue.

Cue - signal for a lighting change to occur.

Cross fade - as one area fades out, another area comes up simultaneously.

Dead Spot - a place onstage which lacks illumination.

Dim - to decrease the intensity of the lights by adjusting the dimmer control.

Down light - a light pointing straight down.

Fill - light which is added to the other lights to blend areas.

Focus - to adjust the direction and spread of the lighting instrument so that the desired area is illuminated.

F.O.H. - front of house.

Hard Focus - adjusting the focus of the lighting instrument so that the edge of the beam can be seen.

Hook-up List - a record of the equipment used in the production listing dimmer and instrument connections.

"Kill" - turn off a light.

Light cue sheet - a list of all light changes and settings which is used by the lighting technician and prepared by the lighting designer.

Light Plot - a description and layout of all the lighting instruments and their relationship to the set.

Lighting Tech - a rehearsal devoted to focusing and adjusting lights.

Lighting Technician - the person who hangs, focuses, and gels the instruments, and who also runs the light cues.

Soft Focus - adjusting the focus of the lighting instrument so that the edges of the beam become fuzzy and indistinct.

Shutter Cut - when the sharp edge of the "shutter line" can be clearly seen in the light beam.

Spill - light which projects outside the appropriate area. Usually caused by improper focusing.

Throw - the distance that a lighting instrument projects a light beam.

Toning - modifying the color in light.

Wash - general spread of colored light over an acting area or background.

Wash out - the fade of color in the set, costumes, and make-up caused by the lights.

The lighting principles above must be adapted to each individual situation. The light plot or plan for any production depends upon five factors.

1. the physical arrangement of the theatre and the stage.
2. the play.
3. the set design.
4. the lighting equipment available and the budget.
5. the individual wishes of the director and designer.

A basic light plot for a proscenium stage is outlined below. A minimum number of instruments are used. More instruments and dimmers may be added as needed. It is appropriate at this point to mention the contributions of Jean

Rosenthal (1912-1969), a remarkable woman and a pioneer in lighting design. Miss Rosenthal was not only a gifted lighting artist, she originated techniques of lighting organization and notation, plots, hook-up lists, and cue notations which have had a tremendous impact on lighting design and practice.

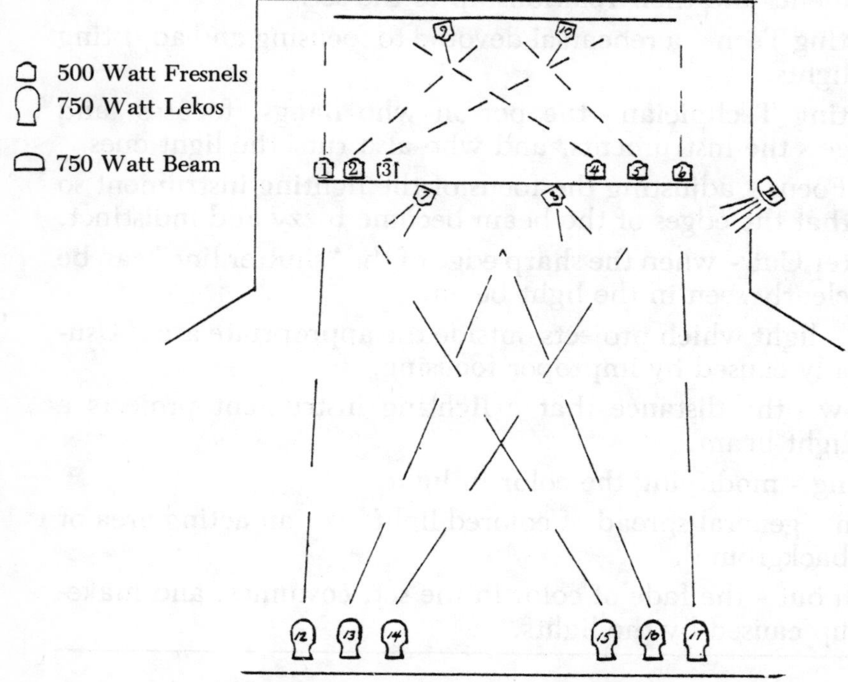

LIGHT PLOT FOR A PROSCENIUM STAGE

HOOK-UP LIST

Dimmer	Position and Number	Type	Area	Color
1	Front of House pipe 12, 13, 14	750 watt lekos	1, 2, 3	light blue
2	Front of House pipe 15, 16, 17	750 watt lekos	1, 2, 3	straw
3	1st electric 1, 2, 3	500 watt fresnels	6, 5, 4	light blue
4	1st electric 4, 5, 6	500 watt fresnels	6, 5, 4	straw
5	1st and 2nd electric 7, 8, 9, 10	500 watt fresnels	fill	lavender
6	Stage Left Boom (sunlight special) 11	750 watt scoop	window	amber

Illustration 8-1

The light plot diagrammed above provides general illumination. Atmosphere can be created by adjusting the intensity and color of the lights. However, many plays require several acting areas which can be lighted and controlled separately - faded out or brought up as needed. The following plot is for a play using three separate acting areas - Stage Right, Stage Left, and Center Stage.

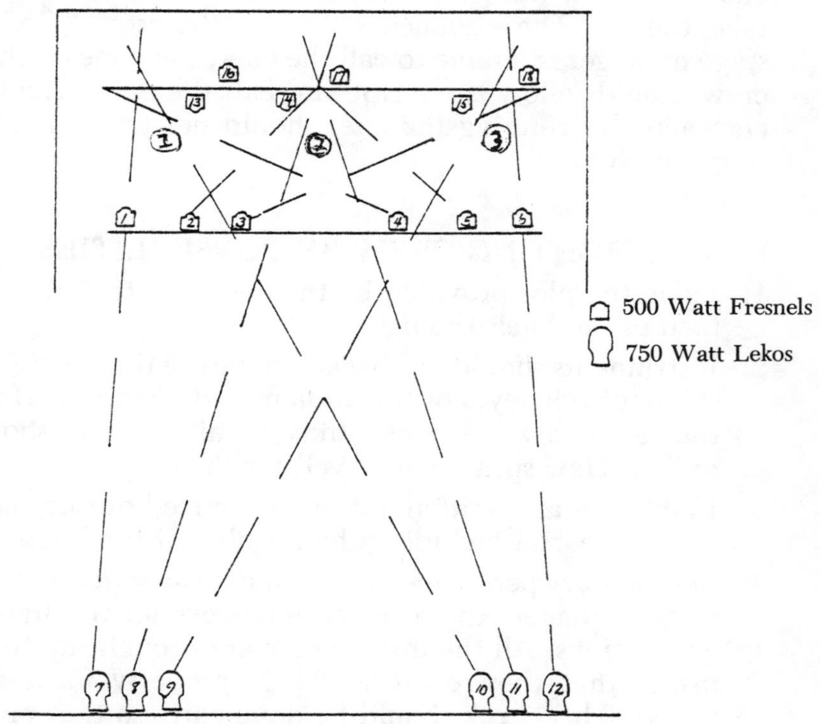

HOOK-UP LIST

Dimmer	Position and Number	Type	Area	Color
1	1st electric and front of front of house pipe 1, 7, 13	500 watt fresnels/ fresnels/ 750 watt lekos	1	light blue
2	" - 2, 8, 14	"	2	light blue
3	" - 3, 9, 15	"	3	light blue
4	" - 4, 10, 16 + 2nd electric	"	1	straw
5	" - 5, 11, 17	"	2	straw
6	" - 6, 12, 18	"	3	straw

Illustration 8-2

Although the lighting designer establishes the cues and their timing, the stage manager and the lighting crew are responsible for running the light cues. Different theatres have different arrangements, but usually the stage manager "calls" the cues or tells the crew when to take the cues. The stage manager "warns" the light crew of an upcoming cue a page before it will occur. "Ready" is called immediately before the cue and when the stage manager says "Go" the technician takes the cue. The sequence is "Warn," "Ready," "Go." If the stage manager is unable to call the cues, someone on the light crew should follow the script and call the cues. The technician actually running the cues should not try to follow the script as well.

LIGHTING CREW RESPONSIBILITIES

1. Using the plot provided by the designer, the crew hangs, focuses, and gels the lights.
2. Instruments should be checked to insure that no lights will shine into the eyes of the audience. Reflective surfaces on the set such as mirrors, shiny furniture, etc. should be dulled. Hair spray works well for this.
3. Light cues are written out and practiced during the technical rehearsal including the running of the house lights.
4. Before every performance and under the supervision of the stage manager, the light crew checks all the lights and connections. All the instruments are brought up to full to insure that they're all working, properly focused, and gelled. This check should be done early so that problems can be corrected before the audience arrives. Spare lamps and fuses should be available. Cables and wires should be securely taped down.
5. During the run of the show, the crew should be attentive and concentrate on the job. Late light cues or lights up too soon can mar an effective scene.
6. After the production, the crew strikes and stores all instruments, cables, and other equipment.

SAMPLE LIGHTING CUE SHEET

Cue	Count	Dimmer
1	10	2, 3, 4↑ 7*
2	15	2, 3, 4↓ X (Cross-Fade) 5, 6,↑ 8
3	7	1↑ 10 2, 3, 4↑ 10
4	--	1, 2, 3, 4, 5, 6↓ BLACKOUT

*Indicates dimmers 2, 3, 4 are brought up to an intensity of 7.

MAINTENANCE AND SAFETY

Lighting equipment and lamps require good maintenance and care in handling and in storage. Instruments should be kept free of dust and moisture and stored where they will not be bumped. All cables should be coiled, tied, and hung out of the way. Lamps can be kept in the instruments unless the instruments are being moved. In that case, the lamps should be removed and packed securely.

Working with electricity and lighting requires conscious observance of good safety habits. The following safety rules will help make your lighting experience safe and accident free.

SAFETY RULES

1. Work in pairs while hanging lights. One person to hand the instruments up the ladder and steady the ladder, and the other person to hang the instruments.
2. Tie the adjustable crescent wrench used for tightening and loosening the instrument to your belt loop to insure that the wrench does not drop on someone and to give you two free hands.
3. Before plugging or unplugging connectors, make sure that the circuit is dead.
4. Use gloves to protect your hands when adjusting and focusing lighting instruments.
5. Check for an overload before replacing a blown fuse. Replace the fuse with one of the same ampere rating.

6. Do not overload dimmers. Always compute the wattage and the amperage.
7. Repair or have an electrician repair any defects in wiring or loose connections.
8. Make sure all dimmers are turned off and unplugged after each rehearsal and performance.

The lighting techniques discussed thus far have centered on visibility, atmosphere, and environment. Lighting can be used to create special effects which enhance the production and foster the theatrical illusion. Listed below are several methods for achieving special effects. Most of the equipment listed is readily available for renting or purchase from theatrical supply houses.

SPECIAL EFFECTS EQUIPMENT

SCENIC SLIDE PROJECTOR

This projector projects photographic slides or hand-painted slides. It is useful for creating a background for the action.

LINNEBACH PROJECTOR

Invented by Adolf Linnebach, this instrument is a simple shadow projector. It projects a general colored light pattern over a wide area from 5 to 15 feet.

ULTRAVIOLET LIGHT "BLACKLIGHT"
Striking effects can be achieved with blacklight and luminous fabric, paint, or paper.

GOBOS
Gobos are templates designed for use in ellipsoidal spotlights. The template is usually made of stainless steel and fits in the "gate" of the spotlight. Many patterns are available - windows, leaves, trees, skyline, stars, etc. Custom patterns can also be made from original artwork. This effect is especially useful because it does not require special equipment.

SCRIM
Disappearances, dream sequences, and creation of atmosphere are just a few of the uses for a scrim. A scrim is a loosely-woven cloth hung from a batten. When it is lighted from the front, it is opaque, and when lighted from the back, it is translucent. The scrim can be used as a backdrop and as a special effect.

A properly-lighted production should provide visibility, atmosphere, and environment and at the same time the lighting should be unobtrusive and in harmony with the entire production. The "living light" bathes the actor and the set and unites with them to form the world of the stage.

EXERCISE #34

Read and analyze a one-act play. Design the lighting for the play. Do a light plot, a hook-up list, and a cue sheet. Since the assignment is "on paper" you have a choice of lighting equipment and physical arrangements to use. Provide a written justification for your lighting choices. Share your design with the class.

QUESTIONS FOR REVIEW AND DISCUSSION

1. Discuss the ways in which lighting enhances a theatrical production.
2. What are the primary objectives of the lighting designer? How are these objectives achieved?
3. What are the basic lighting principles?
4. What are the responsibilities of the lighting crew? What safety rules should be observed?
5. What "special effects" can be created with light?
6. Discuss the emotional and symbolic significance of light.

VOCABULARY

See pages 180-181

limelight
wattage
amperage
voltage
fuse
living light

SUGGESTIONS

- Read and report on THE MAGIC OF LIGHT by Jean Rosenthal.
- Visit an art gallery and observe the use of light in paintings.
- Plan the lighting for an improvisational group. The lighting must be flexible and responsive to various moods.
- Do a light plot for a realistic play performed on a thrust stage or an arena stage.
- Observe the lighting techniques used in live productions.

Chapter 9

Play Production

To insure that a play is a "hit," not a "turkey,"* care must be taken in all facets of play production. Play production brings together the performing and technical aspects of theatre. When these two elements are combined with the audience, they form a cohesive unit which creates the art of theatre, the goal of all play production.

PRODUCTION STAFF

Play production, from conception to culmination, involves many people performing a variety of functions. Because of the nature of theatre, everyone depends on and supports one another. Just as a script has a form and structure, the production elements of a play also have a form and structure. If there is a weakness in a script's basic form, the performance may be seriously flawed. In the same way, if there is a weakness or a missing link in the production elements, the structure may begin to break down. To help eliminate weaknesses a production staff, resembling a business organization, is formed. The staff includes:

- Director/Producer
- Designers
- Technical Director
- Stage Manager
- Set Construction
- House Manager
- Cast
- Lighting
- Properties
- Sound
- Costumes/Make-up
- Publicity
- Box Office Manager

---

*A "turkey" is a show that is a failure usually due to poor organization. In his book SUPERNATURAL ON STAGE, Richard Huggett explains that the term "turkey" is taken from the Broadway play CAGE ME A TURKEY which set the all-time record for the shortest Broadway run. It closed opening night before the final act!

The various staff positions are defined in the following paragraphs. Some of these positions may be filled by the same people, and overlapping positions may occur. For example, everyone, cast included, often helps with set construction and painting, but it is important that direct responsibility for seeing that the job gets done is assigned to a specific person.

DIRECTOR/PRODUCER

The Director/Producer, usually the theatre arts teacher, is responsible for the total concept and execution of the play. He or she brings together all the diverse elements to form one working unit. The Director/Producer schedules the performances, holds auditions, selects the cast and technical staff, manages the budget, holds production meetings with the staff to plan and organize work, stages the play, rehearses the cast, approves designs, and guides the technical work.

SET, LIGHTING, COSTUME, POSTER/PROGRAM/TICKET DESIGNERS

With the advice of the Director/Producer and the counsel of the art teacher, the designers sketch out their creative concepts. After their designs are approved, the designers do a final rendering. The final designs are given to the technical director who is responsible for seeing that the designs are executed.

Posters, programs, and tickets may repeat the same design — giving the production an artistic unity.

TECHNICAL DIRECTOR

The technical director works with the set construction crew, the sound crew, lighting crew, properties crew, wardrobe, and make-up crews. All of the production details are the responsibility of the technical director. He or she may also be responsible for ordering and maintaining supplies.

STAGE MANAGER

The stage manager is the director's extra eyes, ears, and hands. The stage manager attends all rehearsals, assists the director, writes all blocking and business in the script, and is responsible for running the show during performances. The stage manager also makes up the following:

1. List of cast and crew members complete with telephone numbers. Copies go to the director, the technical director, and crew heads.
2. Master calendar for the entire production schedule. Included on the calendar are rehearsals, meetings, deadlines for learning lines, set construction, painting, etc. The stage manager constantly updates and adds to the calendar. He keeps in touch with the director, technical director, and crew heads. (See sample calendar - Illustration 9-1.)
3. Prompt Book. Generally a loose-leaf binder containing a copy of the script, blocking and business notations, a copy of lighting and property plots, and all lighting, sound, set, and actor cues. (See sample prompt book page - Illustration 9-2.)
4. Weekly rehearsal schedules. The stage manager distributes copies of the schedule to the actors, and contacts the actors if there are any last minute changes.

SET HEAD AND CREW

The set construction crew builds, paints, and installs the set. The set crew also performs set changes during the performances when required.

LIGHTING HEAD AND CREW

After receiving the designer's lighting plot, the lighting head and crew hang and focus lights, maintain them in working order, and are responsible for operating the lights during the rehearsals and performances.

SAMPLE MASTER CALENDAR - Six-Week Production Schedule

	MONDAY	TUESDAY	WEDNESDAY	THURSDAY	FRIDAY	SATURDAY
WEEK #1	Prod. Meeting 4:00 Rehearsal - 7:00 (Act I)	Rehearsal - 7:00 (Act II)	Rehearsal - 7:00 (Act III)	Rehearsal - 7:00 (Selected Scenes)	Rehearsal (Individual Work) 4:00	
WEEK #2	Prod. Meeting 4:00 Rehearsal - 7:00 (Act I)	SET CONSTRUCTION → Rehearsal - 7:00 (Act II)	Rehearsal - 7:00 (Act III)	Rehearsal - 7:00 (Selected Scenes)	Rehearsal (Individual Work) 4:00	→
WEEK #3	Prod. Meeting 4:00 Rehearsal - 7:00 (Act I - lines due)	SET CONSTRUCTION → Rehearsal - 7:00 (Act II)	Rehearsal - 7:00 (Act III)	Costume fittings Rehearsal - 7:00 (Acts I & II) Lines Due Act II	Costume fittings Rehearsal 4:00 (Act III)	→
WEEK #4	Prod. Meeting 4:00 Rehearsal - 7:00 (Act I)	Begin "putting in" set → Rehearsal - 7:00 (Act II)	Rehearsal - 7:00 (Act III) Lines Due Act III	Hang lights - 4:00 Rehearsal - 7:00 (Act I)	Rehearsal - 4:00 (Act II & III)	Open for set work if needed →
WEEK #5	Technical Week Runthrough with all technical elements - 6:00	Runthrough - 6:30 Set cues - redo cues as needed	Runthrough - 6:30	Selected Scenes - Polish - 7:00	Runthrough - 4:00	
WEEK #6	FULL TECH FULL DRESS CALL: 6:30	FULL TECH FULL DRESS CALL: 6:30	FULL TECH FULL DRESS CALL: 6:30	PERFORMANCE CALL: 6:30	PERFORMANCE CALL: 6:30	PERFORMANCE CALL: 6:30 STRIKE!

Illustration 9.1

SAMPLE PROMPT BOOK PAGE

LC#1-"Special" - Prospero enters from DR, X's to DSL faces scrim back to audience, raises arms - "Tempest" begins
WARN SC#1

SC #1 - Begin when Prospero raises arms - (Tempest music continues throughout scene)
Warn LC #2

The Tempest

ACT I

Scene I. [*On a ship at sea.*]

LC# 2 - Lights up behind scrim

A tempestuous noise of thunder and lightning heard. Enter a Shipmaster and a Boatswain. — swinging on boat ladder

UL - with lantern

Master. Boatswain!

Boatswain. Here, master. What cheer?

Master. Good,°[1] speak to th' mariners! Fall to't yarely,° or we run ourselves aground. Bestir, bestir!

Exit. - UR

Enter Mariners. - UR

mariners adlib shouts and calls throughout

Boatswain. Heigh, my hearts! Cheerly, cheerly, my hearts! Yare, yare! Take in the topsail! Tend to th' master's whistle! Blow till thou burst thy wind, if room enough!°

Enter Alonso, Sebastian, Antonio, Ferdinand, Gonzalo, and others. from L+R

Alonso. Good boatswain, have care. Where's the master? Play the men.°

Boatswain. I pray now, keep below.

Illustration 9-2

SOUND HEAD AND CREW

The sound head and crew are responsible for the sound effects and sound cues. Depending on the play, the sound may be pre-recorded. Pre-show and intermission sound requirements are also the responsibility of the sound crew.

PROPERTIES HEAD AND CREW

The properties head and the properties crew find, maintain, and store all props, in addition to placing and organizing props during rehearsals and performances. The properties head prepares a master property list of all props needed. After all props have been found, the property head prepares a property plot (a description of when, where, and by whom the props will be used during the play). A master list of all props, a property plot, and a well-rehearsed crew are essential for a smooth performance. The master list and plot should be posted backstage. Copies should be given to the stage manager, so that if the property head or a crew member is unable to make a performance, someone else can take over the function.

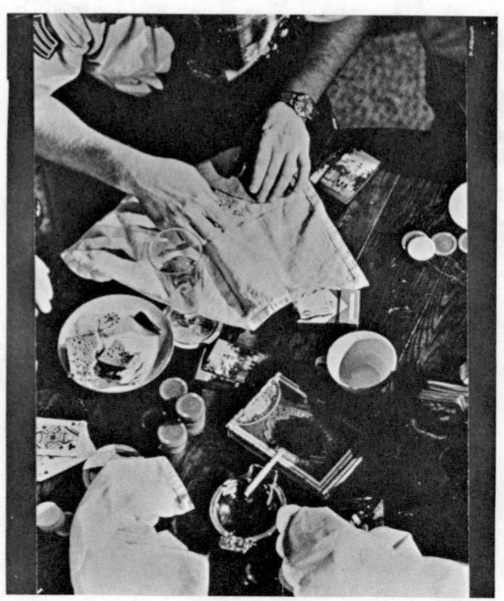

All of the properties on the table above must be maintained, placed, and stored by the properties crew.

COSTUME HEAD AND CREW

Constructing costumes, fitting costumes, helping actors with changes, doing necessary adjustments and repairs, seeing that costumes are clean and stored properly are all the responsibility of the costume crew. During rehearsals and performances, the Wardrobe Mistress/Master is in charge of all costumes.

MAKE-UP HEAD AND CREW

The make-up crew sets out all the make-up and sees that supplies are maintained. Actors should learn to apply their own make-up, but the make-up crew offers assistance in arranging hair and applying make-up when needed.

PUBLICITY

The publicity head is in charge of publicizing the play using posters, flyers, newspaper articles, radio and television announcements, scene previews at school assemblies, and any other effective means. The publicity head may also coordinate printing of tickets, posters, and programs.

BOX OFFICE MANAGER/HOUSE MANAGER

The box office manager is responsible for advance ticket sales and sale of tickets at the performances. The House Manager is responsible for greeting the audience, supervising the ushers, and notifying the stage manager to begin the show.

The organization of the production staff is shown in Illustrations 9-3 and 9-4. Illustration 9-3 shows the chain of responsibilities during production, and Illustration 9-4 indicates the chain of responsibilities during performance.

Effort should be exerted to keep all communications open and regular. One method of doing this is to have weekly production meetings. The first production meeting is called by the Director/Producer. All of the designers, the technical director, the stage manager, and the crew heads attend the meeting. The following items are discussed:

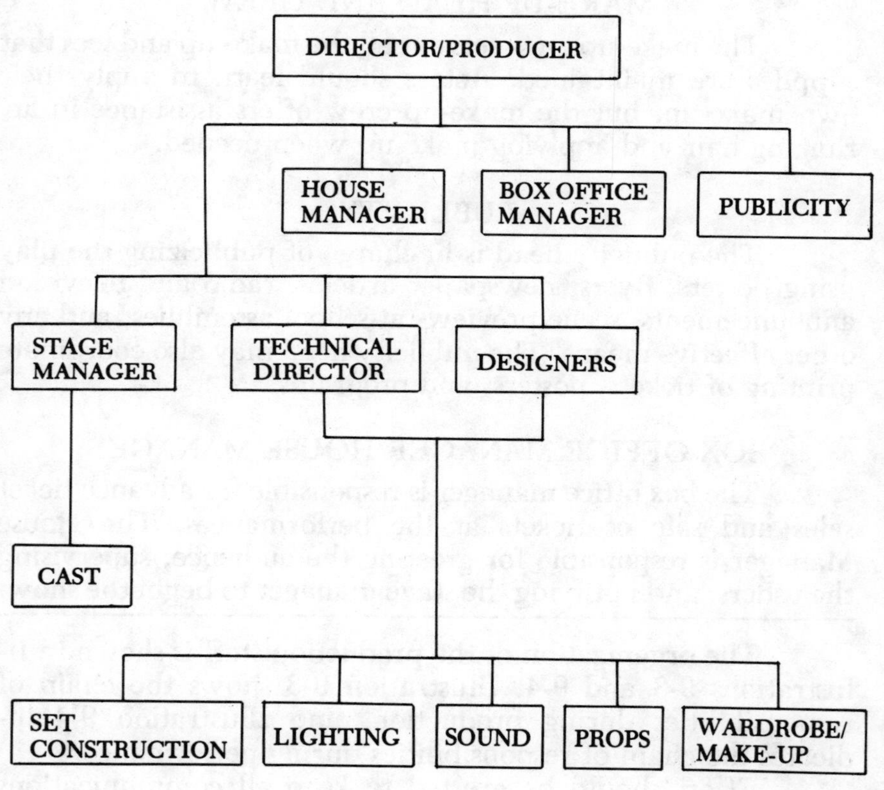

Illustration 9-3

PERFORMANCE ORGANIZATION

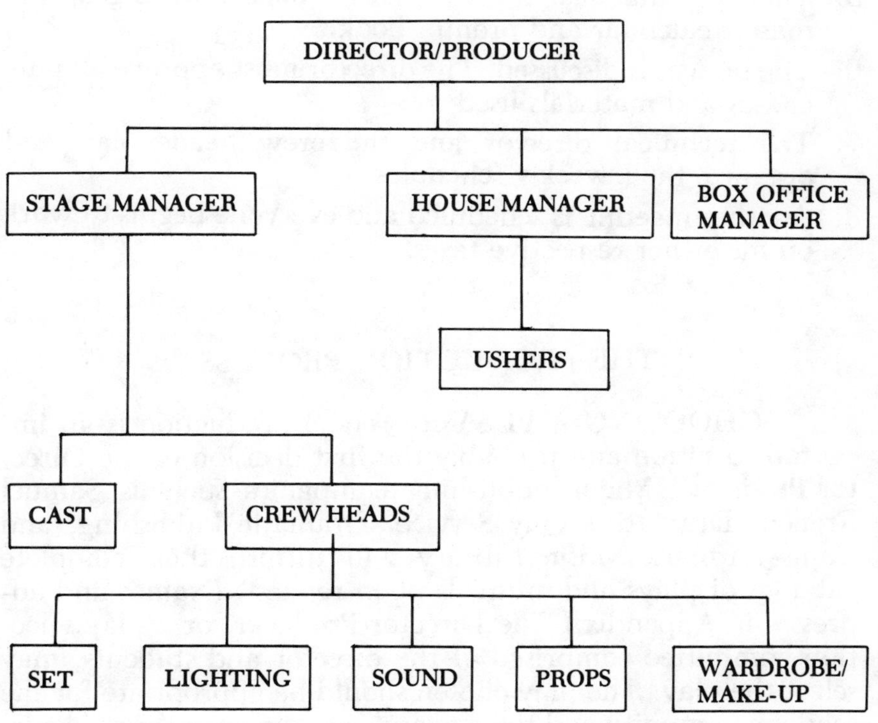

Illustration 9-4

1. The Director/Producer identifies the concept and style of the play.
2. Each designer discusses each design concept.
3. The technical director, stage manager, and crew heads add their own views and discuss any construction or facilities limitations.
4. The staff arrives at a compatible design concept.
5. The stage manager takes notes and begins making up the master calendar and prompt book.
6. The budget is discussed. The director must approve all purchases and materials used.
7. The technical director and the crew heads plan and organize their weekly schedules.
8. Another meeting is scheduled and everyone begins to work on his or her respective tasks.

THE PRODUCTION PROCESS

CHOOSING A PLAY for school production is an important decision and probably the first decision of the Director/Producer. Major publishing companies such as Samuel French, Dramatists Play Service, Dramatic Publishing, and Tams-Witmark Music Library will furnish their complete catalogs of plays and musicals upon request. (Names and addresses in Appendix.) The Director/Producer, or a play selection committee comprised of the director and students, may select the play. The play chosen should be appropriate for the school community and the age and experience of the students. Number of characters, technical requirements, and budget should all be taken into consideration.

OBTAINING THE ROYALTY RIGHTS is the next step. Before announcing auditions and crew sign-up, the Director/Producer writes to the publisher and secures permission to present the play. If a play is being performed professionally in your area, the rights often will not be given to an amateur group. If a play is in the public domain (no royalty payment required) such as Shakespeare's plays, anyone may perform the play without obtaining permission.

HOLDING AUDITIONS to select cast members and selection of crew members is a crucial step in play production. Auditions should be announced and publicized at least a week before they are held. Posters announcing the time and place of auditions, the title and author of the play, the number and type of characters, and any special requirements (e.g. singing, dancing) should be placed in prominent places around the school. Auditions should be held for two to four days depending upon the number of people auditioning and the need for "callbacks." If a director has difficulty casting a particular part, several actors might receive a "callback" to audition for the role.

When actors and prospective crew members arrive at an audition, they fill out a 3 × 5 card or information sheet. The card might look like this:

Name ____________ Height ________ Weight ________
Phone ______________ Hair ________ Eyes ________
Grade ________ Age ________

Acting ________ Crew ________ Crew Preference ________
(Check one or both)
Previous Experience (Acting or Crew) ________________

Do you sing? ____ Dance? ____ Play an instrument? ____
Do you have any conflicts with the schedule? ____________
Will you be able to devote time to the production and also maintain your school work? ____________________
Director's Comments:

After actors have filled out the audition forms, the audition begins. The director gives a brief description of the play and the characters. Students are then asked to audition for parts. Here are a few suggestions to make auditioning a little less painful.

1. Try to relax. Take deep breaths and concentrate on the script and the director's instructions.
2. Put energy and vitality into your voice. An enthusiastic reading is a great asset, but avoid overacting.
3. Listen closely to the director's instructions. If you are asked to read the part a different way or to improvise a scene, don't complain or say you can't. At least give it a try. You may surprise yourself.
4. Try to relate to the person auditioning with you. Look away from the script as much as possible, and keep your head and eyes up so that the director can see your expressions.
5. Don't talk or create any distractions while others are auditioning.
6. If you are not sure about the way a scene should be played, ask the director to clarify it for you.

Keep in mind that the director is not only looking at your total appearance - movement, voice, body type, energy, ability to relate to others, flexibility, directability, and enthusiasm - but the director is also trying to form a compatible ensemble of actors. If you are not cast for a particular play, or if you are not cast in the role you wanted, it does not necessarily mean that you are a poor actor. Perhaps you are wrong for that particular play. You may be too tall, have the wrong voice type, or you might not be experienced enough for a major role. If you are cast in a small role or a walk-on, remember Stanislavsky's advice: "There are no small parts, only small actors." Make the most you can of your moment or moments on stage.

REHEARSALS

At the first rehearsal the director makes sure that everyone is acquainted. The director also gives a brief talk about the play - its theme, style, and type and answers any questions. The production staff should be introduced, and the stage manager shows the ground plan to the cast. The stage manager also outlines the rules that the group will follow. These rules vary from group to group, but some basic rules are as follows:

1. Be punctual! If rehearsal is at 7:00, be at the theatre at 6:55. Sign in with the stage manager when you arrive.
2. Bring your script and a pencil to rehearsal. Make all blocking notations and business and character suggestions in your script with pencil.
3. Be prepared for each rehearsal. Have lines learned when they are due.
4. Leave outside concerns (boyfriends, girlfriends, problems with parents, etc.) outside the theatre.
5. Do not give direction to your fellow actor. That's the director's job. If another actor is upstaging you, or stepping on your lines, speak to the director or the stage manager.
6. If you have to miss a rehearsal, arrange this with the director well in advance so that work may be scheduled around you. If you are inadvertently delayed for rehearsal, call the director or the stage manager to let them know you will be late.
7. When you are not on stage rehearsing, work quietly by yourself.
8. When the director gives you a direction, do not argue or apologize. Simply do what is directed. If the business or blocking is uncomfortable, try it a few times, and if it is still uncomfortable talk to the director.
9. If you have ideas to enhance the production or your part, share them with the director.
10. Be willing to work diligently, enthusiastically, and courteously, and you will have a positive rehearsal experience.

Rehearsal schedules vary from show to show and group to group, but a six-week schedule is usually adequate for a straight play. Eight weeks may be required for a musical. A sample master calendar for a six-week rehearsal of a straight play is shown in Illustration 9-1.

"Polishing" rehearsals are necessary to set timing and business.

PERFORMANCE

On opening night the director "gives" the show to the stage manager who assumes full responsibility for the running of the show. While the director sits in the audience sensing the audience's responses and noting any changes that need to be made for the next performances, the stage manager is busy backstage with the following duties:

1. Makes sure all actors and crew members are signed in.
2. Checks with each crew head to make sure lights, sound, props, set, wardrobe, make-up are all in order.
3. Keeps everyone quiet and calm, and deals with any last-minute problems.
4. Calls one-half hour to curtain, fifteen minutes, five minutes, and when the House Manager gives the signal to begin, the stage manager tells actors to go to their Places for Act I.
5. Calls all cues if the theatre is equipped with an intercom system. If the theatre doesn't have such a system, each crew is responsible for its own cues.
6. Makes sure everything is stored and ready to use for the next performance.

7. Makes up the "strike" assignments and supervises strike. Traditionally, the set is taken down and stored immediately after the last performance and before the cast party, insuring that everyone will help dismantle and store (strike) the sets, lights, props, costumes, and make-up.

Before every theatrical performance, professional and amateur, a wealth of tradition and superstition pervades the atmosphere. Actors often ritualize their preparations *before* the show in an attempt to exercise some order and control over situations *during* performance that sometimes get out of control! They might trip, the door may stick, a button pop off a shirt, but many actors feel that if they apply their make-up in the same way every night, or have a drink of water immediately before they go onstage every night, somehow this ritual, this control, will extend to the performance. Some actors wear a medal of St. Genesius, patron Saint of actors, to insure a successful performance, some wear special good luck charms, and some wear a favorite piece of clothing.

Tradition states that if actors wish one another "good luck" before a performance they will be certain to have bad luck. Instead actors tell one another to "Break a leg!" - "Have fun!" - "Play pretty for the people." - or "Fall flat on your face!"

Many actors feel that whistling backstage tempts fate and is sure to ruin a performance. This superstition is a carry-over from the eighteenth and nineteenth centuries when Navy seamen were employed to handle the ropes and rigging of the theatres. Since sophisticated intercom systems had not been invented, the stage manager communicated with his "seaman" crew by whistling. An actor innocently whistling his way to the dressing room might cue scenery to raise or lower - sometimes on his head!

All the traditions and superstitions, however, will not guarantee a successful show if organization has been lacking. If the actors' preparations have been thorough, and if the technical staff has prepared and performed its job with care and attention to detail, the show will proceed with everyone, audience included, confident of a successful outcome. This confidence, this feeling that no matter what happens the cast and crew have the resources to cope, is essential for a positive theatrical performance.

POST PERFORMANCE

Many of you after working on and performing in a play will suffer from a dread disease called P.P.D. (Post Play Depression). The only known cure is to do another show! Your depression may be relieved in part by allowing the moments to live again in your memory through discussion and evaluation of the production. Each person involved with the production should ask: "What could I have done to make my contribution more effective and more creative?" -"What have I learned?" -"How will I apply what I have learned in future productions?" Everyone involved might meet for an afternoon or an evening to share experiences and discuss and evaluate the production.

Play production is a continuing creative process from beginning to end. The culmination of the process is the creation of an art form - the theatrical performance. Actors may take the bows, but they and everyone else involved know that a fine performance is the result of the best efforts of *all* the members of the theatre group.

QUESTIONS FOR REVIEW AND DISCUSSION

1. What topics are discussed at the first production meeting?
2. Be able to list the duties of each member of the technical staff.
3. What factors should be taken into consideration when choosing a play for production?
4. What are some techniques to make auditions go smoothly?
5. Discuss the basic rules to follow during rehearsals. What rules might you add to the list?

VOCABULARY

prompt book
call backs
master calendar
property plot
"turkey"
places
strike

SUGGESTIONS

- Read and give a report on SUPERNATURAL ON STAGE by Richard Huggett.
- Find out why St. Genesius is the patron Saint of actors and report it to your class.
- Put together a prompt book for a one-act play.
- Research and report on American producers such as David Belasco, Alexander H. Cohen, David Merrick, and Harold Prince.
- If there is a professional or community theatre in your area, interview the director and the producer. Report back to the class.

Part III

THEATRE CRITICISM AND THEATRE HISTORY

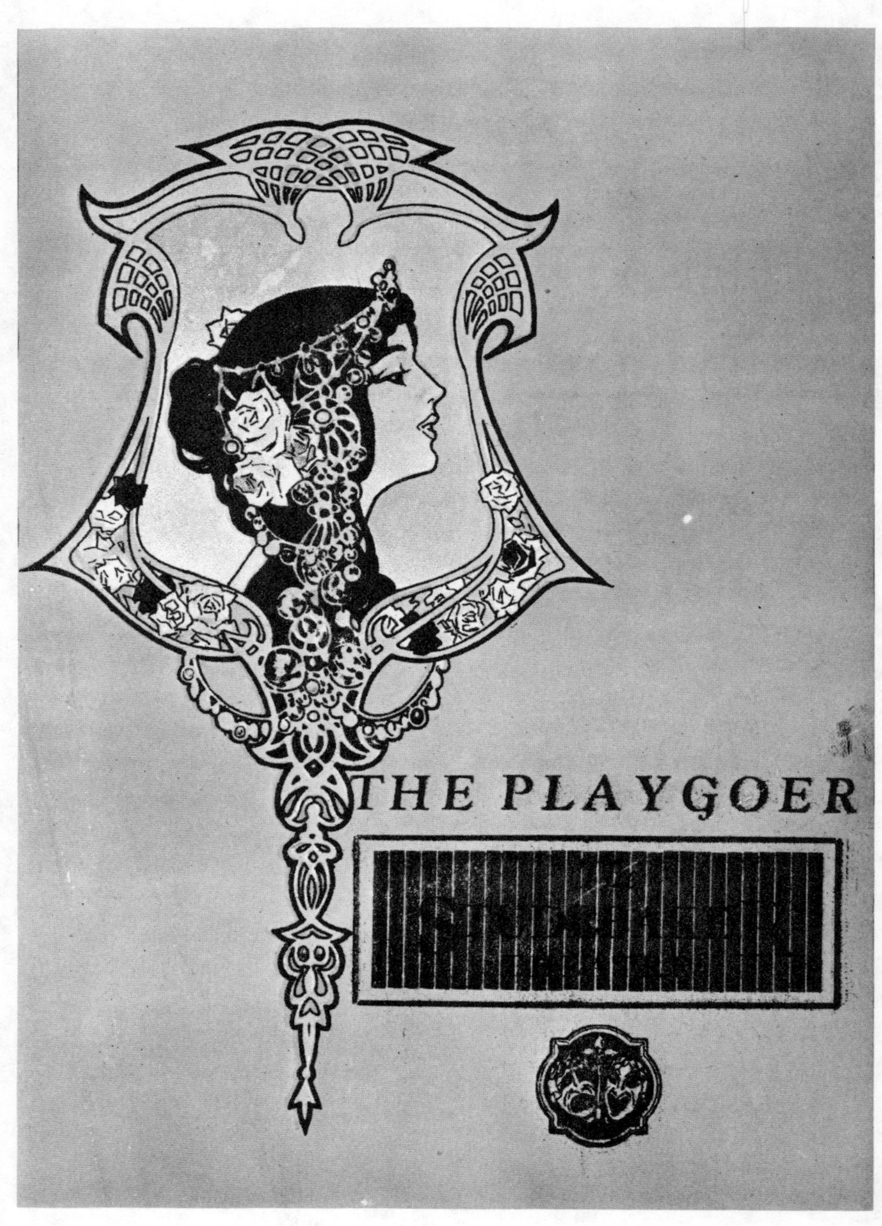
THE PLAYGOER

Chapter 10

Theatre Criticism

Theatre is ephemeral and immediate. The joy of theatre lies in this immediacy, but the sadness of theatre is that the joy is fleeting, ephemeral. Theatre lives in memory, and in the written words of theatre critics, those members of the audience who record their response to the theatrical production. A discerning critic can help sustain the theatre experience by writing about it for others to read. Through the works of critics such as Aristotle, John Dryden, George Bernard Shaw, Stark Young, and Eric Bentley we have a better understanding of theatre and its development. We can read plays; this is literature. A good critic, however, captures the immediate theatrical performance in all its aspects.

The audience and the critic are the final collaborators in the collective process of making theatre. The audience is not chosen, or cast, or hired; the audience simply gathers through choice. The audience is an unknown element, bringing diverse standards, experiences, and emotions to a performance. These diversities unite in the theatre and help shape the theatre experience. With each new audience, the experience changes. Unlike other arts such as film, painting, or sculpture, which are permanently frozen in time, with each new audience theatre creates itself afresh. Although the play, the literature of theatre remains the same, the interpretation of the play in production before an audience is ever-changing. The critic is present to chronicle the new creation, offer insights, evaluate quality, and sharpen appreciation and understanding of theatre art.

Unfortunately, critics and criticism are generally referred to in a negative way. Perhaps this stems from the word "criticize" which is usually interpreted as "finding fault." This meaning is somewhat narrow and does not reflect the broad aspects of criticism. Webster defines *criticism* as "the act of making judgments: analysis of qualities and evaluation of comparative worth; esp. the critical consideration and judgment of literary or artistic worth." A *critique* is defined as "a critical analysis or evaluation of a subject . . ." and a *critic* is "a person who forms and expresses judgments. . . ." The larger meaning of criticism and critic includes the concept of praise as well as "finding fault." A critic is a specialized audience member; but an audience made up of persons with critical skills is a better audience. A knowledgeable, aware audience can make the theatrical experience richer and fuller, not only by giving more, but by demanding more. Every student of theatre should be aware of the role of the critic, be equipped with critical skills, and be able to discuss and evaluate the theatrical experience in a written critique.

To evaluate theatre and to determine what is quality theatre, a critic must not only be informed of all the aspects of production, but be cognizant of theatre history and drama, the literature of theatre. As you have discovered, every aspect of theatre involves choices. The critic evaluates the choices that were made *in terms of the production.* Obviously a performance of a comedy must be evaluated with different criteria than a tragedy. Categories of styles and types of theatre are created primarily for purposes of convenience; types and styles overlap and distinctions blur. Theatrical styles are discussed in Chapter 11 (Theatre History). Polonius, in HAMLET, gives a humorous review of the various types of drama

> "The best actors in the world, either for tragedy, comedy, history, pastoral, pastoral-comic, historical-pastoral, [tragical-historical, tragical-comical-historical-pastoral,] . . ."

The two major types of drama, however, are tragedy and comedy. A *tragedy* is a serious play in which the hero suffers a tragic flaw in his nature and atones for his guilt. Through the suffering of the hero, the audience experiences a catharsis. Other serious plays include history plays, which give an account of real, historical figures, and "problem plays" or social dramas which discuss and debate social issues. *Comedy* may have serious themes, but the outcome or resolution is happy, and the action or dialogue provokes laughter. A *farce* is a form of comedy which has a great deal of physical humor, and the play often contains complications of mistaken identities and unlikely plot twists. Comedy which emphasizes morbid or cynical humor is called *"black comedy." Comedy of manners* is comedy revealing or ridiculing the social customs of a society. These two major types of drama rarely occur in "pure" form, but often intermingle.

A good critic goes to the theatre equipped with a knowledge of the types of drama, styles of production, theatre history, and production techniques. Implicit in the ability to make judgments is a basis of comparison. The critic must be a frequent theatre-goer, and assess as many different productions as possible. An ability to respond with honesty, sensitivity, and perception is an important critical attribute. An open mind and spirit willing to suspend disbelief and enter the world of the theatre is vital. But just as the actor maintains a conscious objectivity, the critic maintains a conscious awareness of the practical aspects of production. The critic evaluates the choices that were made while participating actively in the process of making theatre - as part of the final collaboration between audience and production. This duality of active participation and active judgment is essential for criticism to occur.

The process of criticism is a response to choices and a questioning of the choices. The critic begins with the production as a whole and asks:

What *type* of drama is being presented?

What is the *style* of production?

What is the controlling idea or theme of the production? (Note: Theme does not mean a didactic statement or moral. If so, the theme of MACBETH would be "crime doesn't pay." All the parts of a production contribute to the controlling idea or theme which usually embodies a comment on the human condition.)

As you discovered in earlier chapters, each production element is the result of careful choices. The choices work together to form a cohesive, artistic whole. The failure of a production usually rests with a lack of unity and poor choices.

The critic must be knowledgeable of *all* the aspects of production - technique, performance, and literature - because a theatrical production is not just the play, or the actors, or the setting, or the lighting, but it is all elements coalescing to form the holistic art of theatre.

The critic evaluates the elements of theatre and asks the following questions, keeping in mind that each production must be evaluated on its own terms within the framework of the type, style, and theme. Since the characters convey the sense and sensibility of the play through their words, actions, and feelings, they should be considered first. The actors playing the characters are the playwright's means of communicating. The actors are a living link with the audience.

CHARACTERS

Who are the characters?
Do you care about them?
Do they communicate with you or touch you in some way?

Are the characters three dimensional and fully realized?

What do the characters do?
What do they say?
What seems to motivate each character?

What is revealed through the actions and speech of the characters?
Do the characters change?
In what way?

How do the characters embody or reveal the theme of the play?

ACTORS

Are the actors convincing?

Are the characterizations fully and completely realized?

Are the actors concentrating and in character at all times?

Do the actors interact and respond believably and appropriately?

Are the actors motivated? Do they understand their characters?

Is genuine emotion produced?

Are the actors' voices and speech clear, audible, and right for the characters?

Are movement and gesture appropriate?

Does the acting reflect and illuminate the type, theme, and style of the production?

THE PLAY

What was your overall reaction? Were you moved? shocked? puzzled? entertained? Explain your reactions.

How is the play structured? Does it build to a climax?

Is the dialogue interesting? appropriate?

Are imagery and symbols used? In what way?

EXTERNALS (Make-up, Hairstyle, Costume)

Are the externals suitable for the production?

Do the externals help to reveal character?

Do the externals serve to reflect or illuminate the theme, style, and type of the production?

SET

Is the set workable and usable?

Is the design compatible with the production as a whole? Is the set distracting in any way?

Does the design reflect the theme, style, and type of the play?

Are the artistic qualities of unity, balance, line, texture, mass, color, and emphasis employed effectively?

Does the set provide atmosphere and environment?

Is the set a symbolic image or representation of the action of the play?

Are set changes handled efficiently and effectively?

LIGHTING

Is the lighting appropriate? Does it set the atmosphere? establish environment?

Are lighting cues and changes handled smoothly?

Is illumination sufficient?

Is the lighting distracting in any way?

Does the lighting harmonize with and contribute to the entire production?

OTHER PRODUCTION ELEMENTS

Are sound effects and special effects appropriate and executed smoothly?

Are properties appropriate and handled properly?

Is the staging effective? Does the staging seem natural? contrived?

Is the pace and tempo of the production effective and appropriate?

OVERALL

Do all the elements of the production fit together?

Does the production work? That is, does it hold your attention? Does it move you in some way? Was something communicated? Was the production worthy of presentation?

These questions are guidelines only. Each production stimulates responses which provoke different questions. The wonder of theatre is the multiplicity of responses and reactions possible. Perhaps the characters move you, or maybe you are fascinated with the language, or the structure of the play interests you, or the technical effects captivate you. Whatever your interest, something in the production will suggest itself as the focus of your criticism and written critique. You might ask the purpose of a written critique. Why can't one just go to the theatre, enjoy the production, and leave it at that? Without the critical written response to productions we would have no record at all of theatre. The critic can help playwrights, directors, designers, and actors discover more effective means of production. Try-outs of plays before critical audiences are also effective in shaping good theatre. In addition, the discipline of writing down thoughts and reactions helps us form artistic standards and helps us communicate more clearly and precisely. Even more important is the increased enjoyment and appreciation of theatre gained through critical analysis.

The first step in communicating your critical response is to trust your own reactions and feelings. They are your primary tools as a critic. The second step is determining *why* you had a particular reaction. The guidelines will help here. Keep in mind that out of many possibilities certain choices were made and the choices affect your reactions. For example, at the end of A DOLL'S HOUSE by Henrik Ibsen, Nora leaves her husband and children. The stage directions simply say "She goes out." Now, there are many ways to "go out" depending upon how the character of Nora is played. Nora may pick up her suitcase, walk quickly and forcefully to the door, and exit, slamming the door behind her, never looking back. Or she may slowly pick up her suitcase, walk to the door, turn and take one last look at the room and Torvald, her husband, then turn and exit - and so on. As a critic it is your job to determine if the choices made were good ones and if the choices made are compatible with the overall style and concept of the production.

After you have seen the production, defined your critical response, and determined the production's type, style, and theme, you are ready to write a critique. Although there are many methods of writing a critique, the following method is offered as a guide.

1. BEGIN the critique with a discussion of the type, theme, and style of the production. Include the title of the play, the playwright, and the director.
2. FOCUS your critique on an element or elements which interest you. Show how the elements convey the production's theme and style (or how they fail to do so).
3. USE concrete examples and evidence from the production to support your point of view. Avoid general statements which are unsupported. Your opinion is valid if you support your opinion with evidence.
4. AVOID extensive plot summary. Write a critique, not a summary of the story.
5. END the critique with a summary of your major points.

As an aid for your memory, take a notepad with you to the theatre and jot down your reactions and observations during intermission. Discuss the play with your friends during intermission and after the play. Discussion stimulates you to think about and verbalize your reactions and observations. Before you can write a critique, you must have something to say - your critique must have a point. After you have determined the focus of your critique, you might write an outline, or you might begin writing spontaneously, letting your ideas flow. The act of writing often leads into fresh insights. When you read what you have written, be critical of your wording.

- Are you saying exactly what you mean to say?
- Are your focus and purpose clear and relevant?
- Are you using concrete examples?
- Do your ideas link together or do you jump from one thought to another?
- Have you proved your point?

Revise what you have written and read it aloud. How does it sound? Do your thoughts flow? Is the structure clear? Is the critique unified? Note that a good critique, just like a good production, must be unified and constructed with care and attention to detail. Put your revised critique aside for a day or two and then come back to it, and read it as if you were reading it for the first time. Correct and clarify as needed, proofread for spelling and grammatical errors, and recopy.

Your critique, a record of the theatrical experience, can help preserve and sustain the ephemeral art of theatre. Of course, a critique cannot capture the spontaneous, invisible bond between actors and audience - the bond which shapes the nature of the performance, but it can help you recall and relive in your memory the feelings you shared and experienced as an audience member, a collaborator in the process of making theatre.

QUESTIONS FOR REVIEW AND DISCUSSION

1. What is the role of the critic?
2. Define the two major types of drama. Discuss plays that you have seen and determine which type they are.
3. Discuss positive and negative experiences that you have had as a member of a theatre audience. What made the experience positive or negative?
4. How does an audience shape a performance?

VOCABULARY

criticism
critic
critique
tragedy
comedy
farce
"black comedy"
comedy of manners

SUGGESTIONS

- Read the work of critics such as Stark Young, Walter Kerr, John Simon, Richard Gilman, and Martin Gottfried.
- Write a critique of a school production for the school newspaper.

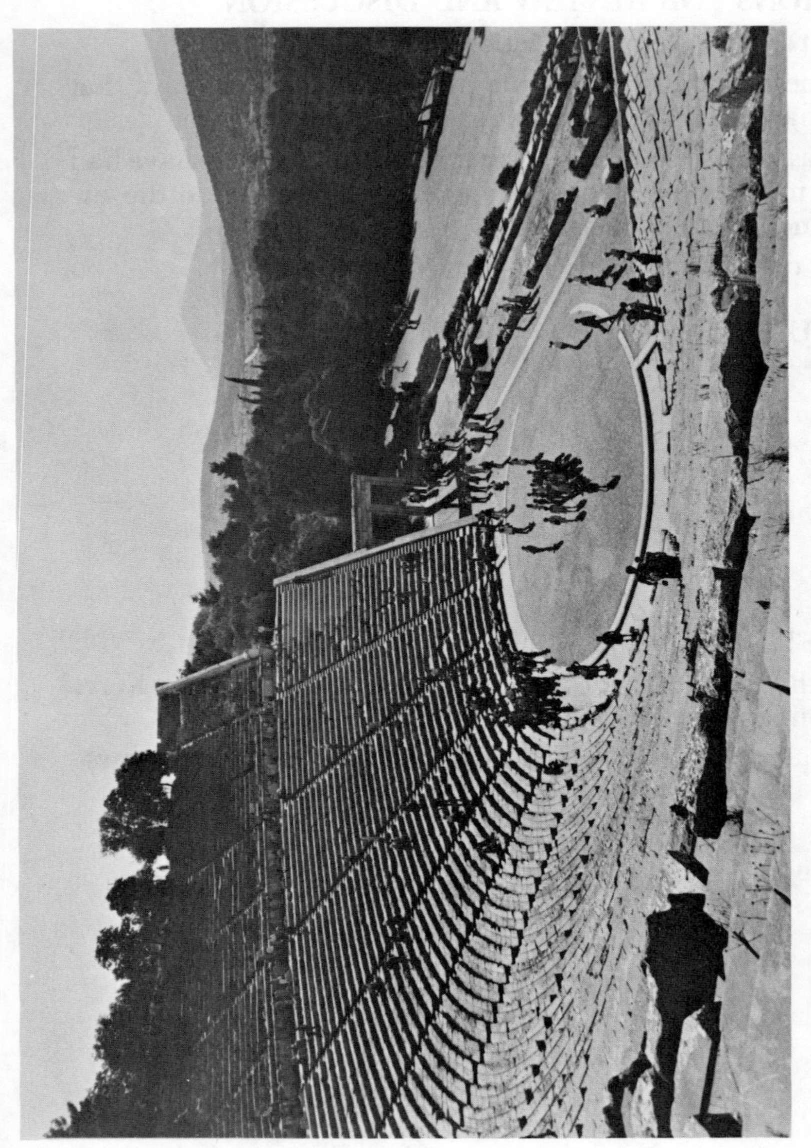

Epidaurus Theatre — is the best preserved of all Greek theatres and one of the best preserved Classical buildings in Greece, dating from the fourth century B.C. The annual Epidaurus Festival is held here with performances of ancient Greek drama: tragedies and comedies. The acoustics are perfect in the 14,000-seat amphitheatre. Epidaurus was originally built as a sanctuary to Apollo.

Chapter 11

Theatre History

Theatre history, in a sense, is one long tour of the art of entertainment. Even though theatre has its roots in religion and ritual, it is first and foremost artistic entertainment of the mind and the spirit. This fusion of art and entertainment in theatre has given rise to the great plays of the Greeks, the golden age of theatre in Elizabethan England, the popular Italian commedia dell'arte, the comic genius of Molière in France, the wit of the Restoration playwrights, the birth of realism, and twentieth-century eclecticism.

The study of theatre history is a study of a living, breathing, vital art shaped by people who were faced with choices. The nature of the play, the playing space, the players, and audience were formed by conscious choices of theatre people in each historical period. The modern theatre is the sum of all the choices that were made in the past. As Shakespeare says "What's past is prologue." But we, too, are faced with choices, and through the study of theatre history we gain a knowledge of where we have been and where we are going. And, because of the immediacy of theatre, its existence in the "now," we gain a picture of the times.

Theatre embodies magic and illusion and a willingness to believe. Theatre began with a celebration of magic and mystery. Primitive man imitated the forces of nature in an attempt to order and control his life. He created the illusion of reality in an attempt to understand reality. But in creating illusion, ordinary reality was transcended. This ability to imagine and create illusions was the seed from which the conscious art of theatre flowered.

GREEK THEATRE

The first established theatre as a conscious form was the theatre of the Greeks. Although a tradition of theatre existed before the Greeks in the coronation festivals and dramatic rituals of ancient Egypt, these performances were religious in nature. Greek theatre also grew out of religion and the worship of Dionysus, the god of wine and fertility. The followers of Dionysus chanted and sang a choral ode called a dithyramb in honor of the god. These followers wore goatskins and sacrificed goats to Dionysus. The word "tragedy" originates from this early practice: tragos - goat, ode - song, tragodes - goatsong, thus, we have "tragedy." Performances of the dithyramb, usually by a chorus of fifty men and boys, were held at the Dionysian festivals in Athens. The first recorded date of a theatrical event is 534 B.C. The Athenian state sponsored a dramatic competition at the festival, and the winner was Thespis. Thespis was not only a poet and writer, but in speaking and performing without the chorus, he invented dialogue, and drama was born.

The period immediately following Thespis' innovation is the peak of the Greek theatre. Four playwrights, Aeschylus (525-456 B.C.), Sophocles (496-406 B.C.), Euripides (484-406 B.C.), and Aristophanes (448-380 B.C.), comprise most of Greek drama as we know it. These men were not only playwrights, but actors, directors, and technicians as well - they were "theatre people."

Aeschylus, the earliest of the playwrights, wrote tragedy. Greek tragedy, as defined by Aristotle, had to have a lofty, serious theme in which a noble hero suffers a tragic flaw in his nature and atones for his guilt. Through the suffering of the hero, the audience experiences a catharsis, or purging, of pity and terror. Aeschylus wrote approximately ninety plays of which seven are extant. PROMETHEUS BOUND and the ORESTIA trilogy are the most well-known. In his plays he dealt with the relationship of the gods and man. He won first prize at the Athenian drama festival many times and was certainly popular. He changed the scope of the theatre by adding a second actor, reducing the size of the chorus from fifty to fifteen, improving the mask, and incorporating properties into the action.

Sophocles inherited the theatre that Aeschylus had changed. Aristotle used Sophocles work as a model of good tragedy. Sophocles is said to have written over one hundred plays; seven are extant. ANTIGONE and OEDIPUS REX remain popular today. ANTIGONE deals with the conflict of man's law and god's law. OEDIPUS REX is a marvelous detective story dealing with fate, and the tragic flaw in Oedipus' nature. Freud, of course, made the term "Oedipus Complex" a household term. Sophocles introduced a third actor, stabilized the size of the chorus at fifteen, and used painted scenery. A popular playwright, Sophocles won first prize at Athens eighteen times.

When Euripides first started writing, Athens was at its peak. As the Peloponnesian War developed, Euripides became highly critical and dissatisfied with the government. He was not a popular writer, and persisted in criticizing the gods and the government. Perhaps because of this he won the drama prize only a few times. He wrote THE TROJAN WOMEN, which deals with the aftermath of war, and it stands as one of the greatest anti-war plays ever written. His MEDEA explored the psychological life of a woman - a new development for the Greek drama. According to legend, Euripides was torn to bits by wild dogs - a violent, sensational end for a controversial, powerful playwright.

Aristophanes wrote comedies which usually satirized prominent people and the government. He attacked Socrates in THE CLOUDS, poked fun at Aeschylus and Euripides in THE FROGS, and aired his anti-war views in LYSISTRATA. In this play, Lysistrata leads the women of Athens in a sex strike until their husbands make peace with Sparta. After much comic action, the men concede and peace reigns. The comedy of Aristophanes grew out of phallic songs sung in honor of Dionysus. This comedy was much more realistic than the traditional tragedies. Aristophanes was not bound by traditional material, but was able to draw upon contemporary life.

At first, playwrights acted in their own plays, but soon professional actors began to perform in the plays. Actors were priests of Dionysus and given honors and privileges such as exemption from military service. The Greek actor had to have a powerful voice and an ability to play many different parts. Since there were only three actors playing all the roles, great skill was needed to differentiate between the characters. The tragic actors wore masks which were painted to suggest the character's age, emotion, and social status. Cothurnus, or built-up shoes, were used to add height and importance to the actor. The chiton, a classic dress, was worn with the himation, a long cloak, or the chlamys, a short cloak. The comic actor wore a mask, a short tunic, and a large leather phallus.

The Greek theatre is semi-circular. The theatre developed from a simple acting circle, called an orchestra. The audience stood or sat on the ground. Soon, rude wooden seats and a wooden hut, called a skene, which became the backdrop for the action, were added. Permanent theatres with stone seats and a stone skene evolved from these earlier forms. The skene was used as a backdrop for the action and as a dressing room for the actors. The roof of the skene was used as an acting area. The Greeks developed some clever scenic devices. A crane, or *deus ex machina,* was used for the sudden entrance or exit of gods and heroes. *Deus ex machina* is used figuratively to indicate an event or character who suddenly and artificially intervenes in the action of a play. Since violent action always happened offstage in Greek plays, the results of the violence, dead bodies, were rolled in on wagons called *eccyclemas.* Triangular scenery, *perioktos,* painted on three sides to suggest different locale were revolved as the scenes changed. Stones were poured into brass pots to simulate thunder. Lightning bolts were painted on scenery and revolved quickly. Since the plays started at dawn and were performed out of doors, sun light was the only lighting used.

The audience for the Greek theatre was representative of Greek society. Because the plays were financed by wealthy Athenian citizens, admission was free and thousands of people attended. The cultured and educated mixed with common workers. Although women did not act in the plays, they were allowed to attend. Slaves attended with their masters. The theatre was public and popular. Great art and great entertainment were one.

ROMAN THEATRE

The Roman theatre was greatly influenced by the Greeks. The Romans borrowed from the Greek Phylakes theatre tradition. Phylakes was a popular, slapstick theatre which parodied the tragic theatre. For example, Hercules was often presented as a roaring drunk. Performances were given on simple wooden platforms. Native Roman farce, called Atellan farce, was based on stock characters in comic situations. Plautus (251-184 B.C.), the first Roman comic playwright, was influenced by the Greek playwright, Menander (342-291 B.C.), who wrote comedies dealing with everyday situations and social conflicts. Plautus' comedies were complicated with plot twists and mistaken identity. His plays were a rich source for playwrights such as Shakespeare, Molière, and Giraudoux. Shakespeare's THE COMEDY OF ERRORS is based on Plautus' MENAECHMI. Actors portrayed a variety of stock characters including braggart soldiers, courtesans, and scheming slaves.

Terence (190-159 B.C.), a more refined, less raucous comic playwright, also borrowed from Greek comedy. He refrained from the bawdy jokes and slapstick of Plautus, and consequently was not as popular.

Seneca (4 B.C.-65 AD) was a philosopher and writer of tragedy. His plays were read aloud rather than performed. They were imitations of Greek tragedy, but they lacked the plot and character development of these plays. Nine of his tragedies are extant including MEDEA, PHAEDRA, and OEDIPUS.

The Roman actor never acquired the stature of the Greek actor. The most famous Roman actor, Roscius, whose name has become a synonym for good acting, played both in comedy and tragedy. As the literary tradition in Rome declined, mimes became more and more popular. Unlike their silent modern counterparts, the Roman mimes were performers who displayed juggling, athletic feats, slapstick, and brief, humorous, often obscene skits. Women and men performed as mimes. Nudity and semi-nudity were quite commonplace. Actors were often slaves or freed slaves, and they could become quite successful. The actor had to be a skilled artist, but he had to perform using inferior material. The actor in Roman theatre was highly praised, but playwriting was at its lowest ebb.

The Roman physical theatre consisted first of wooden platforms used in Atellan farce. Since there was an edict against building permanent theatres, the first theatre was not built in Rome until 55 B.C. by Pompey. Pompey circumvented the ruling by placing a shrine in back of the theatre; the building was called a temple, not a theatre. The Romans began to use the orchestra, or acting circle, for seating, and they played closer to the skene. The modern proscenium stage is a direct descendant of the Roman theatre.

The Roman theatre audience was not as educated as the Greek and, lacking the literary tradition, became more and more interested in spectacle and violence. Imitation of violence soon led to the real thing. Slaves and criminals were executed onstage, Christians were thrown to the lions, and the theatre degenerated. After the rise and spread of Christianity, Christian leaders vigorously opposed theatre and actors. But it wasn't until the invasion of the Barbarian Goths that the theatre finally collapsed along with the Roman empire. By 400 A.D., the Roman theatre, which emphasized vulgar entertainment at the expense of art, was lost; and lost with it was the theatre as a conscious art form. It would have to be rediscovered.

THE MIDDLE AGES

During the Middle Ages, although the institution of theatre ceased to exist, elements of theatre survived. The professional actor continued to entertain. The Church's Decree of Council in 300 A.D. stated that an actor could be converted if he gave up the profession. The Council of Constantinople, in 692 A.D., prohibited mimes, performances, dancing bears, the wearing of masks, and anything connected with theatre. Despite the prohibitions, actors continued to travel and ply their trade wherever they could find an audience. Entertainers from the Germanic tradition, the bards, or scopes, who sang stories and sagas and carried current events from place to place, eventually merged with the mimes and formed minstrel troupes. These troupes were professional groups who gravitated toward courts and monasteries. Many of the more popular troupes became permanent members of households. The actor became more and more important and the bard less important. The invention of the printing press and the subsequent printing of ballads and news resulted in the end of the bards. The only thing lacking for the professional actor was "something to act."

A literary drama was being reborn, ironically, in the Church. After the collapse of the Roman Empire, society was structured around the Church. Life was a constant struggle against ignorance, famine, pestilence, and wars. Life was brutal and short, and the one redeeming factor was the hope of salvation. Thus, religion became extremely important. To communicate ideas more effectively, the Church added the liturgy. In the Church, ritual dialogue was used to represent scriptural situations. This dialogue was called a trope. Clerics performed in their clerical robes and presented important events in the life of Christ. The tropes gradually evolved into playlets, and new material was added as a teaching device. A series of short incidents was combined to form complex liturgical dramas which were called cycles. As these became more popular, church attendance increased, but the crowds often became unruly, even cheering the villainous Herod. In 1210, the Pope ordered the plays out of the Church.

Craft guilds took over the production of the plays. Lay people provided money, materials, and manpower, and the Church provided the scripts. Professional actors may have helped to perform and produce the plays, but the theatre was primarily an amateur exercise. Many secular elements were introduced - Latin was replaced by the vernacular, biblical characters became increasingly contemporary and comic, and production elements and spectacle were emphasized.

Two major types of drama developed in the Middle Ages. The plays which had grown out of the liturgy and were based on scripture and the lives of the Saints were known as miracle and mystery plays. The second type, morality plays, was a logical outgrowth of the sermon, or homily. The purpose of a morality play was to represent Christian dogma dramatically. The most famous morality play is EVERYMAN which is an allegory of man's path to salvation. Slapstick and buffoonery crept into the morality plays usually through the evil or vice characters. These characters provided action which the audience enjoyed.

After the plays moved out of the Church and into the towns, several types of stages were used. The processional type of staging, which most closely reflected the processional in the Church, used a series of "sets" or scenes in the town square with the audience moving from scene to scene. Another variation was the construction of permanent sets in one area, different sets depicting different scenes. A third type of staging, which was popular in England, was the pageant wagon. A series of wagons was often used with a different set on each wagon. The audience remained stationary. One wagon would present the first scene to an audience on one corner and then move on to the next corner. Another wagon would pull up to present the next scene. The wagons were quite elaborate. There were three main acting areas on the wagons: the roof, representing Heaven; the main platform representing Earth; and the area under the wagon symbolizing Hell. Trapdoors were used to move from one acting area to another. The entrance of the devil and his pitchfork from "Hell" must have been a crowd pleaser.

Although medieval plays were not produced with entertainment or theatre consciously in mind, amateurs (the word is derived from "one who loves") and the Church did much to rediscover the theatre. Medieval drama continued to be produced into the sixteenth century, but with the Renaissance a new, literary theatre would be born.

THE RENAISSANCE

The Renaissance, the renewal of literature, art, and learning based on the rediscovery of classical sources, began in Italy in the fifteenth century, and moved to all parts of Europe. Great plays were not written in Italy during the Renaissance.

The writers generally copied the Roman structure. The plays were performed for a very select, elite court audience. Theatre was essentially a private operation. While no great literary strides were made, the physical theatre techniques and theatre architecture were greatly improved and enhanced.

The Italian architects built elaborate new theatres based upon their discovery of Vitruvius' treatise on theatre architecture. Perspective in scene painting, sliding wings and movable scenery to suggest different locales, machines to elevate actors, and raked stages were developed. The idea of upstage and downstage comes from this time. On a "raked" or slanted stage, an actor literally had to walk "up" to get upstage and "down" to move downstage. Theatres were completely enclosed, and lighting techniques were improved. Candles were used for illumination, and color in light was achieved through the use of colored liquid and colored fabric to reflect light. The emphasis, however, was on spectacle, not on literature.

The Teatro Olimpico, finished in 1584, is the forerunner of our modern proscenium stage.

At the same time the court theatre was playing to a limited audience, a non-literary actors theatre was emerging - the commedia dell'arte, which means "professional comedy."

The commedia dell'arte lasted from the sixteenth century into the eighteenth century. Unlike the elite court theatre, the commedia was a people's theatre. The commedia actors, men and women, were highly-skilled performers. Plot outlines of the commedia are part of theatre history. The actors worked with the bare outline of a plot and improvised dialogue, jokes, and stage business. Of course, as they performed, the actors became very familiar with their parts and much of the action was standardized. Actors often played the same part all their lives and passed the role on to their children. The characters were of two types - serious and comic. The serious characters, usually the young lovers, were the least interesting, but the plot usually revolved around them. The comic characters included Arlecchino (Harlequin), a group of Zanni, or rascally servants, Pulcinella, a cunning, cruel old man played with a hooked-nose mask (we know him as Punch), Capitano, the boastful, cowardly soldier, Dottore, a stuffy scholarly type, and Pantalone, a greedy, miserly old man. The stock characters of the commedia dell'arte are descendants of the old Atellan farce.

The troupes traveled with a portable stage, costumes, and properties which they could set up quickly and easily. The troupes were a great hit in France, performing at the Hotel de Burgogne, and strongly influencing the French playwright, Molière.

From the middle of the sixteenth century to the early eighteenth century, commedia dell'arte troupes flourished. Their decline and eventual dissolution was due in part to Carlo Goldoni (1707-1793) an Italian playwright, who literally stole the ideas of the commedia and used them in his plays. This literary theatre superseded the theatre of the commedia dell'arte which centered on the actor.

Meanwhile, in England, a new humanism, along with the Renaissance and the Reformation, was sweeping away the Middle Ages. The rediscovery of the classic plays of Plautus, Terence, and Seneca influenced the forerunners of Shakespeare.

Nicholas Udall's RALPH ROISTER DOISTER, written in the middle of the sixteenth century, was the first English comedy. GORBODUC, by Thomas Sackville and

Thomas Norton, was the first English tragedy. Both of these plays borrow heavily from the Romans, but the characters and treatment of the plot are unmistakably English.

Three other playwrights who preceded Shakespeare are important in the development of English drama. John Lyly, who wrote for private groups, introduced prose comedy. In his play, ENDYMION, he presented comedy in high style with graceful language. Thomas Kyd wrote the tremendously popular SPANISH TRAGEDY which was quite melodramatic and full of action. Its revenge theme influenced later playwrights. Christopher Marlowe's tragedy in blank verse, TAMBURLAINE THE GREAT, established blank verse as the meter of tragedy. Based upon his remarkable plays (DR. FAUSTUS, EDWARD II), written before the age of thirty, many critics feel that had he lived, his work would have rivaled Shakespeare's in power and beauty.

Professional companies grew out of the old minstrel troupes, but they still needed "something to act." Schools and universities were teaching the classics and writing and performing plays. Soon these plays and performances moved out of the classroom and into the public sector. The more responsible companies formed ties with a noble's household, but this was generally for patronage and respectability. The groups, however, still moved about the countryside performing in town squares on simple platform stages. Since the companies were professional and wanted to make money, they were drawn to the large inns which were the economic and social centers. They set up their wooden platforms in the innyard, and the audience stood in the yard or watched from the balconies of the inn. Inns attracted the attention of the authorities and were often closed down, putting the companies out of work.

ELIZABETHAN ENGLAND

In 1576, James Burbage, an actor and head of the Earl of Leicester company, built the first permanent theatre in England. It was called, appropriately, "The Theatre." Burbage built the theatre outside the city limits of London to avoid the control of the authorities. It was patterned after the innyard architecture and the old pageant wagons. The

Pictured (from l. to r.) are Jerome Kilty as Sir Toby Belch, Patrick Garner as Sir Andrew Aguecheek, and Davis Hall as Feste in Hartford Stage Company's production of Shakespeare's comedy, *Twelfth Night*.

building was three-storied, a platform stage was used with the back wall as a backdrop, and the audience stood in the "pit" area or sat on the balconies. Other theatres quickly sprung up, and London became a bustling theatre town.

William Shakespeare's theatre, The Globe, and his company, the Chamberlain's Men, which later became the King's Men, was the most prosperous, popular theatre. William Shakespeare (1564-1616) wrote thirty-seven plays for his acting company to perform. It is important to remember that Shakespeare was an actor as well as a playwright and immersed in the living world of the theatre. He wrote for a large, diverse, critical audience. His spirit and plays reflect the pride, confidence, and energy of Elizabethan England which was exploring the world and glorifying the idea of human greatness.

Technically, the Elizabethan theatre was relatively sophisticated. A minimum of scenery was used and the locale was described by the lines of the play. It's interesting to note that the Italian court theatres, with all the elaborate painted scenery and effects, did not achieve the literary heights of the Elizabethans. Although costumes were contemporary dress, modifications were made to suggest character, and properties were used. The stage was quite versatile including trap doors and many acting areas. Since the stage was open to the sky, the lighting was natural sunlight. Candles were probably used for interior scenes. Sound effects such as music, cannons, and fireworks were used to enhance the illusion. In fact, the Globe burned down in 1612 because of fireworks, but was rebuilt the next year.

In Elizabethan England, actors in the established companies gained respect and stature, but the traveling troupes and "fly by night" companies were still considered vagrants. Shakespeare is said to have written many of his great tragic heroes for Richard Burbage, an actor noted for his naturalness and pleasing voice. Women's parts were performed by boy actors. Hamlet's advice to the actors, in Act III, Scene 2 of HAMLET, probably says the most about desirable and undesirable acting styles in this period.

Not since the Greeks had theatre reached such heights. Theatre was again a public, popular art appealing to and

A model of Shakespeare's Globe Theatre.

reflecting a whole society. Art and entertainment, once again, were one.

Several playwrights who were contemporaries and followers of Shakespeare wrote in a changing atmosphere. The theatre as an institution was to be abolished by the Puritans in 1642.

Ben Jonson wrote fine comedies - EVERY MAN IN HIS HUMOUR and VOLPONE are two of his best. With the scenic designer, Inigo Jones, he developed the "masque" which is a form of theatre entertainment combining poetry, music, dance, theatrical spectacle, and allegory. The masque was quite popular especially at the court. Beaumont and Fletcher wrote tragedies, comedies, and tragi-comedies. THE KNIGHT OF THE BURNING PESTLE and PHILASTER are their most famous. Thomas Dekker is noted for his portrayal of middle-class life in SHOEMAKER'S HOLIDAY. John Webster's tragedies, THE WHITE DEVIL and THE DUCHESS OF MALFI, depict a world of intrigue, revenge, and horror. John Ford's 'TIS PITY SHE'S A WHORE deals with abnormal human relationships.

In 1642, Oliver Cromwell, the leader of the Puritan Commonwealth, closed all the theatres. When the English theatres reopened in 1660 (and Charles the II was restored to the throne), they were greatly influenced by the French. Charles the II had spent his exile in France and observed the sophisticated use of scenery and staging techniques and had seen the neo-classical tragedies.

FRENCH THEATRE

French theatre developed along the lines of the Italian and English theatre, but it lagged primarily because France lacked internal stability. Stability came to France with Cardinal Richelieu and both Louis XIII and Louis XIV. French theatre progress was also delayed by the practice of giving a monopoly on theatre productions to one group. The Confrerie (Brotherhood) de la Passion which began producing miracle and mystery plays in 1402 built the first permanent theatre in France, the Hotel de Burgogne in 1550. Later the Hotel de Burgogne merged with the Theatre du Marais and formed the Comedie-Française, the national theatre of France. The

Brotherhood held a monopoly on producing plays in Paris for more than one hundred years. Although they did allow touring companies to perform, and sometimes sold shares enabling other companies to perform, their monopoly hindered not only the production of plays, but the writing of plays.

The history of French theatre begins with touring players and farce, continues through the miracle, mystery, and morality plays, and culminates in the seventeenth century with the neo-classical tragedies of Corneille and Racine and the comedies of Molière.

Pierre Corneille wrote tragedies founded on the principles developed by Aristotle. His finest tragedy, LE CID, broke with the neo-classical rules which led to criticism of the work. Jean Racine's most famous work is not only a fine tragedy, but has a great role for an actress as the title character, PHEDRE. Molière, however, is considered France's greatest comic playwright. Like Shakespeare, Molière was a consummate theatre person. He was an actor, writer, director, and manager. His brilliant comedies (THE SCHOOL FOR WIVES, THE SCHOOL FOR HUSBANDS, TARTUFFE, THE MISANTHROPE, and THE IMAGINARY INVALID) satirize human foibles and attack hypocrisy and injustice with wit and grace.

The physical French theatre in the seventeenth century was quite elaborate. One theatre, the Salle des Machines, held intricate machines for flying backdrops and over one hundred and forty different settings. Scene painting, influenced by the Italian use of perspective, flourished. Scenery, especially for the court audiences, was spectacular.

Molière introduced more natural acting into the French theatre. In the tragedies, actors still tended to declaim, but the style in the comedies was much freer. Women were accepted on the stage and achieved success.

The comedies of Molière, the tragedies of Corneille and Racine, the introduction of women as actors, and scenic spectacles were the primary French influences on the Restoration theatre in England. Charles II also adopted the French idea of giving patents or monopolies to companies for a particular theatre.

RESTORATION ENGLAND

The physical theatre of the Restoration was entirely enclosed. The theatre had a proscenium stage with movable flats and backdrops, and a forestage, or apron which was the primary playing space. Oil lamps, candles, and chandeliers were used for lighting, and the colored lighting techniques developed by the Italians were utilized as well.

Following the lead of the French, women appeared on the English stage for the first time. One of the most popular Restoration actresses was Nell Gwynne who excelled in comedy parts. She left her acting career, however, to become the mistress of King Charles II. The outstanding actor of the time was Thomas Betterton. He played in revivals of Shakespeare's plays and in new plays achieving great success with his natural, unaffected style.

The Restoration comedy of manners, which took as its theme the social mores, manners, and customs of society, was a mirror image of its narrow audience. The subject matter was usually the love affairs and intrigues of the upper classes. The audience which viewed the plays belonged to the court and the upper classes. They came to the theatre to carry on their social affairs, not necessarily to see the play. In fact, two "plays" were being presented in the Restoration theatre, one by the audience, talking loudly, entering and leaving at any moment, and fighting duels while the real "play" was occurring onstage.

Restoration drama was primarily the work of six playwrights. William Congreve wrote THE WAY OF THE WORLD in which the two main characters, Millamant and Mirabell, manage to come together through many complications and much bargaining. William Wycherly's THE COUNTRY WIFE deals with the adventures of Margery Pinchwife, a country girl thrust into decadent London society. THE BEAUX' STRATEGEM by George Farquhar concerns the attempts of Aimwell and Archer to marry women for their money. In THE MAN OF MODE: OR, SIR FOPLING FLUTTER, Etherege characterizes the vain, affected Restoration fop. John Dryden's tragedy ALL FOR LOVE retells the story of Antony and Cleopatra. Dryden was also a critic of Restoration drama, and his essays have broadened our knowledge of this period. VENICE PRESERVED by Thomas Otway is considered one of the greatest tragedies of the seventeenth century.

With the Restoration theatre and its comedy of manners, which appealed only to the upper classes, the theatre was essentially a private club for the upper stratum of society. Fortunately, in the eighteenth century, the theatre became much more public and appealed to the middle class.

EIGHTEENTH CENTURY

The eighteenth century was dominated by actors beginning with Colley Cibber, a playwright as well as an actor, who wrote APOLOGY FOR THE LIFE OF MR. COLLEY CIBBER, COMEDIAN (which is a record of the theatre of the time), Peg Woffington who was noted for her "breeches" parts, Sarah Siddons who was famous for her extremely emotional acting style, and, most importantly, David Garrick who elevated the status of the actor. Garrick was fresh and natural onstage, and became quite successful. With his success, he was able to stop the audience in their practice of sitting on the stage while the play was being performed. He also shortened the apron of the stage so that the actors played more behind the proscenium, and he placed chandeliers over the upstage area illuminating the actors. The stage became relatively bright, and the audience dark. This was a small, but dramatic, change. Garrick also experimented with more realistic settings.

Only four plays of note are left to us from the eighteenth century. Richard Brindsley Sheridan's THE RIVALS with its marvelous characters (including one of the most famous in English comedy, Mrs. Malaprop, who distorts and misuses language), is full of plot twists and confusion of identities. Sheridan's THE SCHOOL FOR SCANDAL exposes the hypocrisy and corruption of London society. SHE STOOPS TO CONQUER by Oliver Goldsmith is a delightful play of love and mistaken identities which ends happily for all. John Gay in his musical play THE BEGGAR'S OPERA satirized government figures characterizing them as thieves.

An eighteenth-century theatre audience captured by artist Thomas Rowlandson.

Eighteenth-century audiences were lively and critical. They felt free to shout their dislike or pelt the performers with rotten fruit. Obviously, to gain the attention of such a crowd, the actors had to be quite compelling. Thus, the eighteenth century has come to be called the "century of great acting."

NINETEENTH CENTURY

The nineteenth century was a time of great change -politically, economically, socially, and scientifically. This change was reflected in the theatre.

Victor Hugo's romantic play HERNANI, which rejected the classic structure, was produced at the Comedie-Française and caused riots. In England, Dion Boucicault (LONDON ASSURANCE) and Tom Robertson (CASTE) were writing realistic dramas of everyday life. Playwrights were moving toward realism, but it was not until the last quarter of the nineteenth century that Henrik Ibsen "the father of modern drama" burst on the scene with his realistic plays THE PILLARS OF SOCIETY, A DOLL'S HOUSE, GHOSTS, and AN ENEMY OF THE PEOPLE. He shocked audiences with his criticism of existing morality, his espousal of women's rights, and his discussion of such taboo topics as venereal disease.

The physical theatre was ready for the presentation of realistic plays. In England, the actress/manager, Madame Vestris, used a box set as early as 1841. For the first time, the actors played within an environment, not in front of it. This idea of environment was extremely important in the realistic plays. Lighting was improved with gaslight and limelight which could be dimmed or brightened. The necessity for historical accuracy in costuming was finally recognized.

Charles Kean, Henry Irving, Ellen Terry, Lily Langtry, and later Sarah Bernhardt and Duse are a few of the outstanding thespians of this period. The Duke of Saxe-Meiningen and his company in Germany explored ensemble acting and performed all over Europe.

Other innovations which had an influence on theatre were Richard Wagner's musical dramas in which he attempted to unite all of the elements of a production, Gilbert and Sullivan's operettas, and the rise of the music hall in London. All of these influenced the development of musical theatre and vaudeville.

As the nineteenth century drew to a close, the new "modern age" was already in view. The twentieth century eclecticism promised a richness and variety which had never been present in the history of theatre.

TWENTIETH CENTURY

Theatre in the twentieth century - the plays and playwrights, the actors, the physical theatres, and the audiences - is the product of a profusion of choices in such a relatively short time span that the effect is overwhelming.

In the early part of the century, theatre styles were more closely defined. A play could be realistic or romantic or expressionistic, but later playwrights synthesized styles and adapted them in new creative ways so that no one style was dominant. In other words, the playwright today uses form creatively to communicate the content and meaning of the play. Style then is the individual form distinguishing a work of art.

The first predominant style - with Ibsen leading the way - was *realism*. Realism attempted to show life as it really was.

George Bernard Shaw (ST. JOAN, ARMS AND THE MAN, THE DEVIL'S DISCIPLE) debated philosophical issues in his plays, and two Russians, Maxim Gorky (THE LOWER DEPTHS) and Anton Chekhov (THE CHERRY ORCHARD) recreated life as they saw it.

Realism was the dominant style, but other modes such as romanticism, symbolism, expressionism, epic realism, and theatricalism were formed in part as a reaction against realism.

Romanticism is best represented by Edmond Rostand's CYRANO DE BERGERAC written in 1897. CYRANO is an affirmation of the romantic view of the world with its heroic spirit, lofty ideals, and poetic language.

The *symbolists* chose to present not the physical world, but the world of the spirit. Maeterlinck, in his one-act play, THE INTRUDER, vividly presents the abstraction of death, the intruder.

Expressionism is a form of theatre in which the world is usually seen through the eyes of a central character. Inner experiences such as thoughts and dreams are depicted, and surface reality is distorted. Eugene O'Neill's THE HAIRY APE is an expressionistic play.

The German, Bertolt Brecht, in the 1920's and 1930's introduced a style of theatre known as *epic realism*. Brecht's plays are generally episodic in nature and broken up by songs, slide shows, and motion pictures. Brecht wanted to alienate the audience from the action, so that they could become more objective and aware of his social themes. His plays which are widely produced today include the THREEPENNY OPERA (an adaptation of John Gay's THE BEGGAR'S OPERA), MOTHER COURAGE, and THE PRIVATE LIFE OF THE MASTER RACE. This epic realism and Brecht's use of media have had a tremendous influence on contemporary theatre.

Theatricalism is a style which states frankly that a play is theatre, not an attempt to mirror reality. Often characters talk directly to the audience, and there is no attempt at physical reproduction of actual locales. Pirandello's

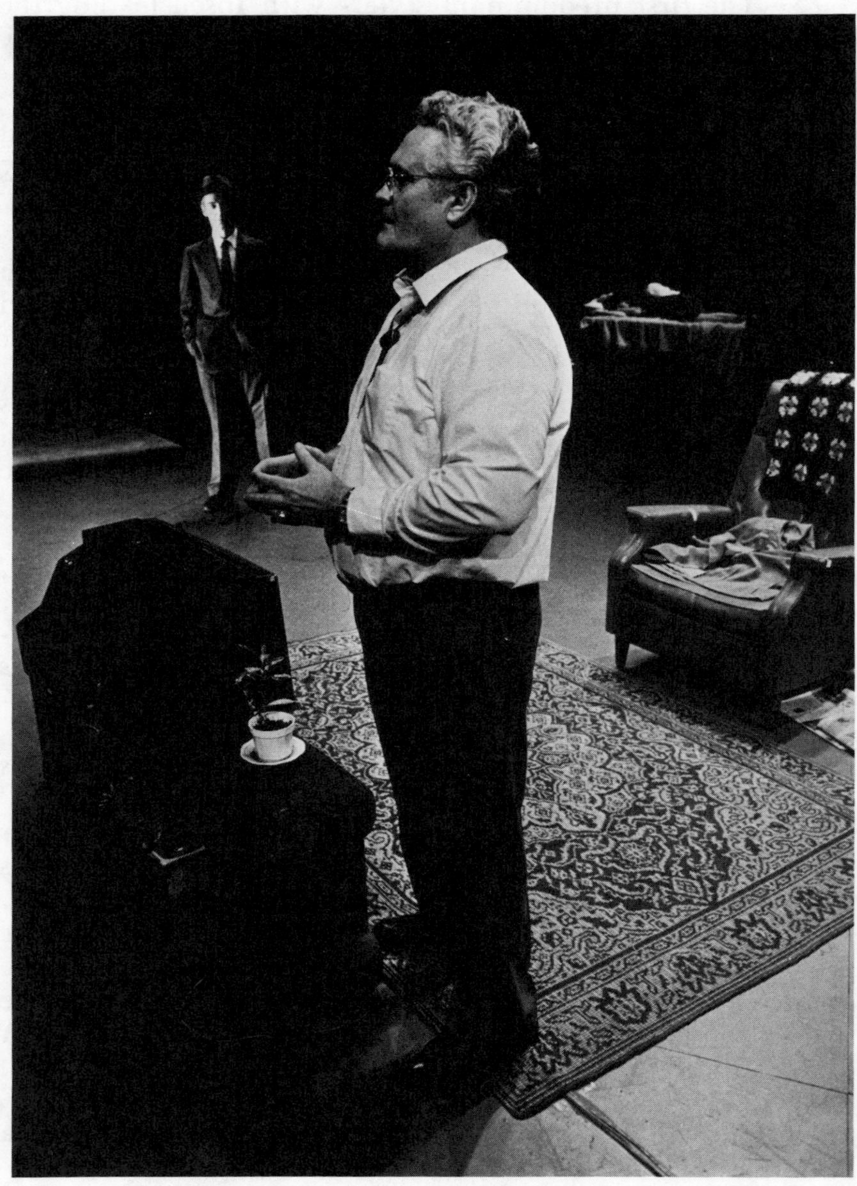

A scene from *No Mercy* by Constance Congdon. Walter Flanagan (right) as Roy and Matthew Lewis (left) as Robert Oppenheimer. The play was developed at the Hartford Stage Company and later produced at the Actors Theatre of Louisville, both resident non-profit professional theatres.

TONIGHT WE IMPROVISE and Thornton Wilder's THE SKIN OF OUR TEETH are theatricalist plays.

Playwrights in the twentieth century have experimented with theatrical styles and kept the theatre in a state of flux. Eugene O'Neill is generally regarded as the greatest American dramatist. His plays include MOURNING BECOMES ELECTRA which is based on the Orestesian tragedy; LONG DAY'S JOURNEY INTO NIGHT, and THE ICEMAN COMETH. The plays of Maxwell Anderson (MARY OF SCOTLAND), Elmer Rice (THE ADDING MACHINE), George Kaufman and Moss Hart (YOU CAN'T TAKE IT WITH YOU) written in the 1920's and 1930's range from historical verse drama to expressionism to realistic comedy. Thornton Wilder wrote two plays which were departures in style - OUR TOWN and THE SKIN OF OUR TEETH. OUR TOWN is presented with no scenery and the set is the stage, but the characters are realistic and moving. Lillian Hellman wrote the powerful dramas THE CHILDREN'S HOUR and THE LITTLE FOXES. Phillip Barry wrote elegant comedies best exemplified by THE PHILADELPHIA STORY. Tennessee Williams (THE GLASS MENAGERIE, STREETCAR NAMED DESIRE), Arthur Miller (DEATH OF A SALESMAN, THE CRUCIBLE), and Edward Albee (THE ZOO STORY, WHO'S AFRAID OF VIRGINIA WOOLF?) have shaped the modern theatre with their distinctive and diverse themes and styles. Harold Pinter (THE CARETAKER), Samuel Beckett (WAITING FOR GODOT), and Eugene Ionesco (THE CHAIRS) with their creative use of language and form have helped mold the contemporary theatre.

Musical comedy, a form distinctly American, and tremendously popular, is a product of the twentieth century. SHOWBOAT, OKLAHOMA!, CAROUSEL, THE KING AND I, GUYS AND DOLLS, MY FAIR LADY, WEST SIDE STORY, FIDDLER ON THE ROOF, HAIR, and CABARET are just a few in a long list of memorable musicals which are continually revived and played all over the world.

Although attempts have been made to categorize and label the diversity and richness of the last half of the twentieth century, unlike other periods of drama the twentieth century

A scene from the popular musical *Oliver!*

defies easy labeling. The styles are individual and reflect the playwrights' points-of-view. Thus, there are as many different styles as there are playwrights. Of course, the playwrights have a tremendous wealth of theatrical tradition and history to draw upon. The choices are unlimited.

The physical theatre and technical innovations have encouraged the development of new styles. Advances in lighting technology, theatre architecture, and construction techniques have stimulated creative approaches to playwriting and production. It is interesting to note, however, that with all the advances in theatre there are movements to go back to "minimal theatre." A theatre pared down to essentials - players performing on a simple platform.

Acting, influenced primarily by Constantin Stanislavsky's teachings in the early part of the twentieth century, continues to explore new techniques aided by teachers and innovators such as Lee Strasberg, Stella Adler, Peter Brook, Jerzey Grotowski, and Uta Hagen. Actor's Equity, a union of actors formed in 1913, has elevated the status of actors, improved working conditions, and negotiated fair compensation. Today, Actor's Equity has approximately thirty thousand active members.

In the late 1940's a small group of theatrical pioneers led by theatre director Margo Jones had a dream - to provide non-profit professional theatre in every major city across the country. Today that dream has come true. Over 250 resident non-profit professional theatres form a national network presenting the classics of world literature, the best work by foreign playwrights, and new plays by contemporary dramatists. The non-profit professional theatre provides an alternative to commercial Broadway theatre and provides a home for playwrights. Margo Jones said in the late 1940's that "If we succeed in inspiring the operation of thirty theatres like ours, the playwright won't need Broadway." Her prophecy has come true. Playwrights like Pulitzer Prize winners Marsha Norman ('NIGHT MOTHER), David Mamet (GLENGARRY GLEN ROSS), Beth Henley (CRIMES OF THE HEART), Lanford Wilson (TALLEY'S FOLLY), and Sam Shepard (BURIED CHILD) all had their plays first produced in the non-profit professional theatre. Some playwrights like August Wilson (MA RAINEY'S BLACK BOTTOM) develop their plays in collaboration with a particular theatre. Others like Eric Overmyer (ON THE VERGE) and Emily Mann (EXECUTION OF JUSTICE) develop their plays with several non-profit professional theatres around the country. Theatre Communications Group (TCG), the national service organization for the non-profit professional theatre, reports that every year over 15 million people attend performances of the non-profit professional theatre.

Theatre audiences are as diverse as the styles and plays. Theatre continues to draw from a broad spectrum of society. School and university theatres, community theatres, resident theatres throughout the country, summer stock, experimental theatres, Broadway, Off-Broadway, and Off-Off-Broadway are flourishing.

Theatre has changed and evolved through time, but one factor has not changed since that first theatrical performance in 534 B.C. - magic, illusion, and mystery created by the art of theatre continue to flower, nourishing the human spirit.

QUESTIONS FOR REVIEW AND DISCUSSION

1. If plays and theatre are a reflection of the times, why do contemporary audiences enjoy, for example, Greek plays or Shakespeare's plays?
2. Who were the major Greek playwrights? What were their contributions?
3. Why did the Roman theatre collapse?
4. How was theatre revived in the Middle Ages?
5. What are the various styles of drama?

VOCABULARY

dithyramb	eccyclema	realism
tragedy	perioktos	romanticism
catharsis	Phylakes	epic realism
Dionysus	Atellan	theatricalism
cothurnus	Roscius	style
chiton	bard	expressionism
himation	miracle/mystery play	Actor's Equity
chlamys	morality play	minimal theatre
skene	trope	
deus ex machina	pageant wagon	

SUGGESTIONS

- Present one of the scenes from pages 245-272.
- Read and report on Mary Renault's novel THE MASK OF APOLLO which deals with the actor in Greek drama.
- Research and write the history of a theatre in your area. How did it begin and how has it evolved? Does it reflect the surrounding community?
- Research and report on an aspect of the Oriental Theatre -the Kubuki or Noh, for example.
- Build a model of a theatre from one of the historical periods.
- Compare and contrast a contemporary tragedy such as Arthur Miller's DEATH OF A SALESMAN with a Greek tragedy.

Acting Scenes from the Greeks to the Present

MEDEA
Euripides
(1 male, 1 female)
RALPH ROISTER DOISTER
Nicholas Udall
(2 male, 1 female)
THE TAMING OF THE SHREW
William Shakespeare
(1 male, 1 female)
MACBETH
William Shakespeare
(1 male, 1 female)
SCHOOL FOR SCANDAL
Richard Brinsley Sheridan
(1 male, 1 female)
A DOLL'S HOUSE
Henrik Ibsen
(1 male, 1 female)
THE BRIDE
Constance Congdon
(1 male, 1 female)

The Medea
Euripides
(Fifth Century B.C.)

(Enter Jason, with attendants.)

Jason

This is not the first occasion that I have noticed
How hopeless it is to deal with a stubborn temper.
For, with reasonable submission to our ruler's will,
You might have lived in this land and kept your home.
As it is you are going to be exiled for your loose speaking.
Not that I mind myself. You are free to continue
Telling everyone that Jason is a worthless man.
But as to your talk about the king, consider
Yourself most lucky that exile is your punishment.
I, for my part, have always tried to calm down
The anger of the king, and wished you to remain.
But you will not give up your folly, continually
Speaking ill of him, and so you are going to be banished.
All the same, and in spite of your conduct, I'll not desert
My friends, but have come to make some provision for you,
So that you and the children may not be penniless
Or in need of anything in exile. Certainly
Exile brings many troubles with it. And even
If you hate me, I cannot think badly of you.

Medea

O coward in every way — that is what I call you,
With bitterest reproach for your lack of manliness,
You have come, you, my worst enemy, have come to me!
It is not an example of overconfidence
Or of boldness thus to look your friends in the face,
Friends you have injured — no, it is the worst of all
Human diseases, shamelessness. But you did well
To come, for I can speak ill of you and lighten
My heart, and you will suffer while you are listening.
And first I will begin from what happened first.
I saved your life, and every Greek knows I saved it,
Who was a shipmate of yours aboard the Argo,
When you were sent to control the bulls that breathed fire
And yoke them, and when you would sow that deadly field.

Also that snake, who encircled with his many folds
The Golden Fleece and guarded it and never slept,
I killed, and so gave you the safety of the light.
And I myself betrayed my father and my home,
And came with you to Pelias' land of Iolcus.
And then, showing more willingness to help than wisdom,
I killed him, Pelias, with a most dreadful death
At his own daughters' hands, and took away your fear.
This is how I behaved to you, you wretched man,
And you forsook me, took another bride to bed,
Though you had children; for, if that had not been,
You would have had an excuse for another wedding.
Faith in your word has gone. Indeed, I cannot tell
Whether you think the gods whose names you swore by then
Have ceased to rule and that new standards are set up,
Since you must know you have broken your word to me.
O my right hand, and the knees which you often clasped
In supplication, how senselessly I am treated
By this bad man, and how my hopes have missed their mark!
Come, I will share my thoughts as though you were a friend —
You! Can I think that you would ever treat me well?
But I will do it, and these questions will make you
Appear the baser. Where am I to go? To my father's?
Him I betrayed and his land when I came with you.
To Pelias' wretched daughters? What a fine welcome
They would prepare for me who murdered their father!
For this is my position — hated by my friends
At home, I have, in kindness to you, made enemies
Of others whom there was no need to have injured
And how happy among Greek women you have made me
On your side for all this! A distinguished husband
I have — for breaking promises. When in misery
I am cast out of the land and go into exile,
Quite without friends and all alone with my children,
That will be a fine shame for the new-wedded groom,
For his children to wander as beggars and she who saved him.
O God, you have given to mortals a sure method
Of telling the gold that is pure from the counterfeit;
Why is there no mark engraved upon men's bodies,
By which we could know the true ones from the false ones?

Ralph Roister Doister
Nicholas Udall
(1505-1556)

SCENE IV

[*Enter*] CUSTANCE. MERYGREEKE, ROISTER DOISTER [*remain.*]

C. Custance. What gauding and fooling is this afore my door?

M. Mery. May not folks be honest, pray you, though they be poor?

C. Custance. As that thing may be true, so rich folks may be fools.

R. Roister. Her talk is as fine as she had learned in schools.

M. Mery. [*Aside to* RALPH.] Look partly toward her, and draw a little near.

C. Custance. Get ye home, idle folks!

M. Mery. Why, may not we be here?
Nay, and ye will ha'ze, ha'ze[1] — otherwise, I tell you plain,
And ye will not ha'ze, then give us our gear again.

C. Custance. Indeed I have of yours much gay things, God save all.

R. Roister. [*Aside to* MATHEW.] Speak gently unto her, and let her take all.

M. Mery. Ye are too tender-hearted; shall she make us daws?[2]
Nay, dame, I will be plain with you in my friend's cause.

R. Roister. Let all this pass, sweetheart, and accept my service.

C. Custance. I will not be served with a fool in no wise.
When I choose an husband I hope to take a man.

M. Mery. And where will ye find one which can do that he can?
Now this man toward you being so kind,
You not to make him an answer somewhat to his mind!

C. Custance. I sent him a full answer by you, did I not?

M. Mery. And I reported it.

C. Custance. Nay, I must speak it again.

R. Roister. No, no, he told it all.

M. Mery. Was I not meetly plain?

R. Roister. Yes.

M. Mery. But I would not tell all; for faith, if I had,
With you, dame Custance, ere this hour it had been bad,
And not without cause — for this goodly personage
Meant no less than to join with you in marriage.

[1]Have us. [2]Fools.

C. Custance. Let him waste no more labor nor suit about me.

M. Mery. Ye know not where your preferment lieth, I see,
He sending you such a token, ring and letter.

C. Custance. Marry, here it is; ye never saw a better.

M. Mery. Let us see your letter.

C. Custance. Hold, read it if ye can,
And see what letter it is to win a woman.

[*He opens letter, and reads. Merygreeke alters the punctuation of the letter and the meaning is changed – quite dramatically!*[3]]

M. Mery. "To mine own dear coney, bird, sweetheart, and pigsney,[4]
Good Mistress Custance, present these by and by."
Of this superscription do ye blame the style?

C. Custance. With the rest as good stuff as ye read a great while.

M. Mery. "Sweet mistress, where as I love you nothing at all —
Regarding your substance and riches chief of all —
For your personage, beauty, demeanor, and wit,
I commend me unto you never a whit.
Sorry to hear report of your good welfare,
For (as I hear say) such your conditions are,
That ye be worthy favor of no living man,
To be abhorred of every honest man,
To be taken for a woman inclined to vice;
Nothing at all to virtue giving her due price.
Wherefore, concerning marriage, ye are thought
Such a fine paragon, as ne'er honest man bought.
And now by these presents I do you advertise
That I am minded to marry you in no wise.
For your goods and substance, I could be content
To take you as ye are. If ye mind to be my wife,
Ye shall be assured, for the time of my life,
I will keep you right well from good raiment and fare;
Ye shall not be kept but in sorrow and care.
Ye shall in no wise live at your own liberty.
Do and say what ye lust, ye shall never please me;
But when ye are merry, I will be all sad;

[3] The letter is punctuated here as Merygreeke reads it.

[4] Coney: rabbit; pigsney: pig's eye. Terms of endearment.

When ye are sorry, I will be very glad;
When ye seek your heart's ease, I will be unkind;
At no time in me shall ye much gentleness find;
But all things contrary to your will and mind,
Shall be done — otherwise I will not be behind
To speak. And as for all them that would do you wrong,
I will so help and maintain, ye shall not live long,
Nor any foolish dolt shall cumber you but I.
I, whoe'er say nay, will stick by you till I die.
Thus, good mistress, Custance, the Lord you save and keep
From me, Roister Doister, whether I wake or sleep —
Who favoreth you no less (ye may be bold)
Than this letter purporteth, which ye have unfold."

C. Custance. How by this letter of love? Is it not fine?

R. Roister. By the arms of Calais, it is none of mine.

M. Mery. Fie, you are foul to blame, this is your own hand!

C. Custance. Might not a woman be proud of such an husband?

M. Mery. Ah, that ye would in a letter show such despite!

R. Roister. Oh, I would I had him here, the which did it endite!

M. Mery. Why, ye made it yourself, ye told me, by this light.

R. Roister. Yea, I meant I wrote it mine own self yesternight.

C. Custance. Ywis, sir, I would not have sent you such a mock.

R. Roister. Ye may so take it, but I meant it not so, by Cock.

M. Mery. Who can blame this women to fume and fret and rage?
Tut, tut! yourself now have marred your own marriage.
Well, yet mistress Custance, if ye can this remit,
This gentleman otherwise may your love requit.

C. Custance. No! God be with you both, and seek no more to me.
[*Exit.*]

R. Roister. Wough! She is gone forever, I shall her no more see.
[*Begins to weep.*]

M. Mery. What, weep? Fie, for shame! And blubber? For manhood's sake,
Never let your foe so much pleasure of you take.
Rather play the man's part, and do love refrain.
If she despise you, e'en despise ye her again.

R. Roister. By Goss, and for thy sake I defy her indeed.

M. Mery. Yea, and perchance that way ye shall much sooner speed.
For one mad property these women have, in fey,
When ye will, they will not, will not ye, then will they.

Ah, foolish woman! ah, most unlucky Custance!
Ah, unfortunate woman! ah, peevish Custance!
Art thou to thine harms so obstinately bent,
That thou canst not see where lieth thine high preferment?
Canst thou not lub dis man, which could lub dee so well?
Art thou so much thine own foe?

R. Roister. Thou dost the truth tel

M. Mery. Well, I lament.

R. Roister. So do I.

M. Mery. Wherefore?

R. Roister. For this thing
Because she is gone.

M. Mery. I mourn for another thing.

R. Roister. What is it, Merygreeke, wherefore thou dost grief take?

M. Mery. That I am not a woman myself for your sake.
I would have you myself, and a straw for yond Gill,
And mock much of you, though it were 'against my will.
I would not, I warrant you, fall in such a rage,
As so to refuse such a goodly personage.

R. Roister. In faith, I heartily thank thee, Merygreeke.

M. Mery. And I were a woman —

R. Roister. Thou wouldst to me seek

M. Mery. For, though I say it, a goodly person ye be.

R. Roister. No, no.

M. Mery. Yes, a goodly man as e'er I did see.

R. Roister. No, I am a poor homely man, as God made me.

M. Mery. By the faith that I owe to God, sir, but ye be!
Would I might for your sake spend a thousand pound land.

R. Roister. I dare say thou wouldest have me to thy husband.

M. Mery. Yea, and I were the fairest lady in the shire,
And knew you as I know you, and see you now here —
Well, I say no more.

R. Roister. Gramercies, with all my heart!

M. Mery. But since that cannot be, will ye play a wise part?

R. Roister. How should I?

M. Mery. Refrain from Custance a while now
And I warrant her soon right glad to seek to you.
Ye shall see her anon come on her knees creeping,
And pray you to be good to her, salt tears weeping.

R. Roister. But what and she come not?

M. Mery. In faith, then, farewell she.
Or else if ye be wroth, ye may avenged be.
R. Roister. By Cock's precious potstick,[5] and e'en so I shall.
I will utterly destroy her, and house, and all.
But I would be avenged, in the mean space,
On that vile scribbler,[6] that did my wooing disgrace.
M. Mery. "Scribbler," quoth you, indeed he is worthy no less.
I will call him to you and ye bid me, doubtless.
R. Roister. Yes, for although he had as many lives
As a thousand widows, and a thousand wives,
As a thousand lions, and a thousand rats,
A thousand wolves, and a thousand cats,
A thousand bulls, and a thousand calves,
And a thousand legions divided in halves,
He shall never 'scape death on my sword's point,
Though I should be torn therefor joint by joint.
M. Mery. Nay, if ye will kill him, I will not fet him,
I will not in so much extremity set him;
He may yet amend, sir, and be an honest man,
Therefore pardon him, good soul, as much as ye can.
R. Roister. Well, for thy sake, this once with his life he shall pass,
But I will hew him all to pieces, by the Mass.
M. Mery. Nay, faith, ye shall promise that he shall no harm have,
Else I will not fet him.
R. Roister. I shall, so God me save —
But I may chide him a-good.
M. Mery. Yea, that do, hardily.
R. Roister. Go, then.
M. Mery. I return, and bring him to you by and by. [*Exit.*]

[5]A meaningless oath: By God's precious stick for stirring a pot.
[6]Scrivener.

The Taming of the Shrew
William Shakespeare
(1564-1616)

Enter KATHERINA.

Good morrow, Kate, for that's your name, I hear.
Kath. Well have you heard, but something hard of hearing:
They call me Katherine that do talk of me.
Pet. You lie, in faith, for you are call'd plain Kate,
And bonny Kate, and sometimes Kate the curst;
But Kate, the prettiest Kate in Christendom,
Kate of Kate-Hall, my super-dainty Kate,
For dainties are all Kates, and therefore, Kate,
Take this of me, Kate of my consolation —
Hearing thy mildness prais'd in every town,
Thy virtues spoke of, and thy beauty sounded,
Yet not so deeply as to thee belongs,
Myself am mov'd to woo thee for my wife.
Kath. Mov'd! in good time! Let him that mov'd you hither
Remove you hence. I knew you at the first
You were a moveable.
Pet. Why, what's a moveable?
Kath. A join'd-stool.
Pet. Thou hast hit it; come sit on me.
Kath. Asses are made to bear, and so are you.
Pet. Women are made to bear, and so are you.
Kath. No such jade as you, if me you mean.
Pet. Alas, good Kate, I will not burthen thee,
For knowing thee to be but young and light.
Kath. Too light for such a swain as you to catch,
And yet as heavy as my weight should be.
Pet. Should be! should — buzz!
Kath. Well ta'en, and like a buzzard.
Pet. O slow-wing'd turtle, shall a buzzard take thee?
Kath. Ay, for a turtle, as he takes a buzzard.
Pet. Come, come, you wasp, i' faith you are too angry.
Kath. If I be waspish, best beware my sting.

Pet. My remedy is then to pluck it out.
Kath. Ay, if the fool could find it where it lies.
Pet. Who knows not where a wasp does wear his sting?
In his tail.
Kath. In his tongue.
Pet. Whose tongue?
Kath. Yours, if you talk of tales, and so farewell.
Pet. What, with my tongue in your tail? Nay, come again,
Good Kate; I am a gentleman —
Kath. That I'll try. *She strikes him.*
Pet. I swear I'll cuff you, if you strike again.
Kate. So may you lose your arms.
If you strike me, you are no gentleman,
And if no gentleman, why then no arms.
Pet. A herald, Kate? O, put me in thy books!
Kath. What is your crest? a coxcomb?
Pet. A combless cock, so Kate will be my hen.
Kath. No cock of mine, you crow too like a craven.
Pet. Nay, come, Kate, come; you must not look so sour.
Kath. It is my fashion when I see a crab.
Pet. Why, here's no crab, and therefore look not sour.
Kath. There is, there is.
Pet. Then show it me.
Kath. Had I a glass, I would.
Pet. What, you mean my face?
Kath. Well aim'd of such a young one.
Pet. Now, by Saint George, I am too young for you.
Kath. Yet you are wither'd.
Pet. 'Tis with cares.
Kath. I care not.
Pet. Nay, hear you, Kate. In sooth you scape not so.
Kath. I chafe you if I tarry. Let me go.
Pet. No, not a whit, I find you passing gentle:
'Twas told me you were rough and coy and sullen,
And now I find report a very liar;
For thou art pleasant, gamesome, passing courteous,
But slow in speech, yet sweet as spring-time flowers.
Thou canst not frown, thou canst not look askaunce,
Nor bite the lip, as angry wenches will,
Nor hast thou pleasure to be cross in talk;

But thou with mildness entertain'st thy wooers,
With gentle conference, soft, and affable.
Why does the world report that Kate doth limp?
O sland'rous world! Kate like the hazel-twig
Is straight and slender, and as brown in hue
As hazel-nuts, and sweeter than the kernels.
O, let me see thee walk. Thou dost not halt.

Kath. Go, fool, and whom thou keep'st command.

Pet. Did ever Dian so become a grove
As Kate this chamber with her princely gait?
O, be thou Dian, and let her be Kate,
And then let Kate be chaste, and Dian sportful!

Kath. Where did you study all this goodly speech?

Pet. It is extempore, from my mother-wit.

Kath. A witty mother! witless else her son.

Pet. Am I not wise?

Kath. Yes, keep you warm.

Pet. Marry, so I mean, sweet Katherine, in thy bed;
And therefore setting all this chat aside,
Thus in plain terms: your father hath consented
That you shall be my wife; your dowry 'greed on;
And will you, nill you, I will marry you.
Now, Kate, I am a husband for your turn,
For by this light whereby I see thy beauty,
Thy beauty that doth make me like thee well,
Thou must be married to no man but me;
For I am he am born to tame you, Kate,
And bring you from a wild Kate to a Kate
Conformable as other household Kates.

End.

Macbeth

William Shakespeare
(1564-1616)

SCENE II

Enter LADY [MACBETH].

Lady M. That which hath made them drunk hath made me bold;
What hath quench'd them hath given me fire. Hark! Peace!
It was the owl that shriek'd, the fatal bellman,
Which gives the stern'st good-night. He is about it:
The doors are open; and the surfeited grooms
Do mock their charge with snores. I have drugg'd their possets,
That death and nature do contend about them,
Whether they live or die.

Macb. [*Within.*] Who's there? What ho?

Lady M. Alack, I am afraid they have awak'd,
And 'tis not done; th' attempt, and not the deed,
Confounds us. Hark! I laid their daggers ready,
He could not miss 'em. Had he not resembled
My father as he slept, I had done't.

Enter MACBETH.

My husband!

Macb. I have done the deed. Didst thou not hear a noise?

Lady M. I heard the owl scream and the crickets cry.
Did not you speak?

Macb. When?

Lady M. Now.

Macb. As I descended?

Lady M. Ay.

Macb. Hark! Who lies i' th' second chamber?

Lady M. Donalbain.

Macb. This is a sorry sight.

[*Looking on his hands.*]

Lady M. A foolish thought, to say a sorry sight.

Macb. There's one did laugh in 's sleep, and one cried, "Murther!"
That they did wake each other. I stood and heard them;
But they did say their prayers, and address'd them
Again to sleep.

Lady M. There are two lodg'd together.

Macb. One cried, "God bless us!" and "Amen!" the other,
As they had seen me with these hangman's hands.
List'ning their fear, I could not say "Amen,"
When they did say "God bless us!"

Lady M. Consider it not so deeply.

Macb. But wherefore could not I pronounce "Amen"?
I had most need of blessing, and "Amen"
Stuck in my throat.

Lady M. These deeds must not be thought
After these ways; so, it will make us mad.

Macb. Methought I heard a voice cry, "Sleep no more!
Macbeth does murther sleep" — the innocent sleep,
Sleep that knits up the ravell'd sleave of care,
The death of each day's life, sore labor's bath,
Balm of hurt minds, great nature's second course,
Chief nourisher in life's feast.

Lady M. What do you mean?

Macb. Still it cried, "Sleep no more!" to all the house;
"Glamis hath murther'd sleep, and therefore Cawdor
Shall sleep no more — Macbeth shall sleep no more."

Lady M. Who was it that thus cried? Why, worthy thane,
You do unbend your noble strength, to think
So brain-sickly of things. Go get some water,
And wash this filthy witness from your hand.
Why did you bring these daggers from the place?
They must lie there. Go carry them, and smear
The sleepy grooms with blood.

Macb. I'll go no more.

I am afraid to think what I have done;
Look on't again I dare not.
Lady M. Infirm of purpose!
Give me the daggers. The sleeping and the dead
Are but as pictures; 'tis the eye of childhood
That fears a painted devil. If he do bleed,
I'll gild the faces of the grooms withal,
For it must seem their guilt. *Exit. Knock within.*
Macb. Whence is that knocking?
How is't with me, when every noise appalls me?
What hands are here? Hah! they pluck out mine eyes.
Will all great Neptune's ocean wash this blood
Clean from my hand? No; this my hand will rather
The multitudinous seas incarnadine,
Making the green one red.

Enter LADY [MACBETH].

Lady M. My hands are of your color; but I shame
To wear a heart so white. *(Knock.)* I hear a knocking
At the south entry. Retire we to our chamber.
A little water clears us of this deed;
How easy is it then! Your constancy
Hath left you unattended. *(Knock.)* Hark, more knocking.
Get on your night-gown, lest occasion call us
And show us to be watchers. Be not lost
So poorly in your thoughts.
Macb. To know my deed, 'twere best not know myself. *Knock.*
Wake Duncan with thy knocking! I would thou couldst!

End

School for Scandal

Richard Brinsley Sheridan

(1751-1816)

ACT II. SCENE I.

A room in Sir Peter Teazle's *house.*

[*Enter* Sir Peter *and* Lady Teazle]

SIR PETER: Lady Teazle, Lady Teazle, I'll not bear it!

LADY TEAZLE: Sir Peter, Sir Peter, you may bear it or not, as you please; but I ought to have my own way in everything, and what's more, I will too. What though I was educated in the country, I know very well that women of fashion in London are accountable to nobody after they are married.

SIR PETER: Very well, ma'am, very well; so a husband is to have no influence, no authority?

LADY TEAZLE: Authority! No, to be sure: — if you wanted authority over me, you should have adopted me, and not married me: I am sure you were old enough.

SIR PETER: Old enough! — ay, there it is! Well, well, Lady Teazle, though my life may be made unhappy by your temper, I'll not be ruined by your extravagance!

LADY TEAZLE: My extravagance! I'm sure I'm not more extravagant than a woman of fashion ought to be.

SIR PETER: No, no, madam, you shall throw away no more sums on such unmeaning luxury. 'Slife! to spend as much to furnish your dressing-room with flowers in winter as would suffice to turn the Pantheon into a greenhouse, and give a *fête champêtre* at Christmas.

LADY TEAZLE: And am I to blame, Sir Peter, because flowers are dear in cold weather? You should find fault with the climate, and not with me. For my part, I'm sure I wish it was spring all the year round, and that roses grew under our feet!

SIR PETER: Oons! madam — if you had been born to this, I shouldn't wonder at your talking thus; but you forget what your situation was when I married you.

LADY TEAZLE: No, no, I don't; 'twas a very disagreeable one, or I should never have married you.

SIR PETER: Yes, yes, madam, you were then in somewhat a humbler style — the daughter of a plain country squire. Recollect,

Lady Teazle, when I saw you first sitting at your tambour, in a pretty figured linen gown, with a bunch of keys at your side, your hair combed smooth over a roll, and your apartment hung round with fruits in worsted, of your own working.

LADY TEAZLE: Oh, yes! I remember it very well, and a curious life I led. My daily occupation to inspect the dairy, superintend the poultry, make extracts from the family receipt-book, and comb my aunt Deborah's lapdog.

SIR PETER: Yes, yes, ma'am, 'twas so indeed.

LADY TEAZLE: And then, you know, my evening amusements! To draw patterns for ruffles, which I had not the materials to make up; to play Pope Joan with the Curate; to read a sermon to my aunt; or to be stuck down to an old spinet to strum my father to sleep after a fox-chase.

SIR PETER: I am glad you have so good a memory. Yes, madam, these were the recreations I took you from; but now you must have your coach — *vis-à-vis* — and three powdered footmen before your chair; and, in the summer, a pair of white cats to draw you to Kensington Gardens. No recollection, I suppose, when you were content to ride double, behind the butler, on a docked coach-horse?

LADY TEAZLE: No — I swear I never did that; I deny the butler and the coach-horse.

SIR PETER: This, madam, was your situation; and what have I done for you? I have made you a woman of fashion, of fortune, of rank — in short, I have made you my wife.

LADY TEAZLE: Well, then, and there is but one thing more you can make me to add to the obligation, that is —

SIR PETER: My widow, I suppose?

LADY TEAZLE: Hem! Hem!

SIR PETER: I thank you, madam — but don't flatter yourself; for, though your ill-conduct may disturb my peace of mind, it shall never break my heart, I promise you: however, I am equally obliged to you for the hint.

LADY TEAZLE: Then why will you endeavour to make yourself so disagreeable to me, and thwart me in every little elegant expense?

SIR PETER: 'Slife, madam, I say, had you any of these little elegant expenses when you married me?

LADY TEAZLE: Lud, Sir Peter! would you have me be out of the fashion?

SIR PETER: The fashion, indeed! what had you to do with the fashion before you married me?

LADY TEAZLE: For my part, I should think you would like to have your wife thought a woman of taste.

SIR PETER: Ay — there again — taste! Zounds! madam, you had no taste when you married me!

LADY TEAZLE: That's very true, indeed, Sir Peter! and, after having married you, I should never pretend to taste again, I allow. But now, Sir Peter, since we have finished our daily jangle, I presume I may go to my engagement at Lady Sneerwell's?

SIR PETER: Ay, there's another precious circumstance — a charming set of acquaintance you have made there!

LADY TEAZLE: Nay, Sir Peter, they are all people of rank and fortune, and remarkably tenacious of reputation.

SIR PETER: Yes, egad, they are tenacious of reputation with a vengeance; for they don't choose anybody should have a character but themselves! Such a crew! Ah! many a wretch has rid on a hurdle who has done less mischief than these utterers of forged tales, coiners of scandal, and clippers of reputation.

LADY TEAZLE: What, would you restrain the freedom of speech?

SIR PETER: Ah! they have made you just as bad as any one of the society.

LADY TEAZLE: Why, I believe I do bear a part with a tolerable grace. But I vow I bear no malice against the people I abuse: when I say an ill-natured thing, 'tis out of pure good humour; and I take it for granted they deal exactly in the same manner with me. But, Sir Peter, you know you promised to come to Lady Sneerwell's too.

SIR PETER: Well, well, I'll call in just to look after my own character.

LADY TEAZLE: Then, indeed, you must make haste after me or you'll be too late. So good-bye to ye. [*Exit*]

SIR PETER: So — I have gained much by my intended expostulation! Yet with what a charming air she contradicts everything I say, and how pleasantly she shows her contempt for my authority! Well, though I can't make her love me, there is great satisfaction in quarreling with her; and I think she never appears to such advantage as when she is doing everything in her power to plague me. [*Exit*]

End.

A Doll's House
Henrik Ibsen
(1828-1906)
Act III

Nora (looking at her watch). It is not so very late. Sit down here, Torvald. You and I have much to say to one another. *(She sits down at one side of the table.)*

Helmer. Nora — what is this? — this cold, set face?

Nora. Sit down. It will take some time; I have a lot to talk over with you.

Helmer (sits down at the opposite side of the table). You alarm me, Nora! — and I don't understand you.

Nora. No, that is just it. You don't understand me, and I have never understood you either — before to-night. No, you mustn't interrupt me. You must simply listen to what I say. Torvald, this is a settling of accounts.

Helmer. What do you mean by that?

Nora (after a short silence). Isn't there one thing that strikes you as strange in our sitting here like this.

Helmer. What is that?

Nora. We have been married now eight years. Does it not occur to you that this is the first time we two, you and I, husband and wife, have had a serious conversation?

Helmer. What do you mean by serious?

Nora. In all these eight years — longer than that — from the very beginning of our acquaintance, we have never exchanged a word on any serious subject.

Helmer. Was it likely that I would be continually and for ever telling you about worries that you could not help me to bear?

Nora. I am not speaking about business matters. I say that we have never sat down in earnest together to try and get at the bottom of anything.

Helmer. But, dearest Nora, would it have been any good to you?

Nora. That is just it; you have never understood me. I have been greatly wronged, Torvald — first by papa and then by you.

Helmer. What! By us two — by us two, who have loved you better than anyone else in the world?

Nora (shaking her head). You have never loved me. You have only thought it pleasant to be in love with me.

Helmer. Nora, what do I hear you saying?

Nora. It is perfectly true, Torvald. When I was at home with papa, he told me his opinion about everything, and so I had the same opinions; and if I differed from him I concealed the fact, because he would not have liked it. He called me his doll-child, and he played with me just as I used to play with my dolls. And when I came to live with you —

Helmer. What sort of an expression is that to use about our marriage?

Nora (undisturbed). I mean that I was simply transferred from papa's hands into yours. You arranged everything according to your own taste, and so I got the same tastes as you — or else I pretended to, I am really not quite sure which — I think sometimes the one and sometimes the other. When I look back on it, it seems to me as if I had been living here like a poor woman — just from hand to mouth. I have existed merely to perform tricks for you, Torvald. But you would have it so. You and papa have committed a great sin against me. It is your fault that I have made nothing of my life.

Helmer. How unreasonable and how ungrateful you are, Nora! Have you not been happy here?

Nora. No, I have never been happy. I thought I was, but it has never really been so.

Helmer. Not — not happy!

Nora. No, only merry. And you have always been so kind to me. But our home has been nothing but a playroom. I have been your doll-wife, just as at home I was papa's doll-child; and here the children have been my dolls. I thought it great fun when you played with me, just as they thought it great fun when I played with them. That is what our marriage has been, Torvald.

Helmer. There is some truth in what you say — exaggerated and strained as your view of it is. But for the future it shall be different. Playtime shall be over, and lesson-time shall begin.

Nora. Whose lessons? Mine, or the children's?

Helmer. Both yours and the children's, my darling Nora.

Nora. Alas, Torvald, you are not the man to educate me into being a proper wife for you.

Helmer. And you can say that!

Nora. And I.— how am I fitted to bring up the children?

Helmer. Nora!

Nora. Didn't you say so yourself a little while ago — that you dare not trust me to bring them up?

Helmer. In a moment of anger! Why do you pay any heed to that?

Nora. Indeed, you were perfectly right. I am not fit for the task. There is another task I must undertake first. I must try and educate myself — you are not the man to help me in that. I must do that for myself. And that is why I am going to leave you now.

Helmer (springing up). What do you say?

Nora. I must stand quite alone, if I am to understand myself and everything about me. It is for that reason that I cannot remain with you any longer.

Helmer. Nora, Nora!

Nora. I am going away from here now, at once. I am sure Christine will take me in for the night —

Helmer. You are out of your mind! I won't allow it! I forbid you!

Nora. It is no use forbidding me anything any longer. I will take with me what belongs to myself. I will take nothing from you, either now or later.

Helmer. What sort of madness is this!

Nora. To-morrow I shall go home — I mean, to my old home. It will be easiest for me to find something to do there.

Helmer. You blind, foolish woman!

Nora. I must try and get some sense, Torvald.

Helmer. To desert your home, your husband and your children! And you don't consider what people will say!

Nora. I cannot consider that at all. I only know that it is necessary for me.

Helmer. It's shocking. This is how you would neglect your most sacred duties.

Nora. What do you consider my most sacred duties?

Helmer. Do I need to tell you that? Are they not your duties to your husband and your children?

Nora. I have other duties just as sacred.

Helmer. That you have not. What duties could those be?

Nora. Duties to myself.

Helmer. Before all else, you are a wife and a mother.

Nora. I don't believe that any longer. I believe that before all else I am a reasonable human being, just as you are — or, at all events, that I must try and become one. I know quite well, Torvald, that most people would think you right, and that views of that kind are to be found in books; but I can no longer content myself with what most people say, or with what is found in books. I must think over things for myself and get to understand them.

Helmer. Can you not understand your place in your own home? Have you not a reliable guide in such matters as that? — have you no religion?

Nora. I am afraid, Torvald, I do not exactly know what religion is.

Helmer. What are you saying?

Nora. I know nothing but what the clergyman said, when I went to be confirmed. He told us that religion was this, and that, and the other. When I am away from all this, and am alone, I will look into that matter too. I will see if what the clergyman said is true, or at all events if it is true for me.

Helmer. This is unheard of in a girl of your age! But if religion cannot lead you aright, let me try and awaken your conscience. I suppose you have some moral sense? Or — answer me — am I to think you have none?

Nora. I assure you, Torvald, that is not an easy question to answer. I really don't know. The thing perplexes me altogether. I only know that you and I look at it in quite a different light. I am learning, too, that the law is quite another thing from what I supposed; but I find it impossible to convince myself that the law is right. According to it a woman has no right to spare her old dying father, or to save her husband's life. I can't believe that.

Helmer. You talk like a child. You don't understand the conditions of the world in which you live.

Nora. No, I don't. But now I am going to try. I am going to see if I can make out who is right, the world or I.

Helmer. You are ill, Nora; you are delirious; I almost think you are out of your mind.

Nora. I have never felt my mind so clear and certain as to-night.

Helmer. And is it with a clear and certain mind that you forsake your husband and your children.

Nora. Yes, it is.

Helmer. Then there is only one possible explanation.

Nora. What is that?

Helmer. You do not love me any more.

Nora. No, that is just it.

Helmer. Nora! — and you can say that?

Nora. It gives me great pain, Torvald, for you have always been so kind to me, but I cannot help it. I do not love you any more.

Helmer (regaining his composure). Is that a clear and certain conviction too?

Nora. Yes, absolutely clear and certain. That is the reason why I will not stay here any longer.

Helmer. And can you tell me what I have done to forfeit your love?

Nora. Yes, indeed I can. It was to-night, when the wonderful thing did not happen; then I saw you were not the man I had thought you.

Helmer. Explain yourself better — I don't understand you.

Nora. I have waited so patiently for eight years; for, goodness knows, I knew very well that wonderful things don't happen every day. Then this horrible misfortune came upon me; and then I felt quite certain that the wonderful thing was going to happen at last. When Krogstad's letter was lying out there, never for a moment did I imagine that you would consent to accept this man's conditions. I was so absolutely certain that you would say to him: Publish the thing to the whole world. And when that was done —

Helmer. Yes, what then? — when I had exposed my wife to shame and disgrace?

Nora. When that was done, I was so absolutely certain, you would come forward and take everything upon yourself, and say: I am the guilty one.

Helmer. Nora —!

Nora. You mean that I would never have accepted such a sacrifice on your part? No, of course not. But what would my assurances have been worth against yours? That was the wonderful thing which I hoped for and feared; and it was to prevent that, that I wanted to kill myself.

Helmer. I would gladly work night and day for you, Nora — bear sorrow and want for your sake. But no man would sacrifice his honour for the one he loves.

Nora. It is a thing hundreds of thousands of women have done.

Helmer. Oh, you think and talk like a heedless child.

Nora. Maybe. But you neither think nor talk like the man I could bind myself to. As soon as your fear was over — and it was not fear for what threatened me, but for what might happen to you — when the whole thing was past, as far as you were concerned it was exactly as if nothing at all had happened. Exactly as before, I was your little skylark, your doll, which you would in future treat with doubly gentle care, because it was so brittle and fragile. *(Getting up.)* Torvald — it was then it dawned upon me that for eight years I had been living here with a strange man, and had borne him three children —. Oh, I can't bear to think of it! I could tear myself into little bits!

Helmer (sadly). I see, I see. An abyss has opened between us — there is no denying it. But, Nora, would it not be possible to fill it up?

Nora. As I am now, I am no wife for you.

Helmer. I have it in me to become a different man.

Nora. Perhaps — if your doll is taken away from you.

Helmer. But to part! — to part from you! No, no, Nora, I can't understand that idea.

Nora (going out to the right). That makes it all the more certain that it must be done. *(She comes back with her cloak and hat and a small bag which she puts on a chair by the table.)*

Helmer. Nora, Nora, not now! Wait till to-morrow.

Nora (putting on her cloak). I cannot spend the night in a strange man's room.

Helmer. But can't we live here like brother and sister —?

Nora (putting on her hat). You know very well that would not last long. *(Puts the shawl round her.)* Goodbye, Torvald. I won't see the little ones. I know they are in better hands than mine. As I am now, I can be of no use to them.

Helmer. But some day, Nora — some day?

Nora. How can I tell? I have no idea what is going to become of me.

Helmer. But you are my wife, whatever becomes of you.

Nora. Listen, Torvald. I have heard that when a wife deserts her husband's house, as I am doing now, he is legally freed from all obligations towards her. In any case I set you free from all your obligations. You are not to feel yourself bound in the slightest way, any more than I shall. There must be perfect freedom on both sides. See, here is your ring back. Give me mine.

Helmer. That too?

Nora. That too.

Helmer. Here it is.

Nora. That's right. Now it is all over. I have put the keys here. The maids know all about everything in the house — better than I do. To-morrow, after I have left her, Christine will come here and pack up my own things that I brought with me from home. I will have them sent after me.

Helmer. All over! All over! — Nora, shall you never think of me again?

Nora. I know I shall often think of you and the children and this house.

Helmer. May I write to you, Nora?

Nora. No — never. You must not do that.

Helmer. But at least let me send you —

Nora. Nothing — nothing —

Helmer. Let me help you if you are in want.

Nora. No. I can receive nothing from a stranger.

Helmer. Nora — can I never be anything more than a stranger to you?

Nora (taking her bag). Ah, Torvald, the most wonderful thing of all would have to happen.

Helmer. Tell me what that would be!

Nora. Both you and I would have to be so changed that —. Oh, Torvald, I don't believe any longer in wonderful things happening.

Helmer. But I will believe in it. Tell me? So changed that —?

Nora. That our life together would be a real wedlock. Good-bye. *(She goes out through the hall.)*

Helmer (sinks down on a chair at the door and buries his face in his hands). Nora! Nora! *(Looks round, and rises.)* Empty. She is gone. *(A hope flashes across his mind.)* The most wonderful thing of all —?

(The sound of a door shutting is heard from below.)

End.

The Bride
Constance Congdon

SCENE FOURTEEN

(BOBBY *and* KEN *meet in their old playing space. They are not in wedding dress or jacket.* KEN'S *football is on the ground. They are as tentative as they were in their first meeting in Part One.*)

BOBBY. This your football over here?

KEN. It's got a leak. Hey, I'm not supposed to see you now. It's bad luck or something.

BOBBY. No, that's just my dress you're not supposed to see. Mom's fixing the bodice, and I got bored in there.

KEN. What is a bodice, anyway?

BOBBY. It's the front—the top front.

KEN. (*Suddenly embarrassed.*) Oh. (*Change of subject.*) You left the rehearsal in a bit of a hurry.

BOBBY. I ran.

KEN. You ran? You *ran*?

BOBBY. You ran first.

KEN. I did not! You did!

BOBBY. Well, maybe I ran because you jerked or something. I saw you make this little jerking movement, and I thought you were taking off to run.

KEN. Jerking movement! Well, if I jerked, it's only because you flinched.

BOBBY. I flinched when I saw your eyes!

KEN. My eyes! You're blaming this on my eyes? I was looking at you! Can't I even look at you?

BOBBY. You weren't looking at me. You were watching me!

KEN. Yes, and that's when I-saw-you-flinch!

BOBBY. A flinch is nothing but a little nervous reaction.

KEN. A little nervous reaction, huh? You flinched completely out of the room!

BOBBY. Well, you didn't exactly stroll out yourself!

KEN. Well, alright!

BOBBY. Alright.

KEN. Okay. (*Pause.*) We're just nervous, okay? Nerves. I mean, we have every right to be. This is no small thing we're about to do. It's a very big thing, and we have the right to be nervous and behave strange.

BOBBY. I think I hate my dress.

KEN. Why?

BOBBY. It's the color.

KEN. White?

BOBBY. Yes, all over.

KEN. It's a wedding dress! Wedding dresses are white!

BOBBY. It makes me feel like something from a bakery.

KEN. Well, how do you think my jacket makes me feel huh? Huh? Like that seedy magician that used to perform at the Y. Like I should have pigeons in my pockets.

BOBBY. Well, then, why don't you just not put it on again. Ever again if it's so awful for you!

KEN. Wait a minute. Wait—a—minute. I see what you're trying to do. You're trying to get me to take off my jacket so you can take off your dress and it'll be my fault.

BOBBY. Kenny, I'm scared. I'm so afraid I'm going to turn out like your mother!

KEN. My mother, huh? Well, I don't want to be like your father, that's for sure!

BOBBY. Kenny, what are we going to do?

KEN. Look, that could never happen to us. We'll never get like that. It could never happen to us. (*Long pause.*)

BOBBY. Let's promise we'll never get like that.

KEN. I promise. (*Pause*) And let's promise to love each other forever in the same way we do now.

BOBBY. I promise. (*Pause.*) And promise to always tell the truth, no matter what. Always.

KEN. I promise. And to never, never hurt one another.

BOBBY. I promise.

KEN. Well, I guess we should get dressed, then.

BOBBY. Yeah, I have to put on all kinds of underwear and nylons and stuff.

KEN. I hope Dad'll help me with my tie.

BOBBY. Oh, Kenny. Every time I put on that dress, I feel like I'm nobody anymore. I feel like one of those little dolls on top of the wedding cake. Like I'm never going to be myself ever again.

KEN. Bobby, it's nerves. It's natural. My father says it's natural when you decide to get married—

BOBBY. When did we decide? Do you remember? It just went by so quickly.

KEN. Well, I don't remember exactly. But the important thing is that we belong together, and it's right, and well, what else is there?

BOBBY. There must be something. A long engagement. Some people do that. Like being married, you know. With everything.

KEN. We could do that. But you'd get pregnant.

BOBBY. Not on purpose!

KEN. No. But eventually. It's natural.

BOBBY. It's natural! It's natural! I know that! It's my body, you know.

KEN. Okay! Alright! It's clear to me that somebody here does *not* want to get married.

BOBBY. Am I the only one? Will you admit that you ran from me? And that you don't want to get married?

KEN. Yes, yes, I ran. (*Pause.*) Oh God, what are we going to do about the guests—all those people waiting. And the reception buffet.

BOBBY. Let them eat the buffet. They were going to anyway, weren't they?

KEN. Oh, Bobby, are we really going to do this?

BOBBY. *Not* get married? I don't know.

KEN. Bobby, will you *not* marry me?

BOBBY. Yes! Oh, yes! (*They embrace.*) Oh God, we have to tell them. I'll tell mine.

KEN. And I'll tell mine. Let's do it quickly, for Godsake. (*They start to exit, stop.*)

BOBBY. Kenny, what about us?

KEN. We'll find a way. There's got to be something—

BOBBY. Some other way. Don't you think so? Some other—

KEN.—arrangement. Something.

BOBBY. We could go to separate colleges.

KEN. Something like that, for a while. After all, we have our whole lives in front of us.

BOBBY. All those years. Yes.

KEN. Yes.

(*They begin their exits, in opposite directions, stop and turn back to each other as if they had something more to say, hold and then turn and finish the exits.*)

SELECTED BIBLIOGRAPHY

Actors on Acting. Ed. Toby Cole and Helen Chinoy. New York: Crown Publishers, Inc., 1949.

Barton, Lucy. *Historic Costume for the Stage*. Boston: Walter H. Baker Co., 1963.

Bongar, Emmet W. *Practical Stage Lighting*, Theatre Student Series. New York: Richards Rosen Press, Inc., 1970.

Brooke, Iris. *A History of English Costume*. London: Methuen & Co. LTD, 1961.

Cheney, Sheldon. *The Theatre: 3,000 Years of Drama, Acting, and Stagecraft*. New York: McKay, 1959.

Coger, Leslie Irene and White, Melvin R. *Readers Theatre Handbook*, Revised Edition. Glenview, Illinois: Scott, Foresman, and Co., 1973.

Corson, Richard. *Stage Make-up*. Fifth Edition. Englewood Cliffs, New Jersey: Prentice-Hall, 1975.

The Encyclopedia of World Theatre. Ed. Martin Esslin. New York: Charles Scribner's Sons, 1977.

The English Drama: An Anthology 900-1642. Ed. Edd Winfield Parks and Richard Croom Beatty. New York: W. W. Norton and Co., Inc., 1963.

Ewing, Elizabeth. *Underwear: A History*. New York: Theatre Arts Books, 1972.

Freedley, George and Reeves, John. *A History of the Theatre*. New York: Crown Publishers, Inc., 1968.

Gassner, John. *Directions in Modern Theatre and Drama*. New York: Holt, Rinehart and Winston, 1965.

Geisinger, Marion. *Plays, Players, and Playwrights*. New York: Hart Publishing Co., Inc., 1975.

Gilder, Rosamond. *Enter the Actress*. New York: Theatre Arts Books, 1931.

Goldman, William. *The Season*. New York: Bantam Books, 1970.

Hagen, Uta. *Respect for Acting*. New York: Macmillan Publishing Co., Inc., 1973.

Ingham, Rosemary and Covey, Elizabeth. *The Costumer's Handbook*. Englewood Cliffs, New Jersey: Prentice-Hall, Inc., 1980.

Knepler, Henry. *The Gilded Stage*. New York: William Morrow and Co., Inc., 1968.

Laver, James. *Costumes Through the Ages*. New York: Simon & Schuster, 1967.

Lewis, Emory. *Stages – The Fifty-Year Childhood of the American Theatre*. Englewood Cliffs, New Jersey: Prentice-Hall, Inc., 1969.

Lister, Margot. *Costumes of Everyday Life*. Boston: Plays, Inc., 1972.

Macgowan, Kenneth and Melnitz, William. *The Living Stage*. New York: Prentice-Hall, Inc., 1955.

McCandless, Stanley. *A Method of Lighting the Stage*. 4th Edition. New York: Theatre Arts Books, 1973.

McGaw, Charles. *Acting is Believing: A Basic Method*. 2nd Edition. New York: Holt, Rinehart & Winston, 1966.

Motter, Charlotte Kay. *Theatre in High School*. Englewood Cliffs, New Jersey: Prentice-Hall, Inc., 1970.

Nelms, Henning. *Scene Design: A Guide to the Stage*. New York: Dover Publications, Inc., 1970.

Parker, W. Oren and Smith, Harvey K. *Scene Design and Stage Lighting*. 4th Edition. New York: Holt, Rinehart & Winston, 1979.

Penrod, James. *Movement for the Performing Artist*. Palo, Alto, California: Mayfield Publishing Co., 1974.

Prisk, Berneice. *Stage Costume Handbook*. New York: Harper & Row, 1966.

The Riverside Shakespeare. Ed. G. Blakemore Evans. Boston: Houghton Mifflin Co., 1974.

Rolfe, Bari. *Commedia dell'arte: A Scene Study Book*. Oakland, California: Personabooks, 1978.

Rosenthal, Jean and Wertenbaker, Lael. *The Magic of Light*. Boston: Little, Brown, and Co., 1972.

Schechner, Richard. *Environmental Theatre*. New York: Hawthorn Books, Inc., 1973.

Smith, Milton. *Play Production*. New York: D. Appleton-Century Co., Inc., 1948.

Southern, Richard. *The Seven Ages of the Theatre*. New York: Hill and Wang, 1961.

Spolin, Viola. *Improvisation for the Theatre*. Evanston, Illinois: Northwestern University Press, 1963.

Stell, W. Joseph. *Scenery*. The Theatre Student Series. New York: Richards Rosen Press, Inc., 1970.

Stern, Lawrence. *Stage Management*. Boston: Allyn & Bacon, Inc., 1974.

Strenkovsky, Serge. *The Art of Make-up*. New York: E. P. Dutton & Co., 1937.

A Treasury of the Theatre, Vol. I & II. Ed. John Gassner. New York: Simon & Schuster, 1967.

Welker, David. *Stagecraft*. Boston: Allyn & Bacon, Inc., 1978.

APPENDIX

Major Publishing Houses which will supply catalogs upon request.

Dramatic Publishing Company
4150 N. Milwaukee Avenue
Chicago, Illinois 60641

Dramatists Play Service
440 Park Avenue South
New York, New York 10016

Samuel French Publishers
25 West 45th Street
New York, New York 10036

Tams-Witmark
Music Library, Inc.
757 Third Avenue
New York, New York 10017

Theatre Careers

For information on college theatre programs and summer theatre programs contact the American Theatre Association, 1000 Vermont Avenue, N.W., Washington, D.C. 20004. For a small fee you can order the Directory of American College Theatres and the Summer Theatre Directory which contain listings and information.

Theatre Publications

DRAMATICS
(Published by the International Thespian Society)
3368 Central Parkway
Cincinnati, Ohio 45225

AMERICAN THEATRE
(a monthly magazine for news, features, and opinions)
Theatre Communications Group
355 Lexington Avenue
New York, New York 10017

PHOTO CREDITS

Alphabetical Order, Long Wharf Theatre, William L. Smith, Photographer, page 8
Hamden Hall Country Day School, pages 16 and 17
Hamlet, Long Wharf Theatre, William L. Smith, Photographer, page 35
Streamers, Vivian Beaumont Theatre, New York, N.Y., page 48
Wichita State University, pages 58 and 82
Cyrano de Bergerac, Long Wharf Theatre, W. B. Carter, Photographer, pages 93-96
The Beach House, Long Wharf Theatre, W. B. Carter, Photographer, page 114
National Gallery of Art, pages 115-122
Southern Connecticut State College, page 146
Biography, Long Wharf Theatre, W. B. Carter, Photographer, page 165
Photographs courtesy of Altman Stage Lighting and Theatre Techniques, Inc., pages 170-174
Yegor Bulychev, Long Wharf Theatre, page 176
Long Day's Journey Into Night, Promenade Theatre, page 179
Hamden Hall Country Day School, page 190
Southbury Playhouse, Southbury, Connecticut, page 194
The Bald Soprano, Hamden Hall Country Day School, Perry Hack, Photographer, page 202
Greek National Tourist Organization Photograph, page 218
Italian Government Travel Office, page 227
Jon Fischer, Photographer, page 232
Boston Museum of Fine Arts, page 237
Oliver! Trinity Players, Washington, D.C., page 242
Greater Tuna, Hartford Stage Company, Lanny Nagler, Photographer, page 24
The Hoffmann Project, Hartford Stage Company, Lanny Nagler, Photographer, page 22
Twelfth Night, Hartford Stage Company, Lanny Nagler, Photographer, page 230
No Mercy, Hartford Stage Company, Lanny Nagler, Photographer, page 240